STRATEGIC MANAGEMENT
IN JAPANESE COMPANIES

THE BEST OF LONG RANGE PLANNING

Series Editor: Professor Bernard Taylor, Henley Management College

The aim of this series is to bring together in each volume the best articles on a particular topic previously published in *Long Range Planning* so that readers wishing to study a specific aspect of planning can find an authoritative and comprehensive view of the subject, conveniently in one volume.

Each volume will contain 10 – 12 articles, and about 120 pages. In due course they will provide a comprehensive and authoritative reference library, covering all important aspects of Strategic Planning.

A Related Journal

LONG RANGE PLANNING★

The Journal of the Strategic Planning Society and of the European Strategic Planning Federation.

Editor: Professor Bernard Taylor, Henley — The Management College, Greenlands, Henley-on-Thames, Oxon RG9 3AU, UK.

> The leading international journal in the field of strategic planning, which provides authoritative information to senior managers, administrators, and academics on the concepts and techniques involved in the development and implementation of strategies and plans.

★Free sample copy gladly sent on request to the Publisher.

STRATEGIC MANAGEMENT IN JAPANESE COMPANIES

Edited by

TOYOHIRO KONO
Gakushuin University

PERGAMON PRESS

OXFORD · NEW YORK · SEOUL · TOKYO

U.K.	Pergamon Press plc, Headington Hill Hall, Oxford OX3 0BW, England
USA	Pergamon Press, Inc, 660 White Plains Road, Tarrytown, New York 10591, NY., USA
KOREA	Pergamon Press Korea, KPO Box 315, Seoul 110-603, Korea
JAPAN	Pergamon Press Japan, Tsunashima Building Annex, 3-20-12 Yushima, Bunkyo-ku, Tokyo 113, Japan

First edition 1992

Library of Congress Cataloging-in-Publication Data
Strategic management in Japanese companies /
edited by Toyohiro Kono. -- 1st ed.
p. cm. -- (The Best of long range planning ; no. 11)
1. Industrial management--Japan.   2. Strategic
planning--Japan.   3. Corporate planning--Japan.
I. Kono, Toyohiro.   II. Series.
HD70.J3S77   1992   658.4′012′0952--dc20   92-3625

British Library Cataloguing in Publication Data
A catalogue record for this book is available from the British Library.

ISBN 0-08-040670-X Hardcover

Printed in Great Britain by BPCC Wheatons Ltd, Exeter.

Contents

Strategic Management in Japanese Companies

Toyohiro Kono, Professor of Business Administration, Gakushuin University, Tokyo

I Foreword

This book is a collection of articles on strategic decision making and the management of organizational change in Japanese corporations. The papers are concerned with strategic decisions and major innovations, not simply operational matters. The articles have been selected because they demonstrate the basic principles of strategic management in successful manufacturing corporations.

The overall framework for the book is shown in Figure 1.

The goals of the corporation and the style of the top management are the foundations on which strategy and strategic decisions are based. Part 1 describes these two areas in Japanese corporations. Part 2 describes their strategies for growth. Part 3 examines the process of changing corporate culture. Strategic planning needs to be supported by a vital corporate culture. The pattern of decision making is an important element of the corporate culture and the organization is the vehicle through which strategy is implemented. Part 5 describes one important aspect of the organization — the computerized information system. Part 6 describes the 'transplanting' of Japanese management systems and attitudes to subsidiaries in foreign countries.

The first paper in *Part 1* analyzes the Japanese management style. Japanese corporations have four key characteristics. They are:

(a) innovative and growth-oriented,
(b) competitive,
(c) flexible and organic, (not bureaucratic) and,
(d) community-oriented.

These features began to take shape after the Second World War.

The second article describes the characteristics of Japanese top-management. They are free from the direct pressures of shareholders. They make their decisions as a group. Professor Kudo and his colleagues compared the behaviour of top managers in Japan and the U.S. They studied their time allocation and their decision making.

The top managers of large Japanese corporations make their decisions as a group. The Management Committee meets once a week and makes decisions on strategies, investments and operations. The decision making tends to be risk-taking. The functional backgrounds of the top managers are in technology and marketing. The salary they receive is low, and they are motivated by the status and satisfaction they obtain through being the leaders of large corporations.

Part 2 examines Strategic Planning in Japanese corporations. Strategic Planning plays an important role in strategic decision making. The company visions are expanded into detailed strategies through strategic plans. This formalised planning is required for group decision making.

There are two recent trends in strategic planning. One is Issue-Oriented Planning; the other is the two-phased planning system. These two processes are described in the two articles in this section.

Part 3 deals with Corporate Culture. Corporate culture reflects the shared values of the management team, their decision making style and their pattern of behaviour. It is largely invisible, but it affects strategic decision making and the way strategy is implemented. The re-vitalisation of a corporate culture is also studied in this Part.

Part 4 examines Research Management and new product development. The first two chapters in this Part deal with research management. Japanese companies in high technology areas are increasing their research expenditure, which is much larger than their capital investment. Japanese

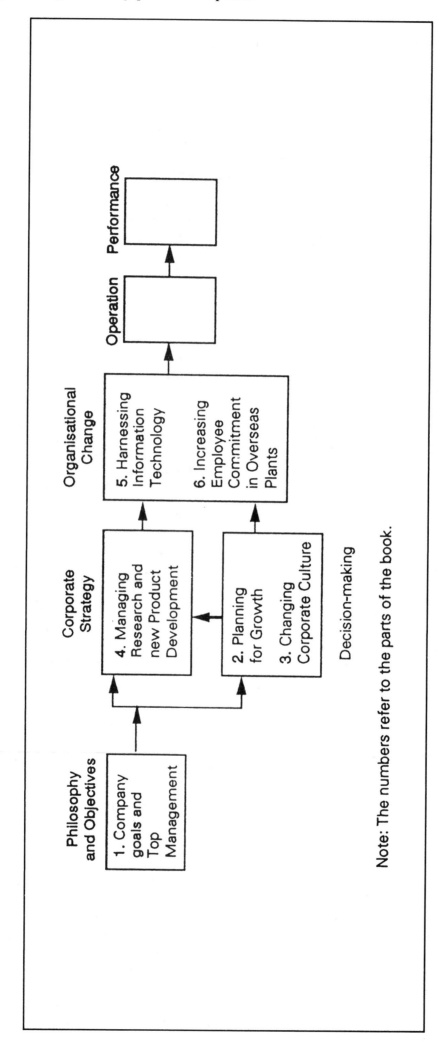

Philosophy
and Objectives

1. Company
goals and
Top
Management

Corporate
Strategy

4. Managing
Research and
new Product
Development

2. Planning
for Growth

3. Changing
Corporate Culture

Organisational
Change

5. Harnessing
Information
Technology

6. Increasing
Employee
Commitment
in Overseas
Plants

Operation

Performance

Decision-making

Note: The numbers refer to the parts of the book.

research laboratories are usually centralized under the head office, the research topics are decided by the long-term corporate strategy, and new product development is given a high priority in resource allocation. These chapters deal with some fundamental problems, such as how to motivate researchers to be creative and how to improve the interface between the different functions involved: Research, Development, Production Engineering, Production and Marketing.

The second two articles in *Part 4* are concerned with New Product Development. New product development has a large impact on company performance. The authors explore the critical factors for success in new product development, the principles that determine the attractiveness of new products, and the steps required to accelerate the speed of new product development.

Part 5 includes cases describing the successful introduction of Computer Integrated Manufacturing systems (CIM). In this process the functions of marketing, designing of products, production schedule and inventory control are integrated through a computer network. The CIM system enables a company to respond quickly to the needs of the customers, and makes the production system more flexible, so that the production department can comply with a variety of customer demands.

Part 6 examines Management in International Companies and the management of Japanese affiliated companies in foreign countries. For these international corporations to succeed, the Japanese style of management has to be transplanted into the subsidiaries. What can be transferred and to what extent the Japanese style can be transplanted overseas are the basic questions to be addressed. The long-term objectives, the emphasis on quality, the flexible or 'organic' organization, and the respect for people are the basic ideas which need to be transplanted. Two successful case histories are presented.

Most of the chapters in this volume have been written at the request of the editor. The editor is grateful for the valuable contributions provided by the authors, and for their co-operation with him in providing revisions of their original papers.

II Summaries

Part 1 Company Goals and Top Management

Japanese Management Philosophy:
Can it be Exported?
Toyohiro Kono
LRP Vol. 15, No. 3

Japanese companies have many characteristics common to innovative organizations. Missions and goals are clearly stated. These motivate the employees and make it easier to introduce innovation. They also encourage a sense of involvement with the organization.

Japanese corporations have growth oriented and long-range goals. This derives from the expectation of life-time employment. Also pressure from shareholders is not as strong as in the U.K. The separation of management from ownership is well advanced with a management committee being in effective control. Group decisions tend to be innovative, in part due to the high number of university graduates. Japanese management thus remains sensitive to new technology and new ideas. Many characteristics of Japanese management do not originate in the uniqueness of their culture but rather in the positive introduction of new theory.

Strategic decisions are made by top management. Formal long-range planning has a very high diffusion among large Japanese companies.

Strategies are competition oriented. There is a long-term co-operative relationship between the final products manufacturer and the parts manufacturers. There is also more use of internal growth and less use of acquisition.

Japanese companies also have many features of the so-called 'soft organization'. Jobs are ambiguous and are not well-defined. Thus it is easy to change jobs and introduce new technologies. Group decision making and participation are popular and there is better horizontal and vertical communication.

Companies respect the welfare of employees and treat them on a length of service basis with frequent promotion and merit increases. Training is emphasized and the individual is respected. Of course, the characteristics of the political and social systems play a part, such as political stability, good co-operation and loyalty towards the organization.

How U.S. and Japanese CEO's Spend Their Time
Hideyuki Kudo, Takeo Tachikawa and Norihiko Suzuki
LRP Vol. 21, No. 6

Corporate behaviour is influenced by environmental constraints and CEO's are likely to have common characteristics based on nationality.

Japanese and American CEO's operate in a dynamic and competitive business environment. Differences in corporate behaviour have produced varied results in corporate business performance. It is assumed that the success rate is directly related to the actions of the CEO.

CEO's in the raw material processing and manufacturing industries in both Japan and the United States were studied in order to ascertain how they spent their time.

The study showed that some commonly held beliefs about the corporate culture in the two countries were not substantiated. Japanese and American CEO's were on average the same age, for instance, contradicting the idea that Japanese CEO's take longer to reach the top. In addition, American CEO's tend to stay in the top position longer than their Japanese counterparts.

American and Japanese top executives manage their daily schedules similarly, although U.S. CEO's work significantly longer hours. This latter group also spends more time reading. For the rest, there were very few differences in the amount of time spent on work related tasks.

In order to understand the decision-making process favoured by CEO's, an analysis of in-house meetings was done. Japanese in-house business meetings were mainly forums for reporting activities and soliciting approval of proposals rather than for discussion and decision-making. Discussions in American meetings focused on the expansion of business and competitive strategy whereas the Japanese tended to concentrate on new product development and new technology.

Part 2 Planning for Growth

Planning for Growth in a Japanese Business
Yoshio Serizawa
LRP Vol. 22, No. 2

Formed as a joint venture of three automotive manufacturers, the Japanese Automatic Transmission Company (JATCO) became an independent company in 1981. Since that time JATCO has expanded the scope of its business, including its product line, customer list, and engineering and marketing capabilities. The planning and control system which was developed is credited with enabling JATCO's transition.

As at many Japanese companies, all corporate activity at JATCO is governed by a few simply stated philosophies and objectives. The primacy of the customer, the continuous search for new products and markets, a commitment to quality, and the preference for co-operation over competition are recurring themes. Strategies which support these objectives are then developed co-operatively by the president and his top management team and disseminated throughout middle management.

JATCO's business planning and budget making process is a blend of three elements: Ford-style financial controls, Nissan's personal business plans for managers, and the Japanese concept of Total Quality Control. Three or four key objectives set by the president form the basis for simultaneous business plans for the long (5 years), middle (3 years) and short term (current year). Of these, the middle range plan is critical in that it is continuously updated to reflect changing conditions.

An analysis of the gap between planned and actual results indicates areas in need of improvement. In particular, a shorter planning period and the gathering of more market information are recommended.

Taisei Corporation Plans for the Year 2000
Hisao Okuzumi
LRP Vol. 23, No. 1

Taisei, one of the leading companies in the important Japanese construction industry, has introduced a series of 5-year plans since 1980 designed to manage corporate restructuring. Taisei's corporate structure is based on a function-focused head office and profit-centre business divisions. As part of the management vision, Taisei has developed a view of the corporation in the year 2000. Strategies are designed within this vision. These are compared with strategies of competitors and are assessed to determine whether they are threats or opportunities. Analyses are performed on various factors and the results are used to form a medium-term 5-year management plan. The goal is to enhance competitiveness, promote product development and create synergistic effects between the various divisions. The Corporate Planning Department then aids in adopting a system in which top-down planning is applied to the 5-year plan, while administration is bottom-up in structure. Taisei's corporate plan has been so successful that both sales and profit goals are achieved within 3 years. In addition, on a qualitative level, the foundation was established from which to launch the transition to a knowledge-intensive industry. Some problems such as setting evaluation standards for qualitative targets have been solved through the use of 'success stories'.

Part 3 Changing Corporate Culture

Corporate Culture and Long-range Planning
Toyohiro Kono
LRP Vol. 23, No. 4

Corporate culture is made up of shared values, decision-making patterns and overt behaviour patterns. There are five different kinds of corporate culture. One stresses innovation and common values, a second follows a strong leader, a third is bureaucratic, a fourth stagnant and the last combines stagnation with autocracy.

The factors that create a corporate culture are those that change culture. Research has shown that a change in top management is the most frequent change factor. Information can also change the attitudes of individuals and groups; thus a change of corporate creed is frequently used. A new experience, for example implementation of a new product-market strategy, can also change attitudes, provided that the new strategy is seen to be successful and is adopted by all the relevant company functions. The process of change requires the company to destroy conventional values; to communicate a new way of thinking which is bolstered by having employees solve problems by themselves, to reward and punish, and to provide experiences which reinforce the rightness of the culture change. Strategic planning can help in this process.

Success Through Culture in a Japanese Brewery
Takanori Nakajo and Toyohiro Kono
LRP Vol. 22, No. 6

Asahi Breweries' 35 year decline can be attributed to a concentration of plants and markets in Western Japan, a focus on the restaurant market and poor product quality. Stagnation in the corporate culture also accelerated the fall in the company's market share.

A new corporate creed was initiated by the new president in 1982, placing emphasis on manufacturing consumer-oriented products and on creating a positive work environment through the distribution of a printed corporate creed and a code of behaviour to all employees, and the organization of a programme of 'away-days' for managers. A Total Quality Control programme helped to remove communication gaps between the production and marketing departments and to improve product quality. Proposals for a new company logo and new products were issued by a Corporate Identity Committee and resulted in the creation of new beers whose success was built on heavy advertising and publicity campaigns, an accurate grasp of consumer requirements and sales activities promoting the rapid rotation of fresh products. A change in the organizational structure enhanced the firm's strategic capability by reinforcing staff departments, improving development research and establishing product divisions.

The rapid expansion in market share caused a change in employee attitudes who then adopted a more positive approach to their jobs.

The Transformation of Nissan—The Reform of Corporate Culture
Yasuhiro Ishizuna
LRP Vol. 23, No. 3

In the early 1980s Nissan was attracting much public attention for its enterprise abroad but its position in the domestic market was failing. This was due to a number of factors, notably the conflict between labour and management. The situation was exacerbated by a deteriorating public image. Following a change of President in 1985, efforts were made to improve labour management relations and to make working practices more flexible.

These efforts were assisted by the sharp appreciation of the yen following the Plaza Accord, which brought unions and management together in an effort to ensure the company's future security. Ultimately a new corporate philosophy was adopted with a focus on customer satisfaction. The drive for reform gradually yielded results with the introduction of new models and a recovery in the domestic market. At the same time, the company started to expand overseas, establishing plants in the U.S. and the U.K. This expansion was accompanied by a programme of 'localization'. Another aspect of Nissan's transformation was the globalization of operations which aimed to expand overseas production while reducing exports from Japan of finished vehicles. The key to success in this will be the construction of a network linking Nissan's global operations. The poles of the network will be North America, Asia and Europe.

Part 4 Managing Research and New Product Development

Planning Research and Development at Hitachi
Yutaka Kuwahara, Osami Okada and Hisashi Horikoshi
LRP Vol. 22, No. 3

Effective planning for research and development at an industrial laboratory poses several strategic issues, including resource allocation, technology transfer and collaboration with domestic and international partners. At a new product intensive company like Hitachi, strategic planning for R & D virtually determines the future of the company. To ensure that its various research activities are co-ordinated with an eye to bottom-line concerns, Hitachi has developed guidelines governing which research is undertaken, how projects are funded and how researchers are rewarded for their contributions.

Hitachi divides R & D into three categories reflecting the position of the research in the product development cycle. For strategically important projects a research 'tokken', or team, will be formed from all three categories. Research planning is short-term (yearly) and long-term (5 years), based on regular interdisciplinary discussion of important technology areas. Good relations are emphasized with global partners to ensure the flow of leading-edge research. Projects are financially assessed at several stages of development and researchers are rewarded partly on their project's contribution to the bottom line. Hitachi feels the system encourages co-operation and dynamic research while contributing to basic knowledge and fostering competition to be the best.

R & D Management at RICOH
Akira Okamoto
LRP Vol. 24, No. 5

The RICOH company has eight research laboratories; this chapter describes research management at the central research laboratory. To promote creative thinking, a number of devices are used. A twenty-four hours' open system and a 'Community Plaza' are examples. Young researchers are appointed as research managers, the screening process for research is simplified, researchers are encouraged to present ideas for the research strategy and a symposium is held. There the selected papers are presented. These measures encourage the creative activities of researchers.

How the Japanese Accelerated New Car Development
Toru Sasaki
LRP Vol. 24, No. 1

New car development is a key factor for success in car manufacturing companies. It absorbs a huge amount of money and requires the co-operation of a large number of specialists. The technical quality and the design are two important areas in development, and design has become more important in recent years. The shortening of the time taken to develop a new car is one of the competitive advantages of Japanese car manufacturers. It is achieved by close-co-operation between research, market testing, product design, production and marketing.

Breakthrough: The Development of the Canon Personal Copier
Teruo Yamanouchi
LRP Vol. 22, No. 5

The special character of new product development in a Japanese corporation is examined. Using the example of the design of a new $1000 personal copier at Canon the company's procedure for product development is explained.

A Canon corporate objective is to achieve the best product possible, by adopting an enterprising approach and by focussing resources on research and development, product planning and marketing. R & D is central to Canon's management culture. In product development as well as in other areas, a project team approach is used. The definition of product concepts is followed by the organization of a feasibility team and a company-wide task force: an independent group appointed by the company president.

The task force is led by the product champion who acts as a link between senior management and the development engineers. An awareness of the market and business environment is crucial throughout the development process. At each stage the process is reviewed by the task force to identify deficiencies in the technology and the product.

A key factor for success in this venture was the exchange of technological information by each group in the task force. The formulation of a team mission and the establishment of a challenging goal also contributed to the successful product launch.

Part 5 Harnessing Information Technology

CIM at Nippon Seiko Co.
Masakatsu Hosoda
LRP Vol. 23, No. 5

The advent of the third generation computer and the Data Base Data Communication system has triggered a boom in the use of Management Information Systems, (MIS). However, many enterprises have returned to Batch Processing Systems.

In the case of Nippon Seiko K.K. (NSK), however, a total MIS system was seen as an essential part of its business strategy for the technological and competitive challenges of the decades ahead. It was used to develop an advanced flexible manufacturing system designated MAGMA, linking marketing, manufacturing and design. The system (and its subsystems) encompass the entire industrial group, directing operations, tracking management resources, estimating and managing the execution process, as well as continually improving cost performance.

The system has yielded a number of significant benefits to the company: reductions in personnel and associated increases in productivity, together with flexibility in production; quality improvements and quality assurance; the shortening of production lead times and a reduction in inventory.

Yamoto Transport Corporation has gone into the parcel business recently and has been very successful, having achieved a high market share in competition with the Post Office.

By the use of a computerized information system, the company provides a quick service with high quality. It offers a pick up and delivery service and uses the retail stores for receiving parcels. Every driver has a small personal point of sale terminal. The company has built its network step by step.

The author participated in an extensive survey of CIM systems of Japanese manufacturing companies, and he describes the critical factors for success and failure.

There is a danger in focussing too much on technical analysis and of neglecting human and organizational factors. CIM increases the flexibility of production systems. By linking marketing with product development and production, it enables the company to respond quickly to changes in market demand.

On the other hand, CIM increases the investment in facilities and software, and so reduces the flexibility of the corporation as a whole. This chapter reviews the success factors and failure factors for CIM based on an extensive field survey.

Part 6 Increasing Employee Commitment and Productivity in Overseas Plants

Bridgestone Corporation of Japan began manufacturing in the United States by taking over a troubled tyre plant from a U.S. corporation. Production, productivity and quality levels were low; profits were non-existent.

Bridgestone took various steps in order to turn the plant around. One was to discover why demand for the tyres was so poor. A survey of customers identified a poor image, derived from poor product quality. Redressing this became the top priority. The first step was to clean up the plant by making each worker responsible for cleaning up after himself. Next was the use of the so-called '4M' approach, addressing problems with machines, materials, methods and manpower. Machines were continuously improved and became preventively maintained. Materials suppliers were subjected to scrutiny on their own process controls and product quality. Adjusting methods to Japanese standards proved more difficult because of the different capital equipment and materials. Not surprisingly, manpower proved to be the most difficult.

Steps were taken to reduce the difference between blue and white collar workers. An opinion poll of the work-force, management seminars and interviews with the President were instituted to help build 'mutual trust'. Training, including visits to Japan, quality control management, mistake reporting, quality circles and management by objectives were all introduced. The net result of these actions was a three-fold increase in output, a doubling of productivity, and a reduction of defective tyres by about half.

When Sumitomo Rubber Industries (SRI) of Japan took over the U.K. tyre operations of Dunlop Group in 1984, it took on a declining operation with ageing plant and equipment and demoralized workforce. By 1986, the venture (now known as SP Tyres U.K. Ltd) broke even and it has increased profit margins every year since. Although changes in the U.K. economy and labour relations climate have helped, the transformation can be credited to SRI management's ability to pinpoint problems and develop solutions co-operatively with their U.K. workforce.

Dunlop employees were receptive to change because they knew the survival of the company depended on it. SRI introduced programmes to upgrade plant and equipment, increase productivity and quality, and improve working conditions. Communications plans, quality circles and suggestion schemes have helped create a sense of teamwork. Harmonization of pay and benefits across all sites has reduced the need for lengthy multi-party labour negotiations. Training programmes include visits to Sumitomo factories in Japan to see in action the SRI philosophy of putting the customer first, and to help inculcate a common set of values across the entire group.

PART ONE

Company Goals and Top Management

Japanese Management Philosophy: Can it be Exported?

Toyohiro Kono, Professor of Business Administration, Gakushuin University

Japanese organizations have three prime characteristics. They are innovative firstly. They are growth oriented and they are sensitive to new opportunity. They are flexible organizations. Jobs are ambiguous and employees are willing to do any related jobs. They are also community organizations and the company will take care of the employees for their life-time. The organizations provide more opportunity for promotion and wage increase with small differentials. These features began to take clear shape after the war. Some of them have their roots in Japanese culture but many are the results of rational judgment, and many were transferred from the U.S. and other countries. It is therefore a misconception to think that these features are too indigenous to Japan to be transferred to other countries.

Introduction

Many papers and books on Japanese style of management are appearing, as Japanese goods are penetrating into the world markets. Many of them state the traits on personnel management or environmental characteristics.

This paper tries to analyse the overall characteristics of Japanese management, with emphasis on strategic level of management practices. There are three characteristics of Japanese management style. (a) Japanese enterprises have traits as innovative organizations. (b) They have features as soft organizations. (c) They have characteristics as community organizations.

(A) Innovative Organization

Organizations adapt themselves to change of environment by a number of models. Organizations may be classified as stagnant, reactive and innovative organizations. Ansoff classified organizations as stable, reactive, anticipatory and initiative.[1] Innovative organization may correspond to the latter two. Innovative organization is growth-oriented and introduces new products at an early stage, and changes strategy and structure frequently. In order to do this, goals are clearly stated and top managements are strong and aggressive.

Stagnant organization is not interested in growth. It is interested in safety, does not change its products, does not undergo any change of strategy and structure. Goals are not clearly shown, and top management is either very autocratic or very weak (power is scattered).[1-6] (For definition see Ansoff *et al.*, 1976; Rowe and Boise, 1973; H. Mintzberg, 1973; Glueck, 1976; Steiner and Miner, 1977; H. Nystrom, 1978.)

Japanese enterprises have many characteristics common to innovative organizations.

(1) Goals
Missions and Goals are Clearly Stated. They may be called the philosophy of management. Many Japanese corporations have a clearly stated philosophy.

Table 1 is an example of Matsushita Electric Co.

Missions and goals have a hierarchy. Missions are the statement of the role the company wants to play in the larger environment. 'To supply the consumer with electric home appliances at a cheap price like water' is a statement of a desired role of the company.

Goals are the highest value of the company, like growth and profit. They have direction (or item), level and timing such as long-term goals and short-term goals.

When missions and goals are clearly stated, they tend to motivate the employee, to increase the sense

Professor Toyohiro Kono is Professor of Business Administration in the Department of Management, Gakushuin University, Toshima-Ku, Tokyo, Japan.

Table 1. Missions, goals and policies of
Matsushita Electric Co.

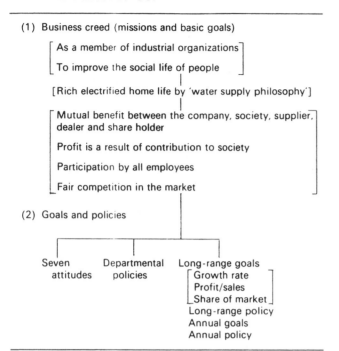

(1) Business creed (missions and basic goals)

[As a member of industrial organizations]
[To improve the social life of people]

[Rich electrified home life by 'water supply philosophy']

Mutual benefit between the company, society, supplier, dealer and share holder

Profit is a result of contribution to society

Participation by all employees

Fair competition in the market

(2) Goals and policies

Seven attitudes

Departmental policies

Long-range goals
[Growth rate
Profit/sales
Share of market]
Long-range policy
Annual goals
Annual policy

of identification with the organization. It then becomes easier to understand the meaning of their work, to understand the relationship between the jobs they perform and the society. If they are not clearly stated, employees may think that 'the company is company and we are we', and that the values of both are different. They may demand easier jobs with higher pay.

When long-range goals and short-range goals are clearly stated, they have the effect of making it easier to introduce innovation into the company, because the workers can understand the new direction of the company. They can orient themselves to the company's new direction. Without clearly stated goals, it is hard for the organization to change direction or the initiative of the employees and with their co-operation.

There are a number of publications in Japan on compiled business creeds, and there is enough evidence to show that many Japanese corporations have stated business philosophies. Many U.S. corporations have stated philosophies, but in the U.K., not so many corporations have company philosophies. It is impossible to find a business creed displayed on a plant site in the U.K. In my interviews with many British executives, they mentioned two reasons for this. One is that the creeds of companies are very similar from company to company, so it may not be very meaningful. Most of them simply state the responsibilities to the society, to the consumer, to the supplier and to the employees.

Another reason is that the values of the employees in the U.K. are more individualistic than the

Japanese. Employees have less sense of involvement with the organization so it does not work if the philosophy is publicly stated. (Some successful British companies do have stated philosophy e.g. ICI, Marks & Spencer.)

Growth Oriented Goals and Long-range Goals.
Japanese corporations have long-range views and growth is an important item of goals. Approximately 80 per cent of large Japanese corporations have long-range planning.[7,8] This is evidence of long-sightedness of Japanese corporations.

Table 2 shows what are the important items of goals in long-range planning, and we find that sales and growth are the most stressed. (In this survey U.K. responding companies have long-range planning, so they are much more growth oriented than the other U.K. companies.)

Why is it that Japanese companies are more long-range growth oriented? There are two reasons. One comes from the expectation of life-time employment. To keep the employee for a life-time, the company has to grow. To provide the employees with wage increases and frequent opportunities of promotion, the company has to grow. Another reason is that the pressure from the shareholder is not so strong in Japan and annual profit or quarterly profit is not important. The ratio of paid-in capital (including stock dividend) accounts for less than 10 per cent of total capital (including current debt).

Japanese corporations borrow most of their money from banks and the banks support the long-term growth of the company, because by so doing the banks can cultivate the market to lend the money. Most of the savings of a family goes to bank deposit accounts and the savings ratio is high. It is approximately 20 per cent, whereas in the U.K. it is about 10 per cent.

Welfare of the Employees is also Important as One of the Goals. In a depression, Japanese companies will decrease the dividend first to protect employment, but U.S. or U.K. companies will lay-off (or make redundant) the employee first in order to maintain the dividend. This shows the different way of thinking. In long-range planning goals, compensation, value added, labour productivity are stressed (Table 2 does not show the full range of the survey of long-range goals). Labour productivity is the precedent of good treatment. (The personnel policies of Japanese corporations will be explained later.)

Top Management and Board of Directors
Top Management. The separation of management from ownership is well advanced. As the size of the company grows, and as the successor of the founder has to pay large amounts of inheritance tax so the further separation proceeds. But this is not a unique

Table 2. Goals stated in long-range planning (by mail questionnaire survey)

	U.K. 74 companies %	Japan 327 companies %
In what specific terms are the goals and policies of your long-range plans stated? (Please tick as many as necessary)		
Basic goals		
(1) Sales	51	88*
(2) Rate of growth (sales or profit)	59	64
(3) Profit		
(a) Amount of profit	53	87*
(b) Profit ratio to total capital (or total assets)	59	42*
(c) Profit ratio to equity capital	18	27
(d) Profit ratio to sales	37	61*
(e) Standard deviation of profit (or limit of profit in the worst case)	0	16*
(f) Earning per share	37	18*
(4) Market share	50	41
(5) Capital structure	41	32
(6) Dividend	30	43
(7) Share price	8	2
(8) Employee compensation	8	39*
(9) Quality level of products	32	13*
(10) Basic policy of growth	49	50
(11) Basic policy of stability	14	34*
(12) Basic policy on profit	47	51
(13) Basic policy on social responsibility	16	19
(14) Other, please describe below	7	—
(15) NA	1	—

Note: Mail questionnaire survey in Japan was conducted by Kono in 1979 and 327 companies were analysed. In the U.K., the survey was conducted jointly by Prof. Stopford of London Business School and by Kono in March 1981 and 74 private companies were analysed here.
*Indicates the level of significance is 10%.

characteristic of Japanese corporations. What is different in Japan is that there is a management committee at the top level. According to a recent survey, 86 per cent of large corporations have management committees.[7] A group decision-making body at the top began to appear in the 1950s. The average number of members of these bodies is approximately 10. They meet once a week, making decisions as a group. The members are usually the chairman, president (managing director) and four to six executive directors. Each member has broad responsibility for corporate decisions covering several departments, receiving reports from these departments and giving advice to them. They are not identical to department heads. They are in charge of general management and strategic decisions.

In the United States, there is a growing tendency to have a group at the top, but the number of members is smaller than in the Japanese case. In the U.K., management committees are not frequently used, but rather the individual managing director or chairman makes the final decisions. If there is a group at the top, the number of members is usually three to five, and it is often an informal meeting.

Group decisions at the top tend to be innovative. There is some misconception that group decisions tend to be mediocre and slow, but a recent survey found otherwise. Group decisions can be innovative. The reasons are three.

Firstly, by group meetings, information is provided by more participants and uncertainty decreases. Where there is uncertainty, people do not like to make decisions. Secondly, there is more diffusion of responsibility. Thirdly, positive opinions tend to dominate negative opinions in group meetings. The high diffusion of management committees may be one of the causes of greater innovation in Japanese corporations.

Creativity is different from innovation. Innovation means the early adoption of a new idea, whether it comes from outside or not, and creativity means the new creation of the idea. I am not, however, saying that group decisions at all levels of Japanese corporations are always favourable to creativity in organizations. This has to be studied further.

Members of the Top Management. Most of the members of Japanese corporations are university graduates and approximately 45 per cent of them are engineering or natural science graduates. (Kono survey on 102 large manufacturing corporations, unpublished.) This percentage is higher in corporations where the products are more technology oriented (for example, 26 technology related companies have 50·6 per cent natural science graduates).

Where there are more university graduates, the decision at the top tends to be more analytical. Where there are more natural science graduates the decision tends to be more aggressive and innovative, because they have a better understanding of new technological development, and they like to do new things. In the U.K., less than 40 per cent of top management are university graduates and a much smaller percentage are science graduates. (About university graduates, see Channon, 1973.)[9] If accountants or financially oriented management are in power, the decision may be more conservative. (The above analysis is based on the directors of Japanese corporations, i.e. the members of the board of directors. In Japan, there are very few outside directors, so the analysis of directors can be the analysis of top management.)

Board of Directors. The board of directors in Japanese corporations plays a small role. It makes decisions on only legally required matters. If the board consists of many outside directors, as is the case with U.K. and U.S. corporations, and if they play a more important role in final decisions, then the strategy must be more conservative, because outside directors are not interested in risky decisions. They tend to put more emphasis on short-term profit.

(3) *Strategic Decisions*
Sensitivity to Opportunities. Innovative organizations are sensitive to change of environment, the scope of research is wider, outside oriented and future oriented. The research is flexible and it does not follow a fixed pattern. The subjects of research need not be very creative, but imitative, and research can lead to innovation, if it is done aggressively at an early stage.

Japanese managements are sensitive to new technology and to new ideas, but they do not necessarily create the original idea. They are quick to introduce foreign ideas and to implement them by conducting development research. For example, Sony produced the small portable transistor radio (1955), television using transistor (1959), video tape recorder (1963), Trinitron colour television tube (one gun three beams) (1968) for the first time in the world, but the original key technology came from the U.S. There is no doubt that Sony is an innovative and successful company. It is introducing a number of new products every year and one division is introducing 100 new products (including improvement) every year.

Scope of research and aggressiveness can be partly measured by R & D activity. Matsushita Electric spend 4 per cent on sales for research (£120m) and it has 10 laboratories with 4000 staff. It has 31,000 patents. Toyota spend 3 per cent on sales for research (£180m), it has two centralized technical centres and one laboratory with 2500 staff.

Taking Japanese industry as a whole, R & D expenditures over sale are 1·48 per cent (electrical appliances, 3·61 per cent), and R & D staff (excluding assistants) over total number of employees account for 3·01 per cent (manufacturing, in case of electrical appliances 5·85 per cent). (White Paper on Science, 1978, by Ministry of Prime Minister.)

Aggressiveness of research can be measured by the performance. Percentage of new products on sale is one of the measurements. Japanese companies are eager to introduce new products. The extent of new products introduced by Matsushita and Toyota is very high and we can confirm this by having a look at the products sold.

Sensitivity to new opportunity is not restricted to technology and Japanese managers are very sensitive to new theories of management.

Theories of organization, methods of planning, methods of production control and methods of quality control were eagerly studied, and experiences were exchanged between companies. At the present, the number of publications on management is quite large, and the study of management is extensive.

Most of the characteristics of Japanese management are not unique, but their implementation of theory goes further than other countries. Japanese businesses grow fast. Many new systems had to be constructed, so it was possible to introduce many new methods and to implement them.

This means that many characteristics of Japanese management do not originate in the uniqueness of their culture, but rather in the positive introduction of new theory and rational decision on continuous improvement.

Interactive Approach. There is a misconception that innovative organizations should have decentralized decision making structures. How can we expect that risky innovative decisions can be done by a bottom-upwards approach.

There is also a misconception that the decision making in Japanese corporations is bottom-upwards. This is not the case with strategic decisions. Top management takes aggressive action in strategic decisions. Strategic decisions involve a large risk, so it is the area where top management should make decisions.

According to my observation, diversified companies in the U.K. and in the U.S., tend to make strategic decisions at lower levels. For example, in GEC there are only 100 personnel in the head office, and most of the strategic decisions are done by the group or at division level.

Generally speaking, when strategic decisions are done at lower levels, they tend to be conservative and incremental to avoid risk, and it is almost impossible that they should decide to discontinue their own operations. Growth-share matrix models try to correct this tendency and aim at centralization of strategic decisions.

Japanese corporations, have very strong head office staff, and decisions are centralized. Matsushita Electric is a diversified company with 40 product divisions, but still there are thousands of people in the head office and strategic decisions are much more centralized than in similar companies in the U.K. and in the U.S.

With the help of strong staff in the head office, top management interchange information and ideas with the staff, and thus decisions are made by an interactive process, and generally speaking, this process is rather of a top-down process.

In the case of Matsushita Electric, key strategic decisions such as product line policy, foreign investment for multi-national management, dropout of unprofitable products, change of organization structure are decided by top management with the strong leadership of the founder.

The interactive approach in strategic decisions of Japanese corporations is shown partly by a survey of the planning process of long-range planning. In the case of Japanese corporations, corporate planning departments play an important role in preparing, and management committees in reviewing, the final decision.

Top-down and interactive processes result in an aggressive and analytical process of decisions.

High Diffusion of Long-range Planning. As was stated already, formal long-range planning has a very high diffusion among large Japanese corporations. There are a number of surveys, and these surveys show that more than 80 per cent of large Japanese corporations have formal long-range planning.[7,8] This high diffusion comes from several reasons: (a) top management is future-oriented, (b) in a high growth economy, it is necessary to forecast the long-term future, (c) long-range national economic plans have been published many times since 1956, which stimulated corporate planning and laid out the bases for long-range planning.

(4) *Strategies*
Competition orientation. Competition orientation means two things. Firstly, with a new product, there are many followers. Companies are willing to enter the area if it is a hopeful product, and new entry is done at an early stage of the life cycle. This results in many manufacturers in the same business. This is an 'I will do if others do' attitude, which is different from 'I will not do if others do' attitude. Secondly, it means the will to increase the share of the market at the expense of others, and to try to drive the competitor out of the market by competition, not by acquisition. This results in a frequent change of share of the market.

Competition between the Japanese corporations is very severe. When I interviewed the corporate planner of Toyota, I asked him the most important reasons for the success of the company, the planner answered immediately that 'we had to survive the domestic competition even when there was a barrier to importing cars'. In every new area of hopeful products, there are many new entries and it is quite usual that 10 companies should produce similar products. For example, even now in the passenger car business where approximately 10 million cars per year are produced, there are six companies; Toyota, Nissan, Toyo, Honda, Mitsubishi and Daihatsu. The two largest have a 70 per cent share, but they are losing that share of the market. In colour television, where 9 million sets are produced, there are seven companies, Matsushita, Hitachi, Sony, Sanyo, Mitsubishi, Sharp and JVC. Even in the computer business, there are six companies.

They are competing with each other in the home market and in the foreign market. Some are losing and others are gaining. There are few mergers and acquisitions of companies, so losing out is fatal to the company.

The number of failures including bankruptcies is 16,000 cases in Japan (1978).

Employees of Japanese companies are willing to identify themselves with the company, cohesiveness is very high, and, as a result, competitive attitudes towards other companies which produce similar products is strong. Under the life-time employment system, the companies have to grow and this tends to intensify the competition.[10]

Competition was an important reason for rationalization of operation, for new capital investment, for introduction of new products.

Vertical Grouping. There is a long-term co-operative relation between the final products manufacturer and parts manufacturers. It is well known in the U.K. that the relations between Marks and Spencer Ltd. and the suppliers to that company are co-operative on a long-term basis. This kind of long-term relationship is very popular in Japan.

Toyota organizes 'Kyoho-kai' which has 172 companies. These parts manufacturers supply parts only to Toyota. In return, they receive supports, e.g. training on quality control and production control, and general management. They receive support on financing. The buying manufacturers will inspect the method of quality control, but will not inspect the parts. Parts manufacturers of the Toyota group will seldom sell their parts to Nissan or other car manufacturers.

By having such a long-term co-operative relationship, the parts manufacturers can plan the production on a mass production basis and improve the quality with lower prices.

These parts manufacturers are independent as a legal entity, are not controlled either by stock ownership or by directors, excepting some key companies, but they enter long-term contract relationships with the manufacturers.

Japanese manufacturers produce parts internally to a lesser extent. GEC used to produce the cabinets for televisions, but Japanese TV manufacturers do not. BL Cars Ltd. produce transmission and steel wheels, but Japanese car manufacturers do not—instead they buy from outside. In this sense, the extent of vertical grouping is more widespread. Sales channels are encouraged to be exclusive. At least, in the case of consumer durable goods the manufacturers try to build an exclusive sales channel. Matsushita has 120 exclusive wholesalers, and 25,000 'national shops' whose sales account for 80 per cent of total sales and 25,000 'national stores' whose Matsushita sales account for 50 per cent. Matsushita provides a number of helps including special discounts to these shops and stores. Exclusive distribution policy is now under challenge from big stores which exhibit many brands, so it may change in the future.

Grouping is the result of the group orientation of Japanese people. Japanese tend to, and try to have stable relationships. Competition is severe, and to meet the competition it is advantageous to form a coalition with the organizations in the form of a complementary relationship.

More Use of Internal Growth, Less Use of Acquisition. Japanese companies seldom acquire other companies for diversification, they would rather use internal development, or joint venture by contract. This is easily evidenced by looking at the history of large corporations, or by looking at the statistics.

The growth of Toyota and Matsushita Electric was done by internal development with few acquisitions. If this strategy is compared with the strategy of U.S. companies and U.K. companies, there is a sharp contrast. When we read Moody's manual, we find that the history of the company is the history of acquisitions.

Growth by acquisition tends to have several problems. Diversification without synergy may be undergone by easy entry using acquisition with the results of failure.

Weak companies which should be driven out of the market might be kept alive by acquisition and the result is a wasting of resources.

Less use of acquisition, and more use of internal development tends to pay more careful attention to the effects of synergy, and results in the

concentration of the company strength. It also results in severe competition and in the application of 'the fittest will survive' principle.

There was a technology gap between Japan and the U.S. and European countries. It was more profitable to buy the patents than to acquire other companies in the home market.

More important reasons are sociological ones. Even in a low technology industry, acquisitions were not used. They were considered to be shameful behaviour. The Japanese are group oriented and members of the company have a deep identification with their company, and they are hard to integrate with the members of other companies. Wages and promotions are determined by length of service to a great extent, so wages of the same profession are not the same. The labour unions are organized on a company-wide basis, so that unions tend to be against acquisition. The companies guarantee lifetime employment and it is not easy to decrease the number of employees after acquisition. These are important reasons for less use of acquisition.

(b) Soft Organization (or Organismic Organization)

Burns and Stalker classified the organizations into organismic and mechanistic.[11] Japanese corporations have many characteristics as an organismic (or soft) organization.

(1) Jobs are Ambiguous
Japanese organizations are comparable to the natural stone walls which are seen at the many Japanese castles. The shape of stones are different from one to another, but they are combined so as to complement each other. Western organizations are comparable to brick walls, which are composed of standardized square bricks.

In Japanese organizations, jobs are ambiguous and they have several characteristics. (a) Jobs are roughly defined, not well defined, and employees are required to do any related jobs, (b) job contents change all the time, (c) employees are expected to present ideas to improve the jobs, (d) rules are less and ignored sometimes.

The opposite model, or bureaucratic models, are as follows. (a) Jobs are clearly defined by contract, (b) change of job is a serious matter, especially when the wage changes and when the membership of the union has to change, (c) it is not necessary to do work other than specified jobs, (d) there are many rules.

It is true that jobs are less defined and less divided in the U.K. than in the U.S., but at the plant site, employees on different jobs wear different colour uniforms. They usually belong to different unions. Operators cannot touch the machines.

The Japanese managers in the U.K. and in the U.S. complain that people there perform only the specified jobs, without willingness to do any related jobs.

In Japanese organizations, sometimes job names are not clear, and wages are paid by status, by performance and by length of service. In this situation employees will perform other duties if required.

There is no problem of job demarcation and there is only one company-wide union.

In the office, people work in a large room. They work as a team. Even the head of department is located in the corner of the large room. This system is quite different from the U.K. or U.S. office layout where each staff member has an individual room and perhaps has a secretary.

Job flexibility is closely connected with job classification. Table 3 is the job classification and grading system of Matsushita Electric.

In this system, operational jobs on the plant site and administrative jobs are more graded by job content, but in other areas, people are graded by their own capability without any relation to the job they perform. Under this system, jobs need not be well defined.

The reasons for this ambiguity spring from several sources. (a) Wages are related to the job to a lesser extent; they are also related to capability and length of service, (b) a union is organized on company basis, (c) the sense of involvement of the employee is very high.

The effects of this system are to make it easy to change jobs and easy to introduce new technology. This system tends to increase the productivity of labour by mutual help.

(2) *Group Decision and Participation*
Group decision making and participation are popular. Meetings within the section and meetings of those who have responsibilities throughout the sections are held frequently. This decision style is different from the system where the responsibility of each person is clear and each person does his job in his room with the help of a secretary.

This decision style has many similarities with the decision making style of system IV by R. Likert.[12]

On the plant site, participation is limited, but group meetings are frequently held and each employee is encouraged to present the idea. In the office, people work in a large room, and group decisions are more popular.

A suggestion system is another means of participation, and in many cases each employee might present more than 10 suggestions a year. Matsushita Electric has to deal with 460,000 suggestions a year. In the U.K., 10 suggestions a month in a whole plant is about the average. Japanese workers are willing to present their ideas.

The reason for group decision or participative decision making may be as follows. People have equal capability and should be allowed to participate, and people are willing to participate because of a high sense of involvement.

The effects of this Japanese style group decisions can be stated as follows. (a) Decisions tend to be slow but implementation is quick because everybody concerned knows the issue well. (b) Decisions are better and errors are less because a lot of information and ideas are collected. (c) Morale is high because of participation.

(3) *Better Communication, Horizontally and Vertically*
Communication from individual to individual tends to be better. This is rather hard to prove, but many Japanese managers of subsidiary companies in foreign countries comment that foreigners do not communicate well with each other.

In the U.K. and the U.S. written memos are frequently used, but in Japan oral communication is more often used. In the relations between individuals, Japanese will communicate better with colleagues and seniors will teach their subordinates well. 'NEMAWASHI' (log rolling) is required before the group decisions. Under the length of service system, people are not competitive with each other, so it is easier to have a good communication system. Under the same system, there is less fear of being out-promoted by a subordinate.

On the plant site, everybody wears the same uniform from plant manager to operator so it is easy for the managers to walk through the plant and to talk with everybody on the site.

In the U.K. office workers never wear uniform, they are provided with a separate lunch room from that of blue collar workers, and in this setting communication tends to be poor.

The above features are similar to the concept of organismic organization by Burns and Stalker.[11] But there are some differences. In the Japanese style, strategic decisions are taken by top-down or interactive approach, because strategic information is held by top level. Authority is not distributed equally in this respect.

Knowledge of the organization itself is emphasized rather than knowledge on specific professional skills. It is rare to find a professional occupation where knowledge is transferable from company to company. Unlike the original concept of organismic organization, people are not loyal to the occupation, but rather to the organization.

(c) Community Organization (*Gemeinschaft*)

Tönnies founded the concept of *Gemeinschaft* (community organization) and *Gesselschaft* (association).[13] *Gemeinschaft* is like a family or a church where members are combined by mutual love. Getting together itself is a source of joy. People love each other, share the good luck and bad luck as well and help each other, trust each other and understand each other.

Gesselschaft is like a pure profit making economic organization. If there is no reward, people will not work. There is no spiritual unity. People are combined by contract, but they are apart, and in a state of tension. They work by division of labour, within the strict limits of the job, and they become one of the atoms of the organization.

Japanese organization is somewhat similar to *Gemeinschaft*, because the company respects the welfare of employees and gives more equal treatment on a length of service system, and in turn the employees devote themselves to the organization willingly.

(1) *Life-time Employment*
Once a person enters the organization, he will devote himself for his life-time, and will stay until 55 or 60 years old. He will not move around from organization to organization. The organization will take care of the employee for his life-time, and will not lightly discontinue the employment. Because of life-time employment, recruiting is usually done from among new graduates from high schools and universities. It is seldom done by advertisement. For the employee, leaving or discharge is a serious damage to his career. There are several misconceptions on life-time employment. It is not a contract. It is a way of thinking on both sides—by the employer and by the employee.

Women employees do not stay for their life-time. They leave the company when they get married. Married women will devote themselves to the family. This is another sort of organization orientation. In the case of small sized companies, mobility is higher than larger companies. The life-time employment system originates from the traditional way of thought by Japanese people that devotion to an organization is a value. But this system was reinforced after the war, because it has merits on both sides.

Closely related with this system is the length of service system which is analysed later. In the life-time employment system, a strict merit system disturbs the order, so length of service with loose merit rating is more appropriate. On the other hand, under the length of service system, it is disadvantageous to change the organization.

The merits of stable employment are many. It is possible to spend a lot of money and time on employee training. This benefits both the organization and employee. There is little fear of losing employees who are well trained and have accumulated knowledge of the operation. The organization can this way obtain a good accumulation of knowledge. It is possible to introduce technological innovation, because employment is assured and there is less resistance to change.

When innovation necessitates a change of job employees are transferred within the company from one job to another, but they are not made redundant. To provide the employee with the job, the company has to introduce innovation in order to grow and has to survive the competition. The company is more concerned with the long-term growth. The company has to establish a long-range personnel plan to increase the productivity of labour. It can not decrease the number of employees temporarily; it has to increase productivity on a planned basis, and this will reduce conflict. Where the company can reduce employees easily, rationalization will not have been planned seriously.

The life-time employment system does not mean that the number of employees cannot be reduced. There are a number of methods to cope with the decreased demand for man-hours. Overtime is decreased first. Suspension of new recruits, early retirement with an increased rate of retirement allowance (flexible retirement system). temporary 'going back to country home' with pay, are frequently used. Voluntary retirement is solicited from aged people. The last resort is to decrease the number in employment. In this case older people will be selected first and younger people will be kept.

(2) *Frequent Promotion and Frequent Increase of Wage by Length of Service and by Merit*
In many cases there are two ladders of promotion, one is the hierarchy of job gradings, another one is the hierarchy of status. In the case of Matsushita Electric, there is only one grading for operational jobs, but for other fields of jobs there are two ladders (Table 3).
Even for operational jobs, when the skill of one person improves, then he is promoted to a higher grade while he is doing the same job. This kind of flexibility changes job grading to status grading. For clerical and technical jobs, each person is evaluated on the basis of job content and capabilities, and ranked on a grade. An employee

Table 3. Grade system of Matsushita Electric

Job groups Grade	Operational	Clerical technical	Administrative	Higher skill jobs Qualification status	Professional status
11				Director class	
10			Head of plant	Junior director	
9			Head of department	Senior manager	Chief engineer Senior manager in charge of _____
8			Head of section	Junior manager	Junior chief engineer Junior manager in charge of _____
7C$_3$	Head, section	Senior leader*	Head of group		
6C$_2$	Foreman	Leader*			
5C$_1$	Supervisor	Junior leader*			
		B$_5$			
4	A$_4$	B$_4$			
3	A$_3$	B$_3$			
2	A$_2$	B$_2$			
1	A$_1$	B$_1$			
Grading based on _____	Job (point system)	Job and person (classification method, each person evaluated)	Job	Person	Person

* = Status.

Notes:

(1) For operational jobs, grading is based on jobs. Jobs were evaluated by point system, but with improved skill, one can be promoted to higher grade while doing the same kind of job. At higher level, one may be shifted to administrative ladder.

(2) For clerical jobs, each person is evaluated on the basis of job content and of capability and placed on the grade. Standard for classification is used. Union member is requested to participate in ranking. At higher level, one may be promoted on status or on administrative ladder.

(3) At higher level, there are three parallel ladders. First is administrative position ladder, second is qualification status ladder, and the third is professional status ladder. Professional status have rather clear definition of jobs, but qualification status is classification of persons. Everybody has qualification status. See following chart.

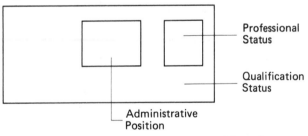

If one person has higher qualification status than the job, he can receive the wage of the rank or status.

(4) Every grade has a rate range. Average amount of annual wage increase is different depending on the grade, higher grades having a larger amount. There is no maximum rate for each grade.

(5) Wages can be increased by two methods, general wage increase and annual wage progression on the wage scale. Annual wage progression is based on merit and length of service.

can be promoted even when he is performing the same job.

For higher levels, there are three ladders, the administrative job grade, the qualification status grade and professional status grade. Everyone is ranked in a qualification status grade, as is explained in Table 3.

The general practice of many corporations is that promotion on the status grading is done by taking into consideration the performance and the capability and the length of service. At the lower level an open test is requested in addition to subjective judgment by the superior.

Subjective judgment is used to a great extent to decide promotion on both ladders. The trade unions do not like subjective judgment but

management believes that as there is maybe a risk on subjectivity of merit rating, it is better to increase the opportunity of promotion and wage increase.

The wage is related to the job and status. A person may be promoted on status grading while he is doing the same job. If there is no vacancy of higher jobs, his status grading may be higher than his job grading. Wages are related to status if the status is higher than the job rating. There is a difference in speed of promotion, but the length of service plays an important role, and therefore there is not a great difference between the employees. The wage is related to status or the job grade, so that promotion on status is accompanied by financial rewards.

Wages in the same job grade or status grade have a wide rate range. Progression on the rate range is done by merit rating and by length of service. Every year the wages are increased to some extent, and, depending upon the performance there is only a small amount of difference among the employees.

Wage scales are drawn up differently according to the grade of jobs and status. The higher the grade, the higher the standard line of wage by length of service (or age), so promotion results in higher wages.

What are the reasons for this unique system? This system was largely developed after the war. Job grading comes from the import of job evaluation and job classification systems. But outright application of imported systems resulted in failure and they had to be modified to meet the special culture of Japanese organizations.

The status system is a unique system, and is largely based on mutual respect. Promotion by length of service is related with the life-time employment where promotion is necessary because people do not move from one organization to another.

The wage increase system by length of service was useful to adjust the wage to the cost of living when wages were very low immediately after the war. Before the war, skilled workers were more mobile, wages were largely determined by job content and wage differentials between blue collar workers and clerical or administrative staff were much larger.

There are many merits of this system. There are frequent opportunities for promotion. Everybody can be promoted eventually to some grade, usually up to fourth or fifth grade from the bottom and this gives people the hope of advancement.

There is a slight difference of speed of promotion among employees and this gives a strong incentive for productivity and creativity. The same effects can be found in wage increases by length of service, with a slight difference of amount of increase for merit.

Some problems have arisen recently with this system. As the average age of employees increases, and as the retirement age is extended from 55 to 60 years old, the wage cost increases under the length of service system. The result has been to decrease the amount of wage increase by length of service, and put more emphasis on merit rating.

(3) Training

Training within the company is very much emphasized, and it pays under the life-time employment system. Matsushita Electric has seven training centres. The training system consists of training for new recruits, training for each functional skill; and training for promotion to higher hierarchical level. A Japanese company will spend a lot of money and time on off-the-job-training.

On-the-job-training tends to be better when people are not competitive with each other, because communication is then better. Under life-time employment, and under the length of service system, communication is easier and better.

Good training is necessary where job content is ambiguous and where employees are requested to do any related jobs. It is also necessary when there are more opportunities of promotion. All of them can be sources of satisfaction to employees.

(4) More Attention to Each Employee

Employees are respected as a partner of the organization. They are not considered as one of the elements of resources for production. Life-time employment is the result of this thought. In a depression, employees are kept on at the expense of dividend and profit. In addition to life-time employment, there are a number of systems which try to do good care for people.

(a) *Good Personal Records and Self-statement system.* Personal records are mainly comprised of personal career and merit rating record. Records are kept even for the blue collar workers and there is no distinction between blue and white collar at all. These records supply information for reviews for promotion and wage increases.

Self-statement is a statement of jobs, annual goals, self appraisal, extent of use of ability, other jobs where ability may be used to a fuller extent. This is sometimes accompanied by an observation sheet from a supervisor, which states job content, qualification, training given, capability to present job, need for promotion or transfer, training needed, characteristics of personality, etc.

(b) *Morning Meeting.* A meeting is held every morning, usually in each section of the plant site. Information is given, and sometimes an employee is asked to give a speech on his or her thoughts and ideas.

Morning meetings are also popular in primary schools and middle schools so this is an easily accepted habit for new employees in organizations. Unions are not against this kind of meeting.

(c) *Group Activity.* Group activity is encouraged on most of the plant sites. The subjects of the activity are selected by the group. They may be quality control, cost reduction, production method, improvement of machines and materials. A group is formed usually within the formal organization, and thus a group activity is to organize an informal group within the formed group. The group leader is selected by the group members. Group meetings are usually held after working hours and overtime is paid for this activity.

Group activity is a kind of job participation. It not only improves the quality of products, but also enhances the sense of identification with the company.

Japanese corporations imported the techniques of quality control and it was accepted enthusiastically. It was implemented as a technical system, but at the same time it was taken up as a subject of group campaign throughout the company, and as a subject of small group activity. Eventually quality control diffused throughout the company, not only as a technique but also as a way of thinking. Here is one of the secrets of the better quality of Japanese products.

(d) *Suggestion System.* Suggestion system is again nothing new. But it is implemented well as a means of participation. In the case of Toyota and Matsushita Electric, each employee presents ten to fifteen ideas a year on the average, so the total number is about 450,000 and 900,000 a year. In the case of a U.K. company, ten suggestions a month for a total plant is usually the case.

(e) *Welfare System.* Housing provided by the company and resort houses are very popular. In the case of Toyota, the company provides houses for 4200 families and dormitories for 17,200 bachelors. There are seven resort houses. It has one hospital and a number of recreational grounds.

Loan for home ownership, stock ownership with partial aid from the company, company deposit with high rate of interest,—these financial benefits are provided by many companies. (Large bonuses are paid during summer and at the end of the year, which account for more than 5 months of pay. This is not a benefit, it is merely a method of payment.)

(D) Some Environmental Characteristics

This is not the place to dwell on the characteristics of political systems and social systems at large, but selected important features will be explained here.

(1) *Political Stability*
Since the end of the war there has been a continuous dominance of the conservative party (Liberal Democrat). The Socialist Party only achieved a majority once (1949). This has meant that a long-term economic policy has been worked out. There are many small groups amongst Liberal Democrats. They compete with and criticize each other, and these small groups helped the conservative party to be viable.

(2) *Good Co-operation between Social Subsystems*
There is good co-operation between political parties and government bureaucrats, government and business, business and labour unions, business and banks, business and universities. There is competition between the organizations which produce similar products, but there is co-operation between complementary organizations.

(3) *Large Number of University Graduates*
There are 400 universities excluding 2-year colleges, and two million university students. Approximately 500,000 university graduates are supplied every year to various organizations. It is not rare that in high technology related companies university graduates total more than 20 per cent of employees.

(4) *Organization Orientedness*
People will select one formal organization, and devote themselves to the organization. Devotion to an organization is a moral value with Japanese people. Individualism which respects the independence of individuals, freedom of individuals and leisure for a private life are not the highest values for the Japanese. Organization orientation springs from the traditional culture of the Japanese people.

The above are the features of personnel management of Japanese corporations. As a community organization, the company respects the employee. It keeps good record of employees, it encourages participation by group decision, by group meetings, by suggestion systems. It provides the employee with a number of welfare programmes. Welfare is one of the goals of the organization. However, the company is not a benevolent organization nor a charity organization. It has to encourage devotion and to enhance productivity and creativity. Incentive systems are used to a greater extent than in organizations in the U.S. or in the U.K.

(E) Universality or Transferability of Japanese Style of Management

It is a misconception that Japanese management is unique, that it is based on a unique cultural background, and that it is neither universally appropriate nor transferable. This is not true and most of the characteristics of Japanese management style were formulated after the war by rational thinking (e.g. status system) and many of them were transplanted from the U.S. or European theories and business practices (e.g. management committee, quality control). Some visitors to

Japanese businesses have said 'there was no new fish, but the method of cooking is better'.

Of course a management system must fit environmental systems such as political, educational, social and economical systems, and also internal management systems must fit each other, so there are some limitations on transferability of any management system from one country to another. Contingency theory emphasizes this.

In order to discover what kind of Japanese management styles are universal, and what can be transferred to foreign countries, there are two methods. One is to observe the practices of Japanese subsidiaries in foreign countries. Another method is to look at the practices of well managed companies and try to find the similarities. Here the latter approach is used.

ICI is undoubtedly a well-managed company, and there are many similarities of management style to Japanese companies. Corporate philosophy is clearly stated, missions and responsibilities are openly declared.

At the top level, there is a management committee which meets once a week and discusses strategic issues. Five out of twelve directors are technology or science graduates. It has a long-range plan which integrates the strategic projects. It does aggressive research (spending £164m, 3·6 per cent, on sales in 1978), aggressive capital investment (£701m, 16 per cent, on sales in 1978). Even in the paint division, there is a good research laboratory, and facilities are on a large scale. Jobs are hard structured, but job enlargement and job rotation are tried among similar jobs after training.

It has only two centralized negotiation units—joint negotiation committee for weekly paid workers and for monthly paid staffs. Wage contracts are thus centralized.

There are works committees on a corporate level, division level, works level and plant level. On the plant level, the committee (managers and shop stewards) meets once a month, and discusses every problem other than wages. Business and investment committees are another form of joint consultation and deal with strategic problems.

ICI respects people. It encourages managers and supervisors to spend 20 per cent of their time on personnel management. There is no time recorder in paint division, for example. It has reduced the number of employees continuously, not by sudden redundancy, but by a longe-range plan, and natural turn-over. It has a profit sharing system. Job grades are many. There are seven grades below supervisor, thus increasing the opportunity for promotion. There is no rate scale for blue collar workers, but there is some extra pay. For white collar workers there are rate scales, and good personal records are held. Job grading and wage scales are standardized all through the company without regard of the union membership.

These features are not necessarily the same as Japanese systems, but there are many similarities and we can see that Japanese systems are not peculiar to Japan.

Transfer of management practice is a kind of organizational change. It is a change of an old balance of sub-systems to a new balance of sub-systems. This change is conditioned by social environment and rigidity of old internal sub-systems.

Generally speaking, management practices which are related to a deep core of cultural value such as individualism or group orientation, and are strongly based on environmental characteristics such as educational systems, are hard to be transferred.

Table 4 lists the transferable practices and hard-to-transfer practices according to the observation of a number of Japanese subsidiaries in U.K., the U.S., Malaysia, Philippines and other countries.

Conclusion

There are three characteristics of Japanese style of management.

It is an innovative organization. The goals of the organization are clearly stated, and growth and employee welfare are considered as important. Top management is a team, they are imitative but are sensitive to new opportunities. They are supported by the staff of large headquarter office.

It is a soft organization. Jobs are ambiguous, and employees are willing to do any related jobs. Most of the decisions are done by participation, so a group decision is the usual type.

It is a community organization. Employees are considered as a partner in an organization. They stay in the organization for their life-time. The organization provides more opportunity for promotion and wage increase with small differentials, which operate as incentives.

Some of these features are rooted in the uniqueness of Japanese culture, but many of them were transferred from other countries and modified; many of them

Table 4. Transferable and hard-to-transfer practices

(I) Japanese management practices universally effective to a great extent, or 'transferable'

   (A) (1) Clear long-range goal, more emphasis on long-term profit and growth
         2-1* Management committee
         2-2 Promotion of engineers to higher ranking
         2-3 Large and strong head office
         3-1* Aggressive capital investment for modernization
         3-2 Positive expenditure for research and development
         3-3 Careful assessment for company acquisition
         3-4* Emphasis on quality control

   (B)
         1-1* Centralized negotiation unit
         1-2* Job enlargement, job rotation
         1-3* Participation on many levels
         2-1* Large rooms
         2-2* Group activities and suggestion system
         2-3* Morning meetings

   (C)
         1* Respect for people
         2* More frequent promotion and wage increase by many grades and rate ranges
         3* Detailed personal records

(II) Japanese management practices hard to transfer

   Generally speaking, the following practices are hard to transfer
   (a) Management practices which have good fit with deep core of cultural value, for example, organization orientation
   (b) Management practices which are strongly conditioned by other environmental features, for example, educational system

   (A) (1) Too much expectation from employees to identify with corporate philosophy
       (2) Sacrifice on short-range profit

   (B) (1) Job ambiguity beyond certain extent
       (2) Too much expectation on group activity

   (C) (1) Life-time employment (but respect for people is universal principle)
       (2) Promotion by length of service and wage increase by length of service
       (3) Some kind of fringe benefits, such as housing, large bonus

*Practices which are actually implemented by many Japanese subsidiaries in the U.K., such as Matsushita, Sony and YKK.

were shaped by logical judgment and so many of them are universally effective and transferable.

References

(1) Ansoff, Declerk and Hayes eds., *From Strategic Planning to Strategic Management* (1976).

(2) Rowe and Boise, *Organizational and Managerial Innovation* (1973).

(3) H. Mintzberg, Strategy-making in three modes, *California Management Review*, Winter (1973).

(4) Glueck, *Business Policy, Strategy Formulation and Managerial Action* (1976).

(5) Steiner and Miner, *Management Policy and Strategy* (1977).

(6) H. Nyström, *Creativity and Innovation* (1978).

(7) Kansai Productivity Centre, *Survey on Business Organization* (1976).

(8) Ministry of International Trade and Industry, *New Indices for Managerial Capability* (1978).

(9) D. F. Channon, *The Strategy and Structure of British Enterprise* (1973).

(10) C. Nakane, *Human Relations in Vertical Society* (1966).

(11) Burns and Stalker, *The Management of Innovations* (1961).

(12) R. Likert, *The Human Organization* (1968).

(13) R. Dore, *British Factory–Japanese Factory* (1973).

(14) R. Gibbs, *Industrial Policy in More Successful Economies— Japan*, NEDO (1980).

(15) T. Kono, *Principles of Management* (1978).

(16) N. Macrae, Must Japan slow? *Economist* (Feb. 1980).

(17) E. F. Vogel, *Japan As Number One* (1979).

(18) Y. Yoshino, *Japan's Managerial System; Tradition and Innovation* (1968).

How U.S. and Japanese CEO's Spend Their Time

Hideyuki Kudo, Takeo Tachikawa and Norihiko Suzuki

Managing Directors (CEOs) in a number of large U.S. and Japanese corporations were asked to write a detailed diary of a typical working day, and they were asked what kind of information was useful for certain kinds of decisions. Some of the results of the survey are described in this article. It was found that the average age of the CEOs in the two countries was about the same—60 years old, but CEOs in the United States stayed longer in the position than Japanese CEOs because they were promoted at a younger age. CEOs in the United States worked a longer day than the Japanese. American chief executives spent about 3 hours longer in meetings than their Japanese counterparts. In Japanese corporations the information is distributed and the negotiating is done beforehand, so meetings tend to be shorter. In America contacts with businessmen outside the company were important sources of information, for strategic decisions in particular.

Although the mechanism of corporate decision-making has been extensively studied, little research has been done on the behaviour of the chief executive officer, a key person in the corporate decision-making process whose personal inclination has a significant impact on decision-making.

The behaviour of the individual CEO and their impact on the corporate decision-making process is a primary concern of our study, and we have analysed the CEO's involvement in the corporate decision-making process by monitoring their behavioural patterns for 24 hours.

The decision-making process includes the following stages:

(1) the information gathering process, and

(2) the decision-making process.

Some CEOs take a systematic approach to information gathering by employing computers; whilst others still use conventional methods, i.e. the human network including discussions with subordinates, guests and clients, etc.

It is also correctly assumed that the CEOs' psycho–behavioural pattern is influenced by sets of environmental constraints which vary among countries. The CEOs' behaviour and their mode of involvement in the decision-making process are likely to have common characteristics based on nationality, which will probably result in different corporate behaviour.

This paper is part of a large study project on the psycho–behavioural model of CEO decision-making and concentrates on the first stage of the above-mentioned processes, i.e. the information gathering behaviour or the CEOs.

Research Setting

CEOs in the United States and Japan have experienced a dynamic business trend during the 1980s, and many firms have been forced out of business whilst others have successfully surmounted the turbulence. Differences in corporate business performance have been observed, even among companies in the same industry, and in order to compare the information gathering behaviour of CEOs in both countries, a questionnaire survey was conducted.

The CEOs are assumed to be making a business decision, whether strategic or tactical, at any moment of his/her daily life. Decisions may be made instantly or over a prolonged period of time, and may be either rational or irrational. The mechanism of CEO's decision-making will therefore require comprehensive observation through continuous 24-hour contact with them. In the questionnaire, the CEOs were asked to describe the details of their activities throughout a typical working day. The dimensions for the analysis and comparison are listed in Table 1.

Hideyuki Kudo and Takeo Tachikawa are Professors in the Faculty of Business, Takushoku University, Tokyo, and Norihiko Suzuki is Associate Professor, Faculty of Arts and Science, International Christian University, Tokyo.

Table 1. The dimensions for the comparison

> *How the CEOs are spending their time*
> 1. Commuting hours between the home and the office
> 2. Travel time between business locations
> 3. Business meetings with subordinates
> 4. Meetings outside the company
> 5. Meetings with visitors
> 6. Desk work for checking and approval of business decisions
> 7. Meetings with guests after work
> 8. Reading, private and sleeping hours
>
> *The usefulness of the time spent*
> 1. Information obtained from inside sources
> 2. Information gathered at in-house meetings
> 3. Meetings outside the company with resource people
> 4. Information obtained from visitors
>
> Subscriptions to reading materials and their contents

All the questions were developed so that the CEOs' activities during 24 hours of a typical working day could be comprehensively traced.

The questions were divided into two parts: (1) a group of questions related to how the CEO spends his/her time, and (2) a group of questions asking the respondents if and in what way their acquired information was used in the decision-making activities.

In summer 1986, 850 Japanese CEOs were selected from large companies listed in the Japanese stock exchanges. 102 CEOs responded to the questionnaire. In the American CEO sample, 350 were screened in spring 1987 from the *Fortune* 500 based on industrial classification. 42 U.S. CEOs responded to the researchers. In order to maintain common characteristics of those responding, CEOs were separated by a working environment classification.

Only the CEOs in raw material processing and manufacturing sectors were used for the study. Table 2 is the summary of the respondents' background.

The CEOs' Profile in Both Countries

The sectoral limitations of the study provided a sample with a lower degree of generalization. The comparison revealed some interesting facts about the CEOs in the two countries and the results seem to contradict typical concepts of Japanese and American executives.

Firstly, it has generally been assumed that Japanese CEOs take longer to reach the top positions due to the slow pace of promotion based on a seniority-oriented promotion system. Our conclusion is that there is no statistically significant difference (except for Japanese CEOs in the raw materials processing industry) in terms of the average age of CEOs. American CEOs in the raw materials processing industry averaged 57·1 years and American CEOs in

Table 2. The profile of the CEOs and their companies

Items	Industry Raw materials processing U.S.	Japan	Manufacturing U.S.	Japan
The number of responding CEOs	17	21	21	33
Average age (years)	57·1	64·5	57·9	59·9
(the oldest)	(71)	(71)	(69)	(75)
(the youngest)	(43)	(56)	(49)	(39)
Years in current position				
Less than 4 years	5	11	7	11
4 to 8 years	4	7	7	7
More than 8 years	8	3	7	14

the manufacturing industry averaged 57·9 years. The average age of Japanese CEOs in the manufacturing industry was found to be 59·9 years.

Comparison of the length of the executive's term in the top position also disclosed somewhat different results from general assumptions: the average time period of presidency for American CEOs assumed was found to be longer than that in the Japanese CEOs' case. More than 40 per cent of U.S. CEOs were found to have been at the top position of the company for more than 8 years, while the corresponding figure was less than 30 per cent in the case of Japanese CEOs.

On the other hand, 41 per cent of Japanese CEOs remained at the CEO's position for less than 4 years while, 30 per cent of U.S. CEOs occupied the top position of the company for less than 4 years.

This evidence enables us to conclude that American CEOs move into the position in their early 50s, staying at the highest position of the company longer than their Japanese counterparts. Although the Japanese CEOs start at more or less the same age they occupy the position for a shorter time.

How the CEOs Are Spending Their Time

Detailed analysis of how CEOs are spending their time suggests that there is little difference in the mode of managing their schedules. However, some of the findings contradict commonly held beliefs of the typical behavioural mode of Japanese and American CEOs. American CEOs worked longer hours than their Japanese counterparts, with less hours left for private and/or sleeping hours. The hard-working behaviour of the U.S. CEOs is particularly striking (see Table 3).

A detailed analysis on the CEOs' time allocation is as follows:

1. *Commuting Between the Home and the Office*
The average time spent commuting by American

Table 3. How CEOs spend their time

	U.S. CEOs minutes	SD*	Japanese CEOs minutes	SD
Commuting	59	(44)	87	(45)
Travel between business locations	80	(95)	78	(55)
Meetings with subordinates	192	(91)	177	(88)
Meetings outside the company	105	(76)	132	(70)
Meetings with visitors	81	(42)	84	(41)
Desk work	129	(68)	126	(59)
Supervising the office/factory	52	(29)	46·5	(22)
Meetings with guests after work	150	(46)	141	(41)
Reading	144	(84)	78	(30)
Private hours	159	(96)	210	(120)
Sleeping hours	345	(164)	420	(53)

*Number in parentheses indicates the standard deviation.

CEOs was assumed to be shorter than for their Japanese counterparts. This was based on the general observation that traffic conditions in major metropolitan areas in Japan are worse than that in the United States. The average time spent commuting was 52 minutes for the U.S. CEOs in raw materials processing, 66 minutes for the U.S. CEOs in manufacturing, 84·5 minutes for the Japanese CEOs in raw materials processing and 90 minutes for the Japanese CEOs in the manufacturing sector.

2. *Travelling Between Business Locations*
Travelling time was found to be longest for the U.S. CEOs in manufacturing (108 minutes), followed by Japanese CEOs in raw materials processing (84 minutes), Japanese CEOs in manufacturing (76 minutes), and by U.S. CEOs in raw materials processing (53 minutes).

3. *Business Meetings With Subordinates*
We assumed that Japanese CEOs spend more time in meetings with subordinates than their American counterparts due to their *nemawashi* (a preparatory meeting with people in related fields in order to get a consensus for the final decision). We found, however, that the American CEOs spent as much time as the Japanese CEOs in meetings within the organization: U.S. CEOs in manufacturing = 3·5 hours, Japanese CEOs in manufacturing = 2·5 hours, U.S. CEOs in raw materials processing = 2·9 hours, and Japanese CEOs in raw materials processing = 3 hours.

4. *Meetings Outside the Company*
The Japanese CEOs in the raw materials processing industry spent the longest time (2·6 hours), and U.S. CEOs in manufacturing followed (2·0 hours). Third, Japanese CEOs in manufacturing spent 1·8 hours, and finally U.S. CEOs in raw materials processing spent 1·5 hours.

5. *Meetings with Visitors*
The CEOs in the survey were found to have spent less than 2 hours on an average meeting with visitors: (1) Japanese CEOs in raw materials processing (1·6 hours), (2) U.S. CEOs in manufacturing (1·4 hours), (3) U.S. CEOs in raw materials processing (1·3 hours), and (4) Japanese CEOs in manufacturing (1·2 hours).

6. *Desk Work in Checking and Approving Business Decisions*
Desk work by CEOs business decisions was longest for the U.S. CEOs in raw materials processing (2·6 hours) followed by Japanese CEOs in manufacturing (2·2 hours), Japanese CEOs in raw materials processing (2 hours), and American CEOs in manufacturing (1·7 hours).

7. *Meeting With Guests After Work*
The Japanese CEOs were assumed to spent a greater amount of time than the U.S. CEOs after working hours in maintaining relations with clients and business contacts. We found however, that no significant difference exists, implying that the CEOs in both countries spend between 2 and 3 hours on such contacts: (1) U.S. CEOs in manufacturing (3 hours), (2) Japanese CEOs in raw materials processing (2·3 hours), (3) Japanese CEOs in manufacturing (2·2 hours), and (4) U.S. CEOs in raw materials processing (2 hours).

8. *Reading, Private and Sleeping Hours*
Hours spent on non-business purposes were compared in terms of reading time, private and sleeping hours. Japanese CEOs in general spent less time than their U.S. counterparts in terms of reading: (1) the U.S. CEOs in raw materials processing (3 hours), (2) U.S. CEOs in manufacturing (1·8 hours), (3) Japanese CEOs in raw materials processing (1·5 hours) and (4) Japanese CEOs in manufacturing (1·1 hours).

As for the private hours spent by the CEOs, the Japanese CEOs spent longer (3·5 hours on the average) than their American counterparts (2·65 hours).

The U.S. CEOs slept less than the Japanese group: (1) Japanese CEOs in raw materials processing (7·1 hours), (2) Japanese CEOs in manufacturing (6·9 hours), (3) U.S. CEOs in raw materials processing (6 hours), and U.S. CEOs in manufacturing (5·5 hours).

The Usefulness of the Time Spent

In the questionnaire, questions were directed to the CEOs in order to measure the 'value' of the time they spent for specific purposes. Usefulness was measured from the CEOs' standpoint of utilizing the time for information gathering.

1. Information Gathering at In-house Meetings

The length of in-house business meetings was 15 minutes shorter in Japanese companies, which appears contradictory to the usually observed modes of business meetings in the two countries; the Japanese spending more time in business meetings than the Americans.

The mode of managing the business meeting was found to be different; in the Japanese business meeting, the major part of it was spent in reporting what had been done by individual departments. This reflects the oft cited custom that meetings in Japanese companies are an occasion for reporting, not for the discussion and decision-making. In-house meetings therefore have a nuance of ceremony and formality; the report is often circulated among managers concerned for their comments and advice prior to the business meeting. This enables the participants to know the nature of agenda at the meeting and to make decisions in advance. The function of the in-house business meeting is therefore that of confirmation/approval of proposals made at the meeting, not the discussion of them. It is understandable, from that standpoint, that the time spent for in-house meetings in Japanese companies is shorter than in the United States.

The contents and/or the agenda at the in-house business meetings are also different. Japanese business meetings discussed new product development and new technology, while the American group reportedly discussed the expansion of business; a wider concept than the discussion of new product or technology, the restructuring and/or withdrawal of declining divisions of business, and the market behaviour of the competing firms. Stated another way, American business meetings are concerned more with the strategy of the company, while the Japanese meeting discusses individual products/technology, a component of the overall corporate strategy.

The department(s) from which proposals come were also found to be different. In Japanese companies it was mainly departments such as marketing, production and sales, i.e. those involved in the front line of the business, that take the initiative. It is supporting division(s) such as planning and/or finance that play a key role in business proposals at the American business meeting. The Japanese emphasis in the proposal tends to be on the satisfaction of the consumers' needs by developing new products. In the American meeting it is on financial strategy centred around return of investment.

2. Meetings Outside the Company With Resource People

The CEO often meets people outside the company, seeking any useful information for decision-making. These resource people vary from representatives from other industries forming an informal circle called *Zaikai*, which plays the role of liaison between the government and industry; or politicians, academicians, regional community leaders, clients, and procurement partners. Both Japanese and American CEOs were found to contact frequently with the '*Zaikai*' people, i.e. top executives in the industry, followed by politicians.

To the question of whether they gained useful information from these people, 24 Japanese CEOs out of 28, 16 of 17 American CEOs replied positively.

Bibliography

Books

Y. Aonuma, *Nihon no Keieiso* (Japanese Top Management), Nihon Keizai Shimbun-Sha, Tokyo **6** (1), 22 (1965).

K. Noda, *Nihon no Juyaku* (Japanese Top Management), Diamond-Sha, Tokyo (1968).

A. Okumura, *Nihon no Top Management* (Japanese Top Management), Diamond-Sha, Tokyo (1981).

Edward T. Hall and Mildred R. Hall, *Hidden Differences; Studies in International Communication*, Bungei Shunju, Tokyo (1987).

T. Kono, *Strategy and Structure of Japanese Enterprises*, Macmillan Press, London (1985).

H. Mintzberg, *The Nature of Managerial Work*, Harper & Row, New York (1973).

James Utterback, Environmental analysis and forecasting, in Charles Hofer and Dan Schendel (eds), *Strategic Management: A New View of Business Policy and Planning*, Little, Brown & Co., Boston (1979).

Journals

Basil W. Denning, Strategic environmental appraisal, *Long Range Planning*, **6** (1), 22 (1973).

James L. KcKenny and Peter G. W. Keen, How managers' minds work, *Harvard Business Review*, May–June (1974).

Henry Mintzberg, Planning on the left side and managing on the right, *Harvard Business Review*, July–August (1976).

PART TWO

Planning for Growth

Planning for Growth in a Japanese Business

Yoshio Serizawa

The author describes the transition of Japan Automatic Transmission Company from a small joint Japanese–American venture company to an independent company with engineering and marketing strength. He outlines the development of the corporate motto, philosophy and vision, and the basic management strategies that were developed, and their achievements. He discusses the management planning system, its characteristics and the process of the plan and operating system: the gap between the plan and the actual result in the middle range—and the problems and lessons to be learnt for future development.

Japan Automatic Transmission Co., Ltd. (JATCO) was a small joint venture company initially formed by Ford, Nissan and Mazda, formally called Toyo Kogyo. It had only one type of automatic transmission (AT) to produce for sale to Nissan and Mazda, Japanese car manufacturers. It had no sales or engineering function, but its business had grown gradually with the expansion of the market.

In 1981, following Ford's withdrawal, JATCO became an independent automatic transmission manufacturer, strengthened its engineering capability, and began to develop new products for sale to other car manufacturers. Now, it is a large company with strong engineering and marketing capabilities (see Table 1). Many changes have contributed to JATCO's growth, one of which is the introduction of a management planning and control system which integrates American and Japanese management thinking and practice.

JATCO has implemented this process and has produced remarkable results. In this article, I will try to explain the basic ideas behind this planning system.

Corporate Motto, Philosophy and Vision

Company Motto

Since it was founded, JATCO has had a clear motto which employees adhere to and value highly. That is: 'People, Cleanliness and Quality.'

More specifically, *People* means individual employees and the best is expected from each one of them. *Cleanliness* means keeping clean in everything, and *Quality* means always striving for the highest quality.

Many Japanese companies have mottos of this kind but the JATCO motto: 'Keep clean in everything' is unusual.

This motto has been reiterated and the company has tried to put it into practice. Since 1984, JATCO has established the 'HSQ Programme', which is the company's version of Total Quality Control (TQC). H stands for *Hito* or *Human*, S stands for cleanliness, in Japanese *Seiketsu*, and Q means *Quality*. The whole is a restatement of the company motto.

Business Philosophy

JATCO's business philosophy is expressed in the following terms.

Customers first. The customer is king. We should serve the king, even if we sometimes have to put customers before company rules or orders. This is necessary and also extremely important. Where an employee has to do this, he should explain the situation and the reasons to his manager for approval afterwards. Also, he must be able to recognize the customer's point of view.

Exchange is preferred to secrecy: co-operation to competition. In an engineering-oriented company like JATCO, it is important to let its customers know

The author is President and Chief Executive Officer of Japan Automatic Transmission Company Ltd.

Table 1. A brief sketch of JATCO

1970. Founded by Ford (50%), Nissan (25%) and Mazda (25%). Technical assistance agreement was executed with Ford, on which royalty was paid to Ford.

1981. Ford sold all of its shares to Nissan and Mazda. New shareholding ratio: Nissan (65%), Mazda (35%).

1984. TQC (Total Quality Control) was introduced under the title of 'HSQ Movement'. Middle range management planning was formally introduced.

Currently, customers are Nissan, Mazda, Isuzu, Fuji Heavy, Mitsubishi, Suzuki and Nissan Diesel. Also JATCO transmissions are sold indirectly to General Motors, Ford and Chrysler.

Total sales volume for 1988 was approximately 800,000 units; cumulatively 8 million units.

Sales value for 1988 was approximately ¥90bn ($720m). Past sales records are as follows.

(Exchange rate: $ = ¥125)

1971	¥8.9bn	($70m)
1975	¥16.0bn	($130m)
1980	¥35.3bn	($280m)
1985	¥62.6bn	($500m)

Total workforce is 1800.

Note: There are only two independent automatic transmission manufacturers (Aisin AW and JATCO) in Japan, one (ZF) in West Germany, one (BEAL) in Australia, and none in the United States. Many car manufacturers make their own automatic transmissions in-house. The market is highly competitive, and production requires high engineering and productivity levels.

---

about its engineering superiority, and to maintain this engineering superiority, management have to get information from many sources. They must keep their minds open not only to their customers but also to their competitors. To JATCO, even its parent companies are competitors. They also compete with one another. To get good information from other companies it is also necessary to give good information yourself.

Therefore, it is a basic company policy to keep our doors open to car manufacturers as well as to our competitors and try to go ahead of them by more intensive effort. While we compete with them, we also seek mutual co-operation. However, we have no interest whatsoever in dealing with companies which try to take advantage of our open door policy.

The Corporate Vision
In 1981 JATCO established a corporate vision, which was expressed in the following terms: 'On the foot of graceful Mount Fuji, we will build a large supply base of automatic transmissions for the whole world.'

Later in 1985, another element of the corporate vision was established. 'There is a large world market for automatic transmissions. Through creating new markets and developing attractive products, we will try to expand, while maintaining control and meeting customers' expectations.' These two visions clearly show the direction in which we, in JATCO management, are intending to go. We aim to involve all our employees through various activities and their achievement.

Basic Management Strategies and Their Achievement

On the basis of the motto, philosophy and vision, basic strategies have been planned, on which more specific strategies and tactics have been developed in the medium range plan and we have recently begun to see some results.

Giving the Highest Priority to Product Development
In order to survive as an independent automatic transmission manufacturer, we must introduce new, unique and superior products ahead of our competitors which will meet the customers' requirements and expectations. To meet this objective we have established the strongest possible R & D group, which will also help to foster innovation in other parts of the company.

In 1983, we strengthened the R & D group. Product engineering staff expanded ten-fold from 30 in 1983 to over 300 in 1988 and Engineering expenditure as a percentage of total sales value was increased four-fold from 1 to 4 per cent. In the company's first 10 years, we made only one type of automatic transmission. Since 1980, this transmission has been completely renewed, and *seven* new types of transmissions have been introduced. They offer customers a wider choice. Increases in the number of customers and in the range of cars and engines have required us to have larger product lines. We aim to become a 'department store' for automatic transmissions, offering a wide assortment.

Putting the Customer First: Improving Customer Service
Since the company's foundation the number of

customers has increased from three to seven. In order to meet our customers' needs, we have upgraded our level of sales and service. We are also striving to meet our customers' most demanding quality requirements with regard to noise, shock and gear-shift point.

Exchange is Preferred to Secrecy: Co-operation to Competition
It is our policy to have frank discussions and to exchange visits with a variety of companies. We have lived up to this policy. We are now recognized as an open-minded company, and we have established relationships with a number of competing car manufacturers. This will help us to build joint ventures with overseas partners, to make our transmissions available to each other and to establish standards which will prove mutually beneficial.

The Logic of Expansion
When the world market is expanding, we must expand the business. When the company stands still we lose business opportunities. We lose market share and we miss a chance for further expansion.

These basic strategies have helped us to achieve a rapid increase in sales, which have nearly doubled over the past 5 to 6 years. This sales growth has exceeded the sales value projected in the middle range management plan (see Figure 3).

Our investment in increasing capacity was not limited to R & D and sales and marketing but extended also to production engineering, corporate planning, cost management and the project promotion function. The staff of these activities are held accountable for making specific expansion programmes in line with the middle and long range perspective. As a part of these expansion programs, some overseas projects are now being developed.

The Origins of the Management Planning System

Management planning at JATCO has been largely influenced by three factors: the management practice of Ford U.S.A., Nissan Motor of Japan and TQC (Total Quality Control).

JATCO has adopted part of the Ford management system. One of the key tools that featured JATCO management while Ford was a shareholder was its budgetary control system. A detailed budget plan has since been made every half a year with the participation of virtually all departments. This budget includes both a capital and an expense budget, on the basis of which the cost of each product is calculated. Added to this is a profit element to be included before arriving at the sales prices. We at JATCO also had to co-operate with Ford in making their own 5-year plan, which was

reviewed and revised every year based on certain assumptions. This included various corporate strategies.

JATCO's system includes some features of Nissan Motor's middle range management plan. Nissan, currently our major parent company, introduced a plan requiring all of its subsidiaries, JATCO included, to develop a 3-year business plan every year. On the basis of Nissan's plan, JATCO also develops and presents, like other Nissan's subsidiaries, its own plan, incorporating its own corporate strategies and taking into account Nissan's basic policies.

JATCO's system features policies which are a central factor of the Japanese-style TQC programme. In 1984, JATCO started a TQC programme under the banner of the HSQ initiative, which was linked to the middle and long range management plan as an important company policy.

The Characteristics of the Planning Process

This section describes the long and middle range management plan, the annual business plan and the semi-annual budget.

(A) *The Long and Middle Range Management Plan*
The long range plan covers 5 years. The middle range plan is a rolling plan covering a 3-year period, to be reviewed and revised every year in a 5-year long range perspective.

In the light of the survey of the market environment and the trends in other competitive companies and their products, demand forecasts are reviewed and revised annually. Top priority is given to new product development above all others. In view of the overall management objectives, specific goals are established in each field of management. A variety of specific management objectives are established in a co-ordinated manner. Middle range corporate policies and functional* policies and policy measures are established.

Reflecting various opportunities and threats, a market forecast is made on three levels (A, B and C) as a basis for planning. On the basis of this market forecast, manpower costs, capital investments and other expenditures are calculated. Then a financial calculation is made and the profit position is established. This process is repeated until all the necessary revisions are made and the overall picture looks good.

Later the annual business plan and budget is produced for the first year of the 3-year period, and the first year portion of the middle range plan is

Note: 'Functional' means lateral or interdepartmental items such as quality assurance, cost reduction, office automation etc.

revised to incorporate any changes. At the same time, revisions are made to the second and third year sections of the plan.

If any further changes take place as a result of strategic decision-making, the plan is revised again, and when the middle range management plan is made for the next year, we make sure that the results of our discussions are reflected there too. These processes are built into the annual business schedule and are carried out systematically. Figure 1 shows the annual planning timetable.

(B) *The Annual Business Plan*
Considering the business situation where the company finds itself each year, the president spells out policies, which consist of three to four items, to be undertaken for the coming year.

In response to the presidential policies and the middle range management plan, specific functional* policies and policy measures, each department manager establishes his own departmental policies and plans. Then in response to this, each section manager, each general foreman and each foreman do the same. The tasks to be covered by these annual business plans usually cover three to five items and they are important enough to require changes in the office or factory system.

The President and other top executives review these individual policies and plans. They also review the ongoing process and the results of these plans. The process of reviewing is called 'top management diagnosis'. The annual business plan is then linked with the annual budget.

(C) *Budgetary Control*
Budgetary control has been a basis of management since JATCO's incorporation. At the start, top management and the accounting staff review the general market trends and draft policies for the short term (6 to 12 months), following the same procedures as are used in constructing the middle range plan. Incorporated into the budget are departmental business policies and plans for the same period.

Two to three months before a new fiscal period starts, we obtain from our major customers a forecast of purchases of automatic transmissions for the following 6 months. We then produce our own sales forecast, to determine the sales volume during the budget period.

Then top management and the accounting staff establish the budget guideline for each item and try their best to induce the operating management to live within their guidelines. The budget plan presented by each department manager is then carefully reviewed, department by department, before top management give their final approval.

The budgeting system whereby sales prices to parent companies and other customers are developed by adding a level of profit to the total costs has undergone considerable changes in recent years. The fact that we have requests coming from customers for more stringent cost reductions than were budgeted and increases in the number of new products with their target price predetermined, has radically altered the original concept and practice. The budget naturally has to incorporate ambitious programmes for cost reduction.

The budget is prepared for two 6-month periods; one for the first 6-month period is firm and put into execution accordingly, and the one for the following 6-month period remains tentative, serving as a guideline. On the basis of this annual budget, revisions are usually made to the first year of the middle range plan. However, the recent change in exchange rates, with their adverse effects on exports and the sharp rise in domestic demand due to the buoyant economy have made it necessary to review the budget again during the course of a 6-month budget in order to cope with new changes.

Total Management Planning System

The plans, which are correlated and put together, are then distributed as the management's plan and control system (See Figure 2).

The matters to be taken into account in operating this system are described below.

☆ It is essential to have a clear management philosophy, vision and strategy.

☆ A middle range management plan has 'functional' policies which integrate activities across the organization.

☆ A middle range management plan includes a process for reviewing the financial position of the company.

☆ The annual policies of each department must be clearly defined.

☆ The annual budget is incorporated into the first year of the middle range management plan.

☆ There is a feedback circuit in every plan.

☆ For successful implementation, the total Management Planning and Control System needs to be integrated across departments.

The Operating System

At the outset, the accounting group was held responsible for putting together the middle range management plan budget and for its control. Later, the Corporate Planning Office and Project Promotion Office were established. Overall responsibility

---

*Note: 'functional' means inter-departmental, or company-wide.

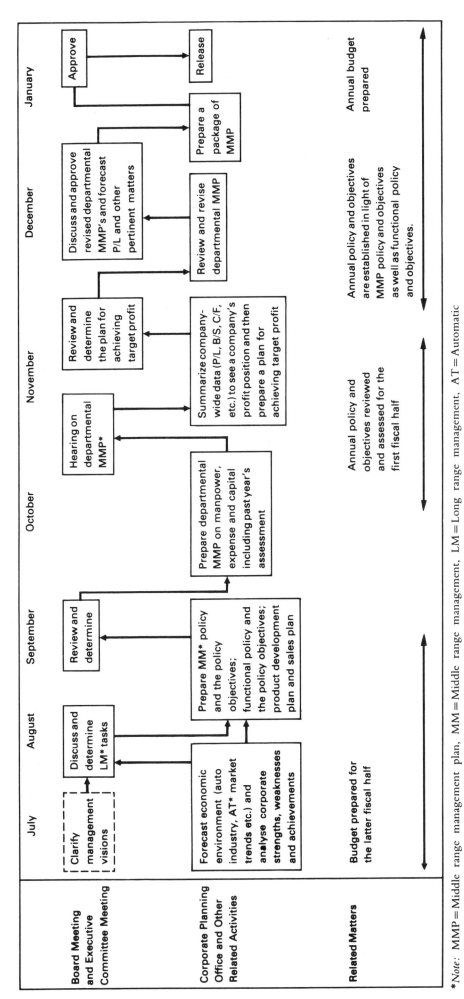

Figure 1. The process of long and middle range management planning

Note: MMP = Middle range management plan, MM = Middle range management, LM = Long range management, AT = Automatic transmissions.

Term	All-Time	Long Range Plan	Middle Range Plan	Annual Plan	Semi-annual Plan
		5 Years and Above	3 Years	1 Year	6 Months
Working Period		July–October	Preliminary October–January Finalized in March	January–April	January–March July–September

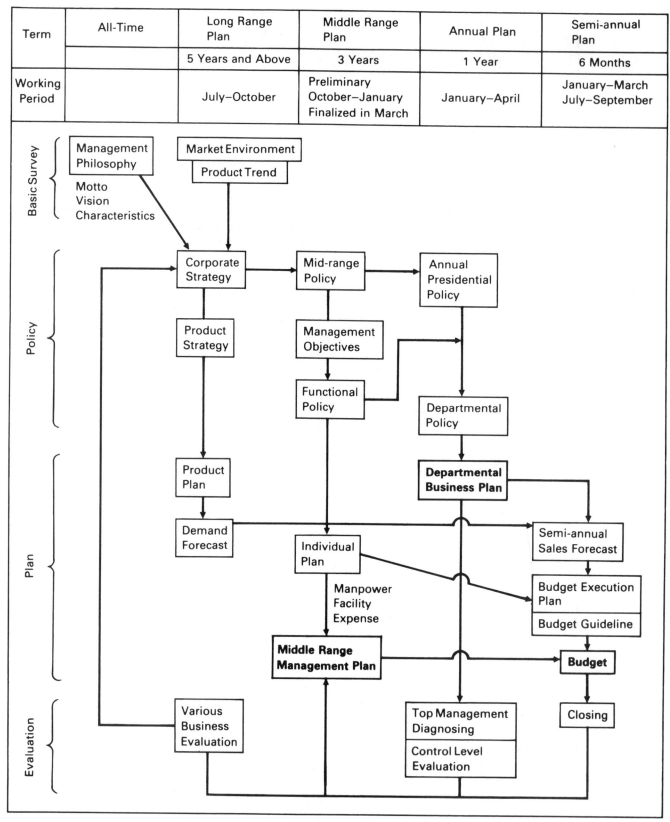

Figure 2. The management planning system

is vested with the Corporate Planning Office for completing the package. The planning, execution and assessment of the policies in the annual business plans are organized by the Project Promotion Office. The Project Promotion Office is a unique organizational arm, which together with the Management Information Systems Department, belongs to the Management Systems Innovation Group, and which is responsible not only for developing management systems by such means as promoting Total Quality Control, Total Preventive Maintenance, Management by Policy, and Top Management Diagnosis, but also for promoting such projects as will put new products into production and sales.

The Corporate Management Office has only four staff members and the Project Promotion Office has seven, all competent staff at managerial level. They handle such projects as will require company-wide execution. Other departments also participate in the planning as their duties dictate.

The Gap Between Plans and Actual Results in the Middle Range Management Plan

We have so far implemented middle range management plans several times (see Figure 3) and an analysis of the actual results compared with the plans shows the following trends.

In terms of sales volume, the actual number of units sold was considerably higher than the Plan B in each business term. The volumes were also sometimes higher than Plan A's which are intended to represent our optimistic view of the market. The reasons for this variation are that the forecast was not sufficiently accurate. It was too cautious. Also our aggressive management attitude and the new products helped to increase the sales of automatic transmissions. In other planned items such as sales value, profit before tax, capital investment and manpower, there was a similar trend, though the gap is not so noticeable.

Figure 3 shows the plan and actual results in sales value, which shows how unpredictible business is in a period of growth.

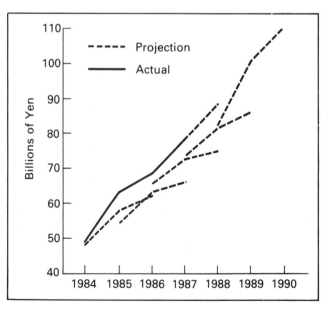

Figure 3. Transition of sales value (projection vs actual)

The actual results of the second and third years have also deviated from the plan, on average the results were fairly close to the forecast. Although the timing may have varied, the plans have been put into effect.

Conclusions

The lessons we have learned from our experiences in improving our middle range management plans are discussed below.

It is necessary to shorten the time taken in planning. In particular we must have an up-to-date demand forecast, and the first year of a middle range management plan should be the same as the annual forecast which is to be developed later.

Computers should be used to standardize processes, shorten the time taken and provide a more sophisticated analysis. Also, a feedback system should be created so that counteractions are taken quickly to deal with any significant changes in the business environment, such as a change in exchange rates.

Discussions and surveys are essential, especially to reflect on past experience and to review the strategy. It is also indispensable to have a follow-up or feedback system and make it work every year.

More market information is needed. Much improvement has been made in this area but we need still better information.

The concept of middle range management planning needs to permeate around the company. It is essential to have policies and directions commonly shared by all the people within the company.

It is necessary to strengthen the organization and staff for middle and long range management planning.

This article has described in outline the management planning system of JATCO. Any comment you may have to improve upon our system is most welcome and appreciated.

Acknowledgement—In closing, I wish to express my sincere thanks to Professor Kono of Gakushuin University for his recommendations and valuable advice.

Taisei Corporation Plans for the Year 2000

Hisao Okuzumi

The escalating competition in the construction industry in Japan has necessitated reorganization within the industry and Taisei Corporation has prepared a long range planning system framed around a vision of the business in the year 2000. Strategies were considered and a company-wide 5-year plan drafted. The strategy implementation was through Division 5-year plans in conjunction with a management plan structure. The effects of the long-range plan are discussed and the problems in promoting the strategy.

(1) The Japanese Construction Industry: Escalating Competition

The Japanese construction market accounts for between 15 and 20 per cent of the nation's gross national product. Due to increased domestic demand, construction investment in 1988 amounted to ¥67tn, equivalent to 18 per cent of the GNP. This massive market is currently supplied by approximately 510,000 construction companies who employ more than 5 million workers. With annual sales of over ¥1tn, Taisei Corporation ranks as one of the leading companies in the Japanese construction industry, although it accounts for only 2·3 per cent of investment in this sector. Japan's current business conditions are characterized by escalating competition, which has led to pressure for the industry's reorganization, especially now, as the construction industry nears full maturity.

(2) Taisei Corporation Organization Chart

The outline of Taisei Corporation is shown in Figure 1. The head office is comprised of functional departments, while the branches and business divisions assume the role of profit centres. Within

Established	1873
Product Mix	Construction and Civil Engineering Housing Development Consulting Construction Machinery and Materials Land, Marine and Air Transportation Building Maintenance and Management Facility Ownership and Management Information Processing Financial Services
Sales	1,270 Billion Yen
Current Profit	42 Billion Yen
Employees	11,400
Operational Units	12
Affiliated Companies	72

Figure 1. Taisei corporation profile (1988)

the head office, the Business Planning and Administration Division, Subsidiaries and Affiliates Division, and Technology Division act as the strategy group. The Marketing and Sales Division, Urban and Regional Development Division, Engineering Division, and Design and Proposal Division function within the Integrated Marketing and Sales Group. The Building Construction Division, Civil Engineering Division, Safety Administration and Machinery Division, and International Division provide support and guidance for the profit centres. In this way, through co-operation between the function-focused head office and business-focused branches and business headquarters, the promotion of management strategy and other objectives is handled primarily through project teams, with the

The author is Manager of the Corporate Planning Department at Taisei Corporation in Tokyo.

39

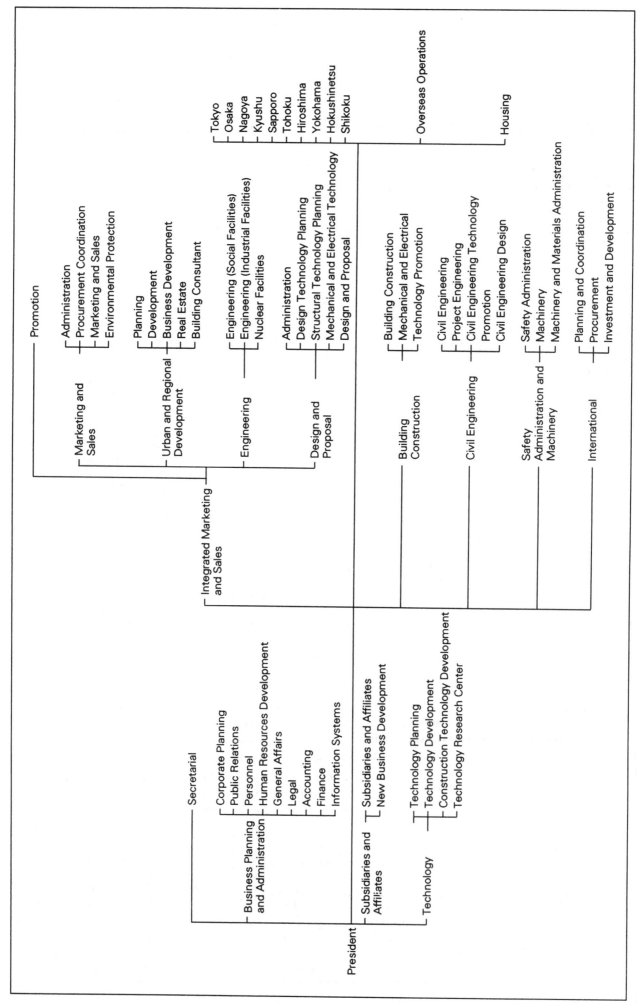

Figure 2. Taisei corporation organization chart (1989)

various functional organizations providing significant co-operation in advancing these efforts.

(3) Changes in the Taisei Long Range Planning System

Prior to 1980, Taisei Corporation planning was implemented through a short-term approach, with the emphasis placed on financial goals.

The Company's first 5-year management plan, which aimed at corporate structure reform, was launched in 1981. Under this plan, a system was introduced in which top management provided policy guidelines, with the various divisions working from this base to plan and implement their own independent strategies. This method failed to generate innovative strategy, and because it was updated every year, revisions of the goals made it difficult to evaluate the performance of individual departments.

After considering the results of the first 5-year plan, the second 5-year plan was drafted in 1985. This second plan clarified the Taisei long-term management vision, and allotted strategic issues to the various organizational functions, which were given responsibility for coordinating the company-wide strategy. Revisions were to be made every 3 years.

The third 5-year plan was introduced while the second plan was still in force, but due to radical market changes it was revised in 1989.

The distinguishing characteristics of the current 5-year management plan are:

(1) expression of the Company's future strategy, clarifying the direction of the 5-year management plan, and drafting a 'Year 2000 Corporate Vision';

(2) setting out the contents of the 5-year management plan through the various strategic business units. Each of the individual unit plans is supported by the management resource strategy, which also serves to clarify each unit's objectives;

(3) clarifying the corporate strategic issues, defining the approaches for the issues, and assigning the implementation procedures to the management divisions as the projects;

(4) specifying the strategy planning and administration format, to realize the optimum strategy implementation plans at each division; and

(5) encouraging the development of special strategic issues (other than designated issues) by individual divisions, thereby heightening the sense of participation in management planning.

(4) Vision of Taisei Corporation in Year 2000

The Taisei management vision has been expressed as: 'An international corporate group, focused on the construction industry and the pursuit of all areas with potential to strengthen the group.' To embody this vision in more concrete form, the Business Planning and Administration Division has drawn up 'The Optimum Stance of Taisei in the Year 2000'. This report specifically focuses on the discovery of 'strategic issues'.

The process of formulating the parameters of this corporate stance is based on:

(1) international relations and economic forecasts;

(2) domestic environment and economic forecasts;

(3) domestic industrial structure and industrial relations;

(4) national lifestyle and values;

(5) status of the construction industry and other

- 1980	Short to Medium Term Plan, Focused on Numerical Goals and Performance
1981-1985	Clarification of Management Ideology, Strategy Development in All Divisions. Too Comprehensive
1986-1988	Expression of Management Vision, Company-Wide Strategy Coordination. Clear Assignment to Departments Responsible for Implementation
1989-	Formulation of Year 2000 Corporate Image, Establishment of Strategic Business Divisions, Project Emphasis.

Figure 3. Strategy management change in stages

materials. Simulation projecting the Taisei environment in Year 2000 was conducted, utilizing both optimistic and pessimistic values.

Next, a scenario was prepared to define the corporate mission within the social environment of the Year 2000, the type of business fields in which the Company should advance, and the optimum management resources and corporate climate at that time. The top management was then asked to choose from the various alternatives presented, from which a final plan was drawn up.

The 'Optimum Stance of Taisei in Year 2000' may be summarized as follows:

(1) strength in the construction industry together with expansion into peripheral industries, and attaining a business scale characterized by an annual turnover of ¥2tn and operating profits of ¥250bn;

(2) positive advances as a social developer both at home and abroad, while functioning in a knowledge-intensive industry, with a focus on engineering and the capability to generate high added value;

(3) development of personnel with a broad range of expertise, who work together to create an innovative and active corporate climate in which entrepreneurial spirit may be manifested;

(4) group integration, to heighten overall strength; and

(5) expanded profit returns to stockholders and employees.

(5) Discovering Strategies

The company-wide 5-year plan based on the 'Year 2000 Corporate Image' functions as a 'bible' for the strategies which should be promoted on a company-wide basis. Therefore, a broad range of

analysis must be used as the foundation for selecting the optimum strategic issues. Figure 4 illustrates the process extending through the strategy proposal, as well as the principal methods of analysis.

(1) *Forecasting the External Environment*
The goal here is to abstract the primary factors of social trends prone to occur in the near future, and forecast the impact of these social trends on industrial trends. Also included is the use of brainstorming and other methods utilized to analyse the impact that social trends will have on the Company's business.

After this, the trends and management policies of competing companies are researched, in order to forecast trends with a high degree of impact on Taisei management. The Company's current status and policies are compared to the primary trends of competitors, with analysis conducted to determine if these trends constitute opportunities or threats. These opportunities and threats are then prioritized according to their impact on the Company.

The impact factors on the Company from the social environment and the impact factors abstracted from the competitive analysis are categorized as being either opportunities or threats. Next, brainstorming and other means are used to study the probability that such elements will occur, with this probability then positioned on a graph as shown in Figure 7. Importance is placed on intensive study of whether these factors constitute opportunities or threats to the Company, as well as the interpretation of the occurrence rate. The factors positioned on the upper and lower right side of this graph are regarded as areas important to the Company, and serve as a data source in determining the direction of the 5-year management plan.

(2) *Recognizing the Company's Abilities*
Taisei business performance trends are categorized by field, region and product, with a portfolio

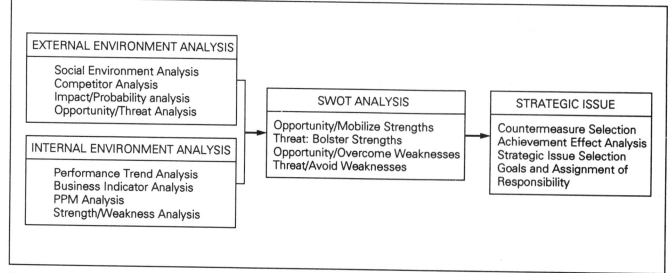

Figure 4. Discovering strategic issues

SOCIAL TRENDS	INDUSTRIAL STRUCTURE	TAISEI BUSINESS
Globalization	Increase of Foreign Investments	Response to Globalization Business Linked with Superior Companies Building Facilities for International Exchange Establishing Intellectual Property Rights

Figure 5. Forecasting the external environment

Competitive Trends	Taisei Trends	Importance
Company A Entrance into Housing and Land Development	Accumulation of Land Development Know-How	◎
Company B Introduction of Flex Time	Trial Stage at Technical Research Center	○

Figure 6. Competitive analysis

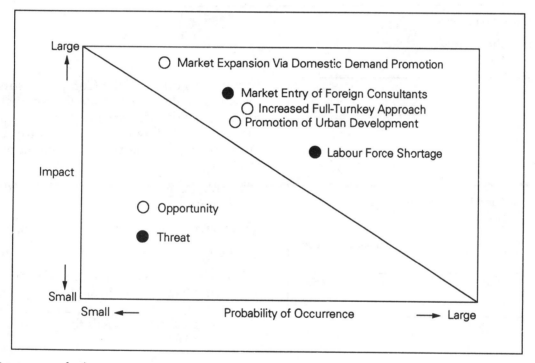

Figure 7. Impact analysis

approach used to analyse growth and profitability in each sector. Portfolio analysis uses the market growth rate and share ratio with competing companies to determine the Company's position in the industry (Figure 8). Comparisons are also run through combining the mutual growth and profitability of in-house business. It is important to gain a clear understanding of which fields are strong and which are problematic.

Along with analysis of the Company's positioning, it is important to conduct an extensive range of efficiency analysis to recognize the Company's strengths. In addition to increasing production and earning efficiency, the changes in the Profit & Loss and Balance Sheet indexes are graphed to clearly grasp any trends. It is important to compare the results of this analysis with competing companies, in order to recognize the Company's strengths and weaknesses.

The Company's strengths and weaknesses abstracted from the positioning and potential analysis are then analysed to find the underlying causes. It is important to obtain an accurate grasp of whether the underlying causes of the Company's strengths and weakness lie in people, commodities, money, technology, information or other management resources, or, in the organization, system or other operational areas.

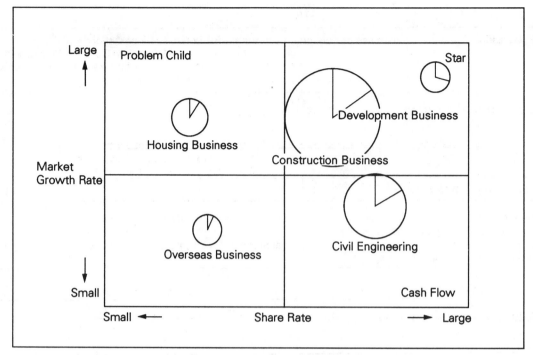

Note: Triangle Shows Market Share.

Figure 8. Portfolio analysis

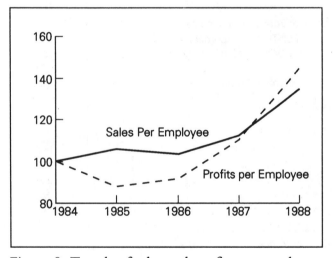

Figure 9. Trends of sales and profits per employee

(3) *Discovering Strategic Issues*
The opportunities and threats to the Company obtained from the external environment analysis and the real causes of the Company's strengths and weaknesses abstracted from the internal environment analysis are arranged on a cross chart (Figure 11). Following this, the proper countermeasures for Taisei are studied from the perspectives of:

(1) mobilizing strengths to take advantage of opportunity;

(2) overcoming weaknesses to seize opportunity;

(3) bolstering strengths to withstand threat; and

(4) avoiding weaknesses in case of threat. Arrangement is performed through the KJ method* and other approaches. These analyses become the strategic issue proposals for the 5-year management plan.

---

*The KJ method is a problem arrangement method developed by Jiro Kawakita. The approach is characterized by the use of group discussions as the base for reaching solutions.

	Management Resources	Organizational System
Strengths	High Social Credibility Large Assets	Highly Functional Departments Excellent Training Systems
Weaknesses	Incomplete Software Technology Management Capabilities of Affiliated Companies	Inadequate Organizational Teamwork Incomplete Long-Term Recruiting Plan

Figure 10. Strength/Weakness analysis

Expanded Domestic Demand Industrial Reorganization Urbanization	Opportunity	Threat	Diversifying Construction Demand Market Entry by Overseas Companies Increased Construction Labour Costs
	Strengths	Weaknesses	
Excellent Performance in All Construction Fields Extensive Technology Outstanding Problem-Solving Skills			Emphasis on Short-Term Profit Promotion of In-House Development Mutual Cooperation Within Group

Figure 11. SWOT analysis

	Opportunity	Threat
Strength	Metropolitan Zone Market Share Expansion	Full Manifestation of Organization's Strength
Weakness	Expanding Joint Ventures With Other Industries	Enhancement of Discriminating Technology Enhancement of Marketing Function

Figure 12. Countermeasure selection

(4) *Determining Strategic Issues*

Each of the strategic issue proposals abstracted from the cross chart analysis is analysed both for effects at the time of achievement and potential for achievement, with each issue then positioned on the graph. As a result of these studies, the strategic issues which are positioned at the upper right of the screen will constitute the areas which must be developed as the 5-year management plan.

(5) *Strategic Issue Systemization*

The strategic issues selected from the effect and possibility analysis are strategies which should be promoted by the Company. The strategies selected are regrouped, further subdivided, and systemized by business domain and goal using the 'objective →goal' sequence. Then the goals are set, and the divisions responsible for each strategy are determined. The strategy system chart which has been prepared is studied again, followed by final coordination of the strategy development balance, the soundness of the goals, and the appropriateness of the implementation division, with the strategies then determined.

(6) *Setting Performance Goals*

The setting of performance goals involves analysis of past performance figures, future market forecasts, and effects of the strategies selected. At this stage, a company-wide Profit & Loss and Balance Sheet simulation is conducted, with an appropriate ratio established for each strategic business unit. The

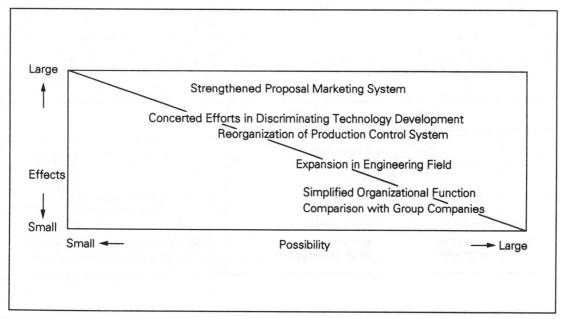

Figure 13. Effect and possibility analysis

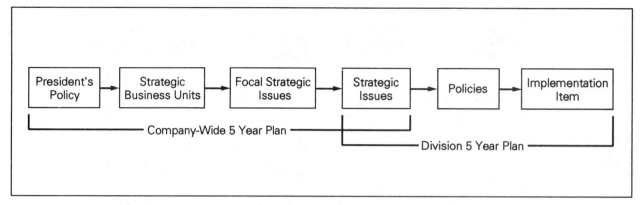

Figure 14. Strategic issue analysis

performance goals do not use real figures, but rather rates—such as growth rate, profit rate, productivity and other fiscal year growth rates. This is to avoid excessive involvement in numerical targets and volume.

(7) *Drafting a Company-Wide 5-Year Plan*
Based on the results of the various types of analysis and studies performed, the Corporate Planning Department plays the focal role in drawing up a medium-term management plan to serve as the company-wide 5-year plan.

The plan consists of the following elements:

(1) the Year 2000 Corporate Vision as a long-term vision;

(2) the President's management policy on the improvement of the principal Taisei sectors, expanding the business domain, strengthening the management resource structure, the com-

pany-wide management scenario and the strategy system chart;

(3) the basic scenario, performance targets, strategic system and issues for each strategic business unit;

(4) management resource strengthening strategy to promote business strategy; and

(5) company-wide performance goals.

The strategic business units are comprised of the six fields of civil engineering, construction, housing, development, international business, and new business. The planning of the management resource strategy is carried out by the staff organization. Each strategic issue is assigned to divisions. A large number of project issues are planned for inter-organization co-operation through project teams.

The major strategies are as follows:

(1) In Taisei's principal sector, the goal is to enhance non-price competitiveness through the strengthening of the commercialization proposal function. Under this method, first in the civil engineering sector the BOT (building operation and transfer) method will be developed to expand the market. Next, in the construction sector the main strategies will consist of product development promotion for the purpose of commercialization proposals and the introduction of TASCOM (Taisei Systematic Controlling Method for Building Construction) to innovate the production control system.

(2) Regarding expansion of the business realm, the Company's development business will be aggressively developed in the areas of housing, international and new business divisions, with a strategy focused on the creation of synergetic effects between the various divisions.

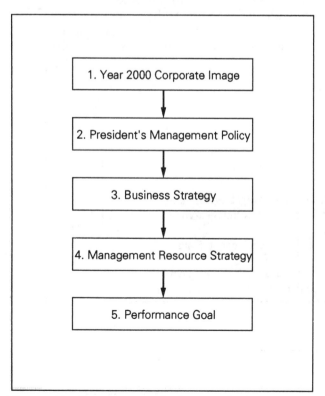

Figure 15. Company-wide 5-year plan

(3) Regarding the strengthening of Taisei's management resources, the main strategies are to innovate the personnel systems in order to activate Taisei employees, and heighten the Company's corporate image. These focal strategic issues are broken down into strategic issues,

with implementation carried out by project teams and functional divisions.

(7) Strategy Implementation Through Division 5-Year Plans

The division 5-year plans are proposed on the basis of the strategic issues designated to the various divisions in the company-wide 5-year plan, as well as the specific strategic issues developed by each division. These plans correspond to the implementation plan for the company-wide 5-year plan, and generally consist of:

(1) the division chief's management policy, as expressed in the division's management policy (and based on the company-wide 5-year plan);

(2) the implementation plan for the designated strategic issues and division strategic issues; and

(3) the implementation plan which breaks down the promotion of strategic issues into fiscal-year plans. These division 5-year plans are edited both by division and by business strategy according to the specific strategic issues, in order to maintain a balance in the promotion of the company-wide strategy.

Division strategy plans are developed for each strategic issue, from policy formulation through fiscal-year implementation. The 'goal→means' form is used, adopting a system in which the implementation item is developed within the business operations (Figure 14). All strategic issues, policies and implementation items are clarified in

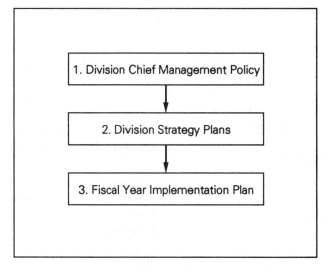

Figure 16. Division 5-year plan

terms of the '4 W's and 1 H' (what, where, who, when and how), with care taken to ensure that the strategic administration loop of 'plan→do→check →action' is carried out clearly.

The division 5-year plans are drawn up by the 14 divisions and 10 operation units, and it is vital for the strategies proposed by each division to maintain uniform content. To ensure this, the division chief policy, strategy plan, and implementation plan formats are standardized, to prevent discrepancies in the various division strategies. In addition, each strategic issue is given a strategic business unit code, to facilitate more effective consolidation. As a point of reference, the strategy planning sheet format is presented in Figure 17.

Category	Key Strategies				Fiscal Year Goals	
	Strategic Issues				Final Goals	
Policy Name	Category	Achievement Goal	Implementation Manager		Process Plan	
Follow-Up						

Figure 17. Strategy planning sheet

(8) Promotion of the Management Plan

(1) *The Role of the Corporate Planning Department*
Promotion and following of the management plan is the duty of the Corporate Planning Department. This department must co-ordinate each division and help them achieve their goals. The Corporate Planning Department consists of the following four sections:

(1) the Planning and Research Section, which analyses the internal and external environments, and researches and analyses the impact factors on the Company's management;

(2) the Project Teams, which promote and help implement the medium-term plans, as well as working to improve organizational function and other aspects of Taisei management resources;

(3) the Auditing Section, which conducts business inspections of the Company and its affiliates, analysing management problems; and

(4) the MTG Section Department, which mobilizes Quality Control methods to provide guidance for problem-solving skills in daily operations.

As noted above, the Corporate Planning Department functions to coordinate and promote all aspects of management planning, and is comprised of 30 staff members who are fully acquainted with all business and functional divisions.

(2) *Autonomous Administration of Division Strategy*
As noted above, the division 5-year plans are comprised of the division chief management policies, strategy plans for each strategic issue, and the fiscal-year implementation plans, with each of these plans administrated at the working level. For the fiscal-year implementation plans, the policy implementation manager (department manager) conducts regular inspections four times a year, checking on the progress of the plan and issuing directions and orders to the manager in charge of implementation (section manager). For the strategic plans, the division managers call for implementation managers (department managers) twice a year, to inspect the progress of strategic issues promotion and give directions and orders. The Corporate Planning Department joins the biannual division chief inspections, thus being kept informed of the strategy promotion status of each division. In other words, a system is adopted in which top-down planning is applied to the 5-year management plan, while administration is bottom-up in structure. This planning model is presented in Figure 19.

(3) *Top Management Administers Company-Wide Strategy*
The Corporate Planning Department checks on the progress of the division strategies and projects, to verify their conformity as business strategies, to see whether the links between the divisions are being managed smoothly, and whether the original goals are attained. The evaluation results are channelled back to the divisions in question, and are also used as reference for the President's inspection.

For the company-wide strategy, the President inspects all of the divisions once a year, and receives strategy progress reports from the various division managers. The President then issues directions and orders, indicating items considered important in terms of the business strategy. The Corporate Planning Department also joins the President's inspection, to verify that the President's specific directions and orders are reflected in the next fiscal year's division strategy plans.

(9) Management Plan Structure

The items contained in the Taisei Corporation 5-year management plan described above are shown in Figure 20.

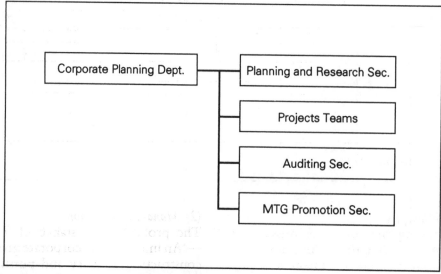

Figure 18. Organization of corporate planning department

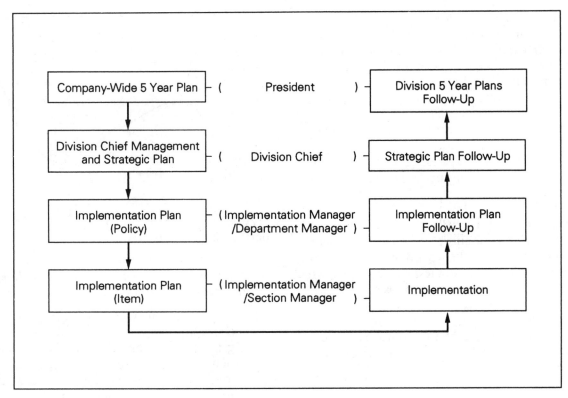

Figure 19. Strategic promotion loop

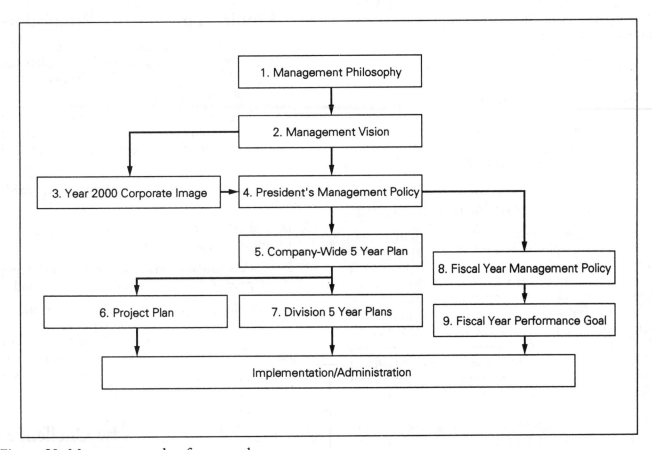

Figure 20. Management plan framework

(1) *Management Philosophy*
An ideology expressing the corporate mission of Taisei Corporation—'Pooling the essence of knowledge and technology, to build an affluent environment through the pursuit of top-flight quality.'

(2) *Management Vision*
The proper future stance of Taisei Corporation —'An international corporate group, focused on the construction industry and pursuing all areas with potential.'

(3) *Year 2000 Corporate Image*
A manifestation of the Company's management vision—clearly defining the social mission, business scale, management resources and other aspects of Taisei Corporation *vis-à-vis* Year 2000.

(4) *President's Management Policy*
The President's 5-year management policy targeting the management vision—'Strengthening the Principal Sector', 'Expanding the Business Domain', and 'Strengthening Management Resources'.

(5) *Company-Wide 5-Year Plan*
A strategy plan (document) based on the President's policy, determining the product-market and management resource strategies, and clarifying the strategy promotion role of each division.

(6) *Project Plan*
One of the components of the company-wide 5-year plan, which requires co-operation of many departments.

(7) *Division 5-Year Plans*
The implementation plans for the company-wide 5-year plan, comprised of the 'Division Chief Management Plan', 'Strategy Plan', and 'Fiscal Year Implementation Plan'.

(8) *Fiscal Year Management Policy*
The President's fiscal year management policy, based on the company-wide 5-year plan.

(9) *Fiscal Year Performance Goal*
The performance goal for each fiscal year, based on the President's fiscal year management policy.

(10) Effects of Long Range Planning

Launched in 1980, the first 5-year management plan changed the corporate culture. It also attempted to introduce cost reduction. However, the Company gradually turned toward an emphasis on sales, and experienced lower earnings. This situation was tackled by drafting the second 5-year management plan, which placed its focus on corporate structure. Under this plan, both sales and profit goals were achieved in 3 years. The third 5-year plan aims at further reform in corporate structure. Current efforts strive for the development of a new strategy.

The effects of strategic planning are broadly categorized into two types: those which can be evaluated quantitatively, and those which can be evaluated qualitatively. In advancing structural change in a company, it is vital to achieve proper evaluation of the qualitative effects. The qualitative evaluations of the second 5-year management plan launched in 1985 are:

(1) clarification of the roles and necessary functions of each organization;

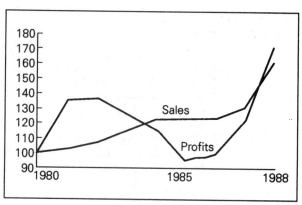

Figure 21. Step 1. Profit performance. Progressive performance index trend

(2) the enhancement of a company-wide strategic mentality and strategic skills;

(3) a shift from hardware technology to software technology, with improvements in latent earning power. In short, the foundation was established from which to launch the transition to a knowledge-intensive industry advocated by the third 5-year management plan.

(11) Problems in Strategy Promotion

Nevertheless, in the promotion of strategic management it is rare to have all factors go as planned. Several problems have merged at Taisei. These problem areas are as follows:

(1) difficulties in maintaining conformity in business strategy promotion, due to the lack of linkage between the strategic business units and the organization format;

(2) difficulties in setting proper evaluation standards for qualitative targets;

(3) lack of effective fusion between strategic issue promotion and everyday operations;

(4) lack of a company-wide system for evaluating the degree of strategic effect attainment; and

(5) lack of smooth resource allotment in strategy promotion. These problems tend to occur in every company, because companies are apt to restrict innovative activity. To change such culture, it is necessary to compile 'success stories'.

(12) Embarking on a New Challenge

Finally, we will examine the distinguishing features of Taisei management planning, and the strategy promotion direction to be adopted from now on. The features of the management plan are:

(1) Clarification of corporate volition and dreams for the future which embody the long-term plan. This gives direction to medium-term 5-year management plans.

(2) The medium-term plans are set for 5 years, and updated every 3 years.

(3) Clarification of strategic issues and goals, which are assigned to divisions.

(4) Broad-scale adoption of project teams, in order to strengthen the ties between divisions.

(5) Establishing the strategy planning format, eliminating discrepancy at the division strategy level.

(6) In addition to corporate strategies assigned to each division, individual divisions may also develop their own peculiar strategies. This heightens the sense of participation in strategy management.

(7) Strategy implementation is formulated as a system which enables development within the realm of daily business activity. Of importance, rather, is the implementation, revision, and improvement of the planning system.

The third 5-year management plan launched in 1988 projects the transition of Taisei toward a knowledge-intensive industry, characterized by its generation of high value-added quantities.

On the threshold of the 115th anniversary of its foundation, Taisei has embarked upon yet another challenge. The ultimate goal of this undertaking is to become a premier global company in the near future.

Bibliography

Igor H. Ansoff, Strategic Management, Macmillan Press (1978).
Tom Peters, Thriving on Chaos, Excel (1987).
Michael E. Porter, Competitive Strategy, The Free Press (1980).
W. Warner Burke, Organization Development, Little Brown (1982).
T. Kono, *Shoki Keiei Keikaku no Jitsurei* (New Cases in Long Range Planning), Dobunkan, Tokyo (1978).
M. Iinuma, *Keiei Senryaku Guide* (Management Strategy Planning Guide), Japan Management Association, Tokyo (1985).
S. Inoue, *Keiei no Susumekata* (How to Advance Management Strategy), Japan Management Association, Tokyo (1985).

PART THREE

Changing Corporate Culture

Corporate Culture and Long-range Planning

Toyohiro Kono

Corporate culture affects the planning and strategic decision-making processes of a company. This article is based on the findings of a research study of Japanese companies and it categorises the types of corporate culture, the factors affecting the culture and the processes for changing a corporate culture.

Corporate culture is composed of three elements —shared values, decision-making patterns and overt behaviour patterns. It may be called organizational climate, corporate style, corporate ethos, and sometimes, beliefs, assumptions, schemas, corporate eye glasses, common maps. (Schein, 1985; Davies, 1984; Killman, 1986; Harris, 1989; Kono, 1988; Umezawa, 1986).

There are two reasons why the corporate culture came to the attention of researchers. Firstly, as the environment changes the strategy has to change, but the culture tends to stay the same and there arises the discrepancy between the strategy and corporate culture. Also the initiatives of individuals have become important for improving the organization's performance in many areas. Researchers need to be creative, marketing personnel need to be alert to changes in consumer behaviour. These initiatives cannot be expected to arise from a situation controlled by rules.

Motivation is a little different from corporate culture, because motivation means co-operating with the responsibilities and goals set by the organization. Corporate culture means looking for new opportunities.

(I) Long-range Planning and Corporate Culture Change

Long-range planning has the effect of changing the culture in the following aspects:

(a) *Unfreezing*
The analysis of the environment and the appraisal of a company's performance usually discloses problems, issues and potential gaps in financial performance. These analyses may evoke a sense of crisis.

(b) *Change*
Regularly every year, the planning process forces management to reconsider the product-market strategy and the personnel management system, and thus to change the corporate culture.

(c) *Refreeze*
Ideas generated from many departments disappear. They are written down, formally authorized, implemented and followed up. This system is different from the informal one, and it provides a situation for refreezing the change. Thus formal planning provides the conditions for culture change.

The initial conditions of corporate culture affects the nature of long-range planning in the following way.

(a) When the culture is lively long-range planning can be built easily. A plan could be detailed (as in the case of Canon), because employees are willing to formulate the strategic plan. On the other hand a plan can be relatively simple (as in the case of Asahi Chemicals), because culture of the company compliments the plan, and employees take innovative action on their own initiative.

The cause–effect will be as follows

Vital culture ⟶ Innovative ⟶ Revitalized
Long-rang planning ⟶ strategy ⟶ culture

Professor Toyohiro Kono is the Journal's Editor for Japan and Southeast Asia, and Professor of Business Administration at Gakushuin University, Tokyo.

55

(b) When the culture is stagnant, culture change and strategic planning have to be carried out simultaneously. There are two approaches.

(1) *A long-range plan*. This approach formulates long-range planning by a top-down approach and tries to change the culture and strategy.

$$\text{Issues finding} \longrightarrow \text{Long-range planning} \longrightarrow \begin{cases} \text{Change of culture} \\ \text{Change of strategy} \end{cases}$$

This process is made possible by strong leadership from top management. The process can be incremental i.e. the plan need not be comprehensive but partial, and strategy change could be incremental. A symbolic change of strategy could affect the culture change (as in the case of an advertising company).

(2) *A cultural change*. This approach is as follows:

Activities to change the culture→Partial change of strategy→Comprehensive long-range planning →Comprehensive strategy change (as in the case of Asahi Brewery and of Nissan Motor).

This process tries to change the culture first and implement a partial change of stategy. After the company culture has become more strategy oriented, then comprehensive planning is installed to promote and refreeze the strategic innovation.

(II) Types of Corporate Culture

Before planning a change of corporate culture, the types of corporate culture which will breed an aggressive corporate strategy are identified.

(A) *Measurements of Corporate Culture*

Corporate culture is composed of three groups of elements:

(1) the values held by the members of an organization,

(2) their method of decision-making or way of thought,

(3) their overt behaviour patterns.

In this study, the author does not define corporate culture as the beliefs or assumptions of its members, but rather as the actual decision making patterns, because these patterns are easier to observe and measure, and they affect the performance of the organization and the satisfaction of its members.

The detailed factors of three groups of measurements of corporate culture are shown in Table 1.

There are seven factors: (1) values that the members believe, (2) information collection, (3) idea generation, (4) evaluation of ideas and risk taking, (5) co-

Table 1. Elements and types of corporate culture

Elements \ Types	(1) Vitalized	(2) Follow the leader and vitalized	(3) Bureaucratic	(4.1) Stagnant	(4.2) Stagnant and follow the leader
General characteristics	Value in innovation. Many ideas presented	Follow the leader	Procedures and rules are respected	Tradition oriented	Follow the leader
(1) Value	Innovation oriented	Following the leader is a value	Procedure-oriented. Safety first	Safety first	Safety of self. Safety first
(2) Information	Information collection is oriented to outside environment	Information comes from the higher ranks	Oriented to technical knowledge	Internally oriented	Top down
(3) Idea Presentation	Many spontaneous ideas presented. Many opposing ideas	Do only as directed. No opposing ideas	Perfect and completed plan is necessary. High level of specialization	Habitual few new ideas. No opposing ideas	Few new ideas presented. Do as directed
(4) Risk taking	Not afraid of failure	Failure is the responsibility of the leader	Afraid of failure	Afraid of failure	Afraid of failure
(5) Cooperation	Little social distance between the leader and the follower. Good teamwork	Follow the leader. Mutually competitive	Hierarchy is necessary. Responsibility and authority are clear	Do not trust the higher ranks. Mutually separated	Large vertical social distance. Mutually separated
(6) Loyalty to the organization	Two extremes	Work for lifetime	Work for lifetime	Quit the company if better opportunities are available	Quit the company if better opportunities are available
(7) Motivation	High sense of responsibility	Little sense of responsibility	Follow the rule	Low sense of responsibility	Low sense of responsibility
Examples	Canon Hitachi Sony	Kyocera Nippon Gakki in early times	Public office. Large manufacturers of materials	Old National Railways. Old ship building companies	Van Jacket at the end

operation, (6) loyalty to the organization, and (7) value of the task to the employee, or morale of the member.

These seven factors describe the decision making process and the overt behaviour pattern. The above table was derived from the results of an extensive survey by questionnaire conducted in November 1987. Questionnaires were sent to 126 companies (908 pieces), and 88 companies and 265 persons responded. One set of questionnaires contained 126 questions, out of which 67 questions are related to the expression of the corporate culture. Each answer had five levels from 'definitely yes' to 'absolutely no'. Answers were analysed by factor analysis by computer, and it was found that the above seven were the key factors. The contents of Table 1 illustrate important elements selected from the responses and classified according to the seven factors.

(B) *Types and Performances*
The classification of corporate cultures is useful in order to identify the position of culture in a corporation. It discovers the relationships between culture and the strategy of the organization, its performance and the satisfaction of its members, because there is a specific cause and effect relationship for each type.

Three axes were used to classify culture, innovative vs conservative, analytical vs intuitive and the social distance between the levels of hierarchy. These axes were assumed to relate to the performance and the satisfaction of employees. It was found that many common expressions describing the corporate culture of a company, such as, 'Matsushita is a merchant', 'Mitsubishi is a lord', 'Sony is an innovator' and other similar expressions can be classified by these three axes. The combination of three pairs with two levels makes 8 kinds of culture, but since there are some correlationships between the levels, the kinds of culture are reduced to five, as is shown in Table 1.

(1) *Vitalized Type*
The vitalized culture type has the following characteristics. Its members put emphasis on innovation, have a sense of one family or one community, and share common values. The goal of organization is clearly understood, and the members understand the meaning of jobs clearly. Information is actively collected from the outside, and is customer-oriented. The organization has good communication both vertically and horizontally.

Ideas for improvement are presented voluntarily, and members perform duties in anticipation of the expectation of others. Opposing ideas towards seniors and colleagues are presented. Members take risks. Also, members feel that there is little social distance between them and their seniors. They do not hesitate to call their seniors by name.

The vitalized culture tends to reproduce new strategies, to implement them well and have a high productivity.

(2) *Follow-the-leader and Vitalized Type*
The feature of this type of culture is that its members follow a strong leader who is often the founder of the company. They trust the ability of their leader, and important information and ideas come from the top management. As long as management makes good decisions, this type of culture works well, but once top management gets older and begins to make the wrong decisions, this type shifts to the (4.2) type described below.

(3) *Bureaucratic Type*
In companies with this culture, rules and standards increase, the behaviour of employees is bound by these rules, and they do not try to take risks. This type is found in old companies and in mass-production material manufacturing companies.

(4.1) *Stagnant Type*
The members of this type of culture repeat old patterns of behaviour, and their information collection is inner-oriented and insensitive to changes in the environment. Also, members do not generate new ideas. This type appears in companies with monopolistic market shares and in public organizations.

(4.2) *Stagnant with Strong Leader Type*
Here top management is autocratic, but their decisions are wrong and the employees who have to obey orders lose their initiative. A company with a type 2 culture might develop into this type, when the top management stays in position for too many years.

Many companies tend to start from type 2 and then shift by the following sequence: (2)→(1)→(3)→(4). To avoid this shift, rejuvenation of the organization's culture is necessary.

The relative performance of these various classifications were examined, and the results are shown in Table 2.

The classification of companies was determined by the gap between the values of answers relating to key elements and the standard values of each type. The survey results show that a type 2 culture has the highest value of vitality, followed by type 1. The best financial performance is also seen in type 2, and again type 1 follows. The reason why the financial performance of type 2 is the best is that many of the companies in this type are newly established and fast-growing companies and they have vital cultures. In contrast, the performances of the stagnant culture companies are the worst.

An analysis of Table 2 shows that the method of classification is meaningful, and that companies

Table 2. Measurements and performances of each type of corporate culture

Types / Elements	(1) Vitalized corporate culture	(2) Follow-the-leader and vitalized	(3) Bureaucratic	(4.1) Stagnant	(4.2) Follow-the-leader and stagnant
Responding companies	34 companies	7 companies	32 companies	8 companies	7 companies
Persons	157 persons	20 persons	161 persons	25 persons	28 persons
(1) Shared values					
(1.1) Take risks, not afraid of failure	55*	58*	47*	38*	40*
(1.2) Take initiative, rather than follow the leader	52*	43*	47*	52	52
(1.3) Know the business philosophy and business creed	53*	54	47*	43*	46
(2) Communications					
(2.1) Much horizontal communication	53*	62*	47*	36*	46
(2.2) Make a decision after collecting enough information	53*	56*	47*	44*	45*
(2.3) Put emphasis on intuition and experiments	51	59*	45*	49	51
(3) Idea presentation					
(3.1) Present opposing opinions to the senior leader	53*	59*	48*	39*	42*
(3.2) Present opposing ideas to colleagues	55*	54	46*	43*	40*
(4) Evaluation					
(4.1) Are not afraid of failure	51	52	50	43*	45*
(4.2) Do not think merit rating is made by deducting system	53*	50	48*	47	42*
(5) Social distance and cooperation					
(5.1) Small social distance between higher level and lower level	55*	42*	49	40*	49
(5.2) Good cooperation between departments	55*	53	47*	31*	45*
(6) Loyalty to the organization					
(6.1) Like to work for lifetime	52*	51	49	43*	48
(7) Motivation					
(7.1) Report mistakes to the senior	54*	58*	46*	43*	41*
(7.2) Eager to work hard	53*	58*	49	38*	43*
(8) Performances					
(8.1) Yearly growth rate of sales (%)	10·4	19·7	7·1	3·2	5·6
(8.2) Rate of return on total asset (%)	7·4	9·4	5·8	3·0	5·2
(8.3) Equity ratio (%)	40·0	44·8	28·0	19·2	26·4
(8.4) Total performance = (1) + (2) + 1/4 (3)	28·3	40·5	20·0	12·5	17·5

Note:
(1) From 1 to 7, the figures indicate the standardized value. The value $Y = 50 + 10t$ $t =$ (values measured − average value) ÷ standard deviation.
(2) Annual growth rate was computed between 1977 and 1986. Return on total assets were computed by averaging the 1980 and 1986 results. Equity ratios were the averages of the 1980 and 1986 figures.
(3) Classification of companies into types of corporate culture are judged by responses to several key questions.
(4) The good performance of type 2 comes from the fact that many young companies are included.
(5) The difference between the averages are almost all significant at the 5 per cent level.

should try to possess a vitalized corporate culture, should try to shift to type 1 if they are at some other group and should aim to remain in a type 1 culture.

(III) Factors that Formulate a Corporate Culture

A corporate culture is formed by four factors——(a) the corporate philosophy; (b) the product-market strategy; (c) the organizational structure and personnel management system; and (d) the attitude of top management as it affects the above three.

The relationship between these factors is outlined in Table 3 below.

There are three factors that affect the personal attitude: (1) infomation or education; (2) learning by experience; and (3) rewards and punishment. These three factors roughly correspond to the above three factors. The corporate philosophy describes the desired values of the corporation and the desired way of thinking, and it thus affects the pattern of behaviour. The product-market strategy determines the job positions which affect the behaviour pattern through experience. The corporate culture varies from industry to industry ensuring that the product-market strategy affects the type of corporate culture. Finally, the organizational structure defines the communication pattern and the responsibilities of each member and the personnel management system stipulates the reward and punishment system. Thus they influence the corporate culture.

As a specific example of how these factors influence

Table 3. Factors affecting the corporate culture

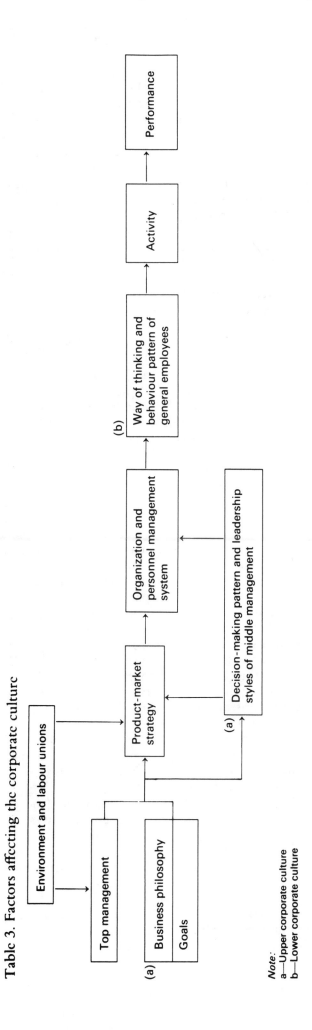

Note:
a—Upper corporate culture
b—Lower corporate culture

a formation of corporate culture, the case of Honda Motor Corporation is described in Table 4.

Honda has a vibrant and energetic culture, which has been cultivated by the leadership of the top management, who retire at the age of 55. Its corporate philosophy puts emphasis on 'dreams and youthfulness'. It aggressively introduces new products at frequent intervals and encourages an innovative atmosphere. The personnel management system is deliberately designed. Its aim is to recruit capabilities from diverse sources, for example, recruiting university graduates from as many universities as possible. Honda utilizes the job rotation of employees on planned schedules until the employees reach the age of 30. It also delegates authority to young people—for example, the designing of new cars is delegated to young development teams to a greater extent than in any other company.

Honda's personnel records are detailed. In particular, all employees are requested to write personal statements (or personal proposals) and superiors are required to write a record of guidance for each subordinate. New recruits are requested to keep a 'diary' in which they write down anything they think useful for the company. Honda also holds a company-wide 'idea contest' every 2 years, costing millions of yen. It has idea rooms, and supports the voluntary study groups financially.

(IV) Factors Changing the Corporate Culture

A corporate culture tends to deteriorate by shifting from (2) the strong leader type to (1) the vitalized type and then to (3) the bureaucratic type and eventually to (4.1) or (4.2) which are the stagnant types. There are several reasons for this deterioration. One is the size of the company: the larger the company, and the more rules, the more bureaucratic the company becomes. Another reason is the average age of employees: the older they are, the more the knowledge and experience of employees tends to become outdated, and the company becomes less vibrant. On the other hand, if the environment changes, the strategy also has to change and the content and direction of culture may not be a good fit with the new strategy. These are the reasons why a change of culture becomes necessary.

The factors that formulate a corporate culture are also the factors that change the culture. We conducted a survey on the important factors which change a corporate culture. Table 5 indicates the results.

A change of top management was the response with the highest frequency (56 responses). A sense of crisis

is also important since this may make possible the 'unfreezing' effect (30 responses). A change of corporate philosophy and the introduction of a corporate identity programme have similar effects (11 and 12 responses). The third is a change in the top corporate culture (9, 12 and 8 responses). The fourth is a change of strategy (15 responses). The fifth is a change of the organizational structure and the personnel management system (25, 8 and 6 responses). At the section level, a change of managers and changes of section members are the most important.

These surveys and the study of cases reveal that four factors are important in changing the corporate culture—that is, information, symbolic product-market strategy, a sanction system and top management. As a process of change, three processes—defreeze, change and refreeze—are important.

(a) *Information Approach*
Imformation can change the attitude of individuals and groups. Max Weber mentions that the ethics of Protestantism gave birth to the spirit of American capitalism. Buddhism and Confucism have created the organization-orientedness of Japanese people. Mass communication is affecting the spirit of people, and of young people in particular. In a corporation, information and training can be a powerful means in affecting the corporate culture.

A change of corporate philosophy or corporate creed is frequently used. The corporate creed has a strong influence on the corporate culture, as Table 5 shows. The corporate creed needs to be changed as the value of stakeholders changes and many companies change it every 5 years. Recently, a team of young managers was appointed to study the new corporate creed. Nissan Motor changed its creed from 'Distinctive Technology' to 'Feel the Beat' meaning that the feeling of the consumer is respected. In this way the corporate culture changed to a consumer oriented one. After that, successful new models started to appear.

Corporate identity reform is used to change the symbol mark, the image of the company, and the corporate culture.

The behaviour (and communication skills) of top management have a symbolic effect in changing the attitude of employees.

A number of channels of communication are used to emphasize the importance of change, and to direct change. The company newspaper, morning meetings, a variety of movements, employee training are used to deliver the new philosophy.

(b) *Learning Through Experience of New Product-market Strategy and the Diffusion of Spirit of Experimentation*
A new experience can change attitudes. A value

Table 4. Factors affecting the corporate culture of Honda Motor Corporation

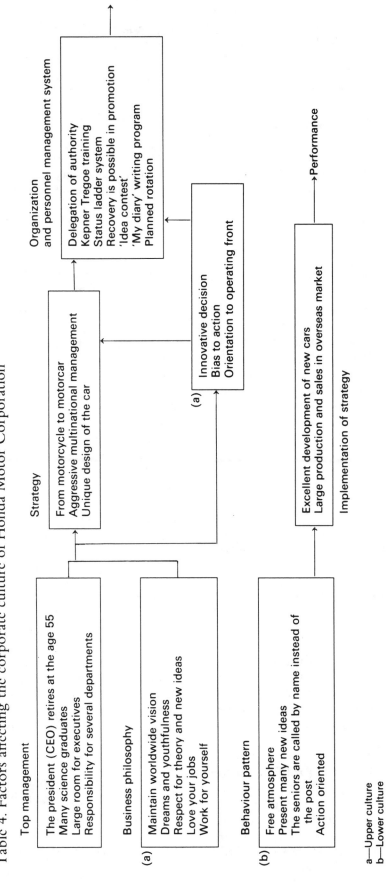

a—Upper culture
b—Lower culture

Table 5. Reasons for the change of corporate culture, in the whole company and your section

Company as a whole		In my section	
(1) Change of top management members and lowered average age	56 (co.)	(1) Change of managers	38 (co.)
(2.1) Increase of sense of crisis by the change of environment and by the deteriorating financial performance	30	(2.1) (Same as the left column)	15
(2.2) Due to improved financial performance, the vitality and enthusiasm of the company have increased	13	(2.2) (Same as the left column)	7
(2.3) Diffusion of corporate philosophy and goals, and enthusiasm of top management	11		
(2.4) Introduction of corporate identity movement	12		
(3.1) Change of attitude of top management towards aggressive and innovative behaviour	9	(3.1) Clear goals for the sections and individuals, management by objectives	11
(3.2) Improvement of daily operations and making efforts to improve the attitude of the members	12		
(3.3) Improvement of administration system	8	(3.3) (Same as the left column)	7
		(3.4) Introduction of quality control movement	5
(4) Introduction of new business and change of product-market strategy	15		
(5.1) Change of organizational structure and delegation of authority	29	(5.1) (Same as the left column)	7
(5.2) Introduction of merit system and improvement of personnel management system	8		
(5.3) Recruiting of new employees	6	(5.3) Change of members and lowered average age	41
		(5.4) Change of jobs and improvement of working place	11
		(6) Others	11

(Free response. 260 persons out of 391 persons responded. Number is the number of persons.)
Note: The meaning of the head numbers.
(1) Top management.
(2) Business philosophy and goals.
(3) Decision making of upper echelon.
(4) Product-market strategy.
(5) Organizational structure and personnel management.

system and behaviour pattern are formed through experiences since childhood. Likes and dislikes towards some foods, patterns of eating foods, attitudes towards readings and towards other people, all are formed through a lifetime's experience.

When an experience is not compatible with an established conception, a person will change his attitude if the new experience is a convincing one. This is explained by the theory of cognitive dissonance. For this reason, success in new product-market strategy will change the confidence of the corporation. For example, the success in new products 'Pulser' and 'Be 1' of Nissan Motor gave a great impact to the culture of the company, and employees realized the importance of consumer orientedness.

There are many cases, however, where the new product did not result in a change of corporate culture. Neither the oil well development nor the operation of a ranch of Teijin Synthetic Fiber, nor the soft contact lens by Toray changed the corporate culture.

What then are the conditions in which a partial change of strategy can influence the corporate culture?

Firstly, the new strategy needs to succeed, and needs to become a symbol of a new culture. It should indicate the new direction of behaviour patterns and it should be supported and authorized by top management through simple praise, through prizes and ceremonies, or be made into a company myth.

Secondly, the experience should be imitated and similar experiences should be sought by other departments. At Nissan, after the success of a new car development, new activities to improve the culture were encouraged, a new components supply system at the production plant was tried, new groups of aged workers were formed and a new way of working for the aged was explored, and many other new experiments were tried.

Thirdly, the transfer of personnel. At Asahi Brewery, 600 people from all departments were mobilized for a sales promotion campaign to let one million consumers on the street try out the new beer. This had the effect of making employees understand the demands of consumers. At Mitsubishi Electric, the managers at one plant who produced a successful new home appliance were transferred to other plants in the same line, the new approach was transplanted, and many new success products were produced as a result. Innovators in one department become opinion leaders. They are scattered throughout other departments and transmit the new spirit. Opinion leaders play an important role in transmitting new ways of thinking, evidenced by new experiences such as new product developments.

(c) *Sanction System*
Changes of organizational structure and personnel management system are the third factors to change the corporate culture. The organizational structure affects the responsibility of the members, and delegation of authority tends to activate the members.

The personnel management system includes recruitment, training and reward systems. Practices by many corporations to activate the corporate culture are collected and listed in Table 6.

Among established practices, the merit assessment system, not the demerit rating, is drawing attention.

A manager tends to see the demerits or failure of subordinates as they are easier to identify. Those who try new innovations sometimes fail. If these failures are punished, nobody will dare to run the risk, and behaviour will become conservative. In order to encourage innovation, real 'merit' rating has to be introduced. Merit rating is to reward the process, not the results. One company gives a prize to a failure, because a new thing was essayed. The company evaluates the effort and the process as well as the result.

In order to install the 'merit' rating, a company needs to have a self-statement system, i.e. a kind of management-by-objective system. Employees are encouraged to make a plan to improve their job, to innovate and to plan for self development. The plan will then be reviewed by the employee and his boss.

In order to activate the employee, there should be many opportunities for rewards. Most Japanese corporations have a status ladder promotion system in addition to promotion on a job classification ladder, and annual wage increase by merit on a wide rate of ranges. These extrinsic reward systems can support the operation of real merit rating.

'The loser recovery system' is another way. If a person is slow to be promoted he will be offered opportunities to recover his position and eventually he could outstrip his colleagues. In order to re-evaluate those who are slow in promotion, the personnel manager will review those who are behind their colleagues, and try to re-evaluate them, and provide them with faster tracks to recover their positions. One company selected 20 per cent of slow movers and re-evaluated them. Another large bank has about 10 interviewers in the personnel department, and they interview about 20 per cent of all employees in a year and listen to their problems. This data is used to provide opportunities for them to recover their impetus.

Table 6. Personnel management system

	Activating system	Stagnating system
(1) Recruiting	☆ Recruit those who like to take risks ☆ Recruit the experienced from outside and mix them with insiders	☆ Recruit the high score students ☆ Promotion from within, pure blood, only
(2) Promotion	☆ Merit appraisal system (Addition only) ☆ Promotion by capability ☆ Loser recovery system	☆ Demerit appraisal system (Deduction only) ☆ Too rigid length of service system ☆ Fast track system
(3) Job assignment	☆ Planned rotation ☆ Assign the capable to key projects	☆ Early specialization
(4) Training	☆ Train decision-making process	
(5) Wage and salary	☆ By merit	☆ Strict length of service system
(6) Personnel information system	☆ Self statement, self evaluation	☆ Evaluation by the senior

(V) Process to Change the Corporate Culture

Change in the cororate culture takes the form of a process of 'unfreeze', 'change', and 'refreeze'. This process is similar to the process of 'brainwashing' applied to the war prisoners held by the communist bloc during the Second World War.

(A) Unfreeze

To unfreeze is to destroy conventional values. To achieve this, people are taught that their conventional values or ways of thinking are erroneous. In the case of an individual, each person is taught to reflect inwardly and confess the error of his ways.

(B) Change

There are three ways to effect a cultural change:

(a) The information approach teaches a new way of thinking. The new management philosophy is established, and is promoted to employees.

(b) The experience approach consists of having employees solve problems by themselves by going through new experiences. This is most effective for creating changes in corporate culture. This is a change in strategy, particularly in the development of new products and their subsequent success.

(c) The approach through reward and punishment involves rewarding preferable actions and punishing undersirable ones and is mainly achieved by changes in personnel management.

(d) Finally there is the 'comprehensive approach'. This includes all three approaches, and requires a replacement of the top management.

(C) Refreeze

In order to 'refreeze' a change, it is necessary continuously to reward and punish, to teach new ways of thinking, and to provide new experiences which reinforce the correctness of the change in culture. Long-range planning has the effect of refreezing, by formally writing down the new strategy and structure. To ensure that long-range planning is used effectively to change corporate culture, the above processes need to be planned and action needs to be taken within a long-range plan.

Summary

Corporate culture is composed of shared values, decision-making patterns and behaviour patterns. There are five types of corporate culture, and it is important to recognize to which type of corporate culture a company belongs.

Corporate culture affects the strategic decision-making and contents of strategy as is seen in the case of Nissan Motor Company.

If the corporate culture is vitalized, the long-range plan can incorporate innovative strategies, and the strategies are well implemented (Case of Canon and Bridgestone).

If the corporate culture is stagnant a change of corporate culture has to be planned. The long-range planning has the effect of changing the culture. It makes clear what threats lie ahead in the future. It forces the company to generate new ideas every year.

However, such innovation is more difficult when the culture is stagnant and the other means of change must be sought.

There are four factors in changing a culture: information, successful implementation of small and symbolic new strategies, sanction and a change of top management. A symbolic new strategy has the highest impact.

There are then three processes to change the corporate culture, that is, defreeze, change and refreeze.

References

In Japanese

J. Ishikawa, Asahi Beer no Chosen (Challenge of Asahi Breweries, Ltd), Japan Management Association (1987).

T. Kagono, Kigyo Paradigm no Henkaku, Change of Corporate Paradigm, Kodan-sha (1988).

T. Kono, Gendai no Keiei Senryaku, Corporate Strategy, Diamond-sha (1985).

T. Kono, Keieigaku Genri, Principles of Management, Hakuto-shobo (1987).

T. Kono, Henkaku no Kigyo Bunka, Change of Corporate Culture, Kodan-Sha (1988).

K. Matsuura, Shafu no Kenkyu, Study of Corporate Culture, PHP (1984). Organizational Science, Special Edition on Corporate Culture, **17** (3) (1983).

T. Nakajo and T. Kono, Success Through Culture Change in a Japanese Brewery, *Long Range Planning,* December (1989).

T. Umezawa, Soshiki Bunka no Shiten kara, View-points on Corporate Culture, Gyosei (1983).

T. Umezawa, Kigyo Bunka no Sozo, Creation of Corporate Culture, Yuhikaku (1986).

In English

S. M. Davis, Managing Corporate Culture, Ballinger Pub. (1984).

Deal and Kennedy, Corporate Culture, Addison-Wesley (1982).

P. Diesing, Non-economic Decision Making, Rowe & Mason, (1955). ed. Strategic Management & Business Policy, Addison-Wesley (1982).

P. J. Frost and others ed., Organizational Culture, Sage Pub. (1985).

S. G. Harris, A Schema-Based Perspective on Organizational Culture, a paper presented at Annual Meeting of Academy of Management, Washington D.C., August (1989).

R. H. Kilman, Five Steps for Closing Culture-gaps; in Beyond The Quick Fix, Jossey Bass (1984).

R. H. Kilman and others ed., Gaining Control of the Corporate culture, Jossey Bass (1986).

R. H. Kilman and others ed., Corporate transformation, Jossey Bass (1988).

R. Likert, The Human Organization, MacGraw-Hill (1967).

G. H. Litwin and R. A. Stringer Jr, Motivation and Organizational Climate, Harvard University (1968).

G. C. Morris, Psychology, an Introduction, Prentice-Hall.

Peters and Waterman, In Search of Excellence, Harper & Row (1982).

Roethlisberger and Dickson, Management and the Worker, Harvard University (1939).

G. Hofsteade, Culture's Consequences, Sage Pub. (1980).

E. Shein, Management Development as a Process of Influence, *Sloan Management Review,* May (1961).

E. Schein, How Culture Forms, Develops, and Changes, in Kilman and others ed. 1985 and Organization Culture & Leadership, Jossey-Bass Publishers (1985).

A. L. Wilkins and W. G. Ouchi, Efficient Cultures, Administrate Science Quarterly, September (1983).

Appendix

Method of Survey

Designing of survey	Toyohiro Kono, Professor of Business Administration Takashi Uchino, Professor of Business Administration Both of Gakushuin University, Mejiro, Toshima-ku, Tokyo.
Date of survey	Mail questionnaires were sent in November 1987.
Number of responses	Mail questionnaires were sent to 126 companies (908 pieces). Responses were received from 88 companies and 391 persons (4.4 persons per one company). Response ratio was 70.0 per cent for company and 43.1 per cent for persons.

Distribution of response by industry

(1) Mining and construction	7 companies	(36 persons)
(2) Food and fisheries	4 companies	(30 persons)
(3) Fibre, pulp and paper	4 companies	(10 persons)
(4) Chemicals and drugs	13 companies	(67 persons)
(5) Petroleum, rubber, glass and stone	8 companies	(34 persons)
(6) Iron, steel and nonferrous metals	4 companies	(14 persons)
(7) Machinery	6 companies	(27 persons)
(8) Electrical appliances and precision machinery	23 companies	(88 persons)
(9) Transportation equipment	4 companies	(19 persons)
(10) Finance and insurance	5 companies	(31 persons)
(11) Commerce and services	7 companies	(23 persons)
(12) Miscellaneous	3 companies	(12 persons)
Total	88 companies	(391 persons)

Success Through Culture Change in a Japanese Brewery

Takanori Nakajo and Toyohiro Kono

The birth, growth and subsequent decline of Asahi Brewery is described up to the appointment of a new president of the company and the introduction of a new management concept. This brought a change in strategic direction and the development of new products. Changes in corporate culture at the top and middle level of management encouraged change in employee culture. Improvements of organizational structure and programmes are described and principles for change in corporate culture are extrapolated.

Asahi Breweries, Ltd. was originally incorporated in 1886 as Osaka Brewery. As a result of a merger with Nippon Brewery and Sapporo Brewery in 1906, the company name was changed to Dai Nippon Brewery Co. The company enjoyed steady growth until 1949, at which time it held more 70% of the market and employed some 3200 persons.

However, in accordance with the Anti-Monopoly Law, Dai Nippon Brewery was divided into two companies in 1949: Asahi Breweries and Nippon Breweries. Thereafter, the market shares of the three breweries in Japan—Asahi Breweries, Nippon Breweries and Kirin Breweries—were 36·1 per cent for Asahi, 38·7 per cent for Nippon and 25·3 per cent for Kirin. In the 35 years that followed, Asahi's share continued to decline until it fell below 10 per cent (i.e., 9·6 per cent) in 1985; meanwhile, Kirin's share soared to 63 per cent in 1976. However, thanks to revolutionary changes in the corporate culture of Asahi, the subsequent success of a new type of draft beer and the introduction of 'Super Dry', Asahi quickly regained much of the market share it had lost, reaching an estimated 21 per cent in 1988.

What were the reasons for the continued 35-year

Takanori Nakajo is Senior Vice-President of Asahi Breweries Ltd. Tokyo and Dr Toyohiro Kono is Professor of Business Administration at Gakushuin University Tokyo and Japan and South-east Asia Editor of the Journal.

decline and the recent recovery? The direct causes for the decline were as follows:

(a) plants, markets, and wholesalers were concentrated only in Western Japan;

(b) emphasis had been placed on the restaurant market with inadequate attention paid to the growing home-consumption market, and

(c) worst of all, a slow sales turnover had contributed to inconsistencies in product quality. In order to increase their sales, the brewery stocked up their wholesalers and retailers. This resulted in a slow turnover of stock and the sale of beer that was relatively old.

The decline of Asahi's market share also brought about stagnation in the corporate culture, which in turn accelerated the fall of its market share—a vicious circle. In other words, Asahi was 'an apathetic group of underdogs with their tails between their legs'. In order to raise sales in the short term, the company often adopted the typical and simple stopgap of pressuring wholesalers to make purchases. Such tactics are resulted in stock accumulation at the retailers' shop room and as a result of the

Table 1. Chronological changes in Asahi's market share, sales and profit

Year	Market share (%)	Sales (¥bn)	Profit after interest and before tax (¥bn)
1949	36·1	2	0·03
1955	31·8	27	1·0
1960	28·2	50	1·8
1965	24·2	89	2·8
1970	17·2	108	2·8
1975	13·5	145	3·0
1980	11·0	185	3·2
1985	9·6	236	3·3
1986	10·4	259	5·3
1987	12·9	345	9·4
1988	20·6	545	15·0

low turnover and long display, the beer's flavour deteriorated.

Until recently, the beer recipe was considered to be solely the responsibility of the R & D Department, the members of which would not heed the advice of the marketing department. For example, the R & D team made a mistake in 1968 when they produced a beer without 'bitterness'. They apparently forgot that 'bitter' is the inherent taste of beer. (For list of problems, see Table 2.)

Table 2. Key problems

> *Strategy*
> ☆ 35 years of declining market share
> ☆ Deterioration in product quality due to slow turnover and overaccumlation of stock at retailers
> ☆ Products not in tune with today's consumers
>
> *Corporate culture*
> ☆ Employees unaware of the critical state of Asahi since the company was getting profit due to the overall growth of the beer market
> ☆ General attitude of apathy
> ☆ Internally-oriented, i.e. lack of consumer or market orientation
> ☆ Lack of communication and cooperation among divisions

A New President and a New Management Concept

After the 17-year reign of Mr Yamamoto, who had served as the president since the breakup in 1949, the office of President was successively occupied by Mr Nakajima, Mr Takahashi and Mr Enmei at 5 year intervals. Meanwhile Asahi's market share continued to fall, a clear indication that a new president does not necessarily mean a new corporate culture or improved profits—unless the corporate system and strategies themselves are changed.

New Leadership

In 1982, Mr Tsutomu Murai, the then senior vice president of Sumitomo Bank and the man who had successfully guided the recovery of Mazda Motors, was appointed the new president of Asahi. His first task was the renovation of the corporate culture. (Please refer to Table 2: Outline of Renovation.) Mr Murai discovered that there was no feeling of 'crisis' at Asahi as had been evident at Mazda. Although its market share had steadily declined, Asahi had not suffered any losses because of the growth of the entire beer industry. Therefore, he attempted to evoke a feeling of crisis, and he appealed for revolutionary changes in awareness by creating a new corporate creed. As the leader of a U.S.-Japan Management Study Mission, Mr Murai had inspected American businesses; he knew that successful companies had definite and distinctive

corporate creeds. In order to establish a new corporate creed at Asahi, he directed the members of the Management Team to begin research and to consult the opinions of those inside and outside the company. The new corporate creed, placed emphasis on: (a) making consumer-oriented products adapted for new life-styles and (b) creating a free and open atmosphere which respects the people in the company.

To disseminate this new creed, all the employees were given a card printed with the corporate creed as well as a code of behaviour. The card was read regularly at morning meetings and posted at many locations throughout the company. The card reads:

> 'Through the manufacture and sale of liquor, beverages, foods and medicines, we shall assist the creation of a healthy and affluent life for all people in Japan and overseas, contribute to society, and develop as a business entity by winning the trust of the society.'

In detail, the cards identified these points: (1) consumer-orientation, (2) quality-orientation, (3) respect for humanity, (4) labour-management conciliation, (5) existing and prospering together, and (6) accepting social responsibility.

At the same time, a code of behaviour comprising 10 articles was completed as a guide for employees' daily behaviour. The corporate creed was summed up in a small booklet that was given to all employees and read aloud at work every morning. Thus, the employees of Asahi came to understand the direction in which the company was heading and acquired a unified standard by which actions and decisions could be measured. This transformed the actions of individual workers into an organizational effort.

Mr Murai then introduced Total Quality Control within Asahi, and began training employees to develop the habit of considering everything on a 'Fact Basis'. In other words, he successfully executed a 180-degree turn in employees' attitudes toward work, where previously they had tended to evade responsibilities, passing them on to other departments, and expressed apathetic attitudes. observing that all the employees including new recruits and female clerical staff were joining the TQC campaign on their own initiative, the top management saw a flicker of hope for the company's future.

In 1984, the Corporate Identity Committee and a task force were formed. With the aim of becoming a consumer-oriented company, a variety of CI activities were performed, and proposals such as the establishment of a new company logo and the development of new products with new tastes and labels were received. Among such activities, the collection of information from outside sources and the development of new products were especially encouraged.

Developing New Beers and a Change in Strategy

At the time that the introduction of CI was bringing about a change in the corporate image, it was further proposed that the beer itself be changed, and not merely the label. Consequently in 1984, Asahi conducted a consumer survey with 5000 samples in order to determine what kind of beer is wanted by the consumers and also the criteria which consumers used to evaluate 'good beer'. This complete change in the content and taste of the beer was extremely risky and required courage. However, based on the views of 5000 consumers, Mr Murai made the necessary decision, and new beer samples were produced.

The market research which guided the creation of the new draught beer was not a mere questionnaire survey, but a thorough interview programme using new Asahi beers offering a variety of flavours and beers of competitors.

Prior to this tasting, the consumers said that they preferred 'a bitter and full-bodied taste'; however, after sampling beer which met this description, they did not say that it was delicious. The Marketing Department analysed this problem and discovered that it is extremely difficult to find appropriate terms to describe the taste of beer. However, they came to the conclusion that a 'rich but smooth tasting beer' is what the consumers really want. In the past, the palates of the technical staff had determined the taste of Asahi beers, but the permeation of the new Corporate Identity throughout the company and a committment to Total Quality Control had led to shift in thinking by both the marketing and technical staff towards giving greater priority to the preferences of consumers.

The result of this research was the creation of the 'rich and smooth' Asahi Draft Beer. Based on the responses from 5000 consumers, the criteria for judging a beer as 'tasty' were determined to be the qualities of 'richness' and 'smoothness'. 'Rich' defines the mellowness of the beer while 'smooth' means its ability to satisfy the palate and give a refreshing aftertaste. 'Bitterness' and 'heaviness' which characterize lager beers were no longer the tastes desired by today's consumers.

The new Asahi Draft Beer, the 'Koku-Kire Beer' (Rich and Smooth Beer), was launched onto the market in February 1986. A major campaign sampled almost 1-million consumers at 110 locations throughout Japan. Asahi Draft Beer was considered 'definitely tasty' and was got off to a smooth start.

Mr Higuchi, who had been appointed president in March 1986, took a bold step by dumping the stocks of the old draught beer. At a cost of more then ¥1bn, he ordered the complete recall of former draught beer stocked at 130,000 liquor stores throughout Japan. This drastic measure also contributed to the establishment of a new policy of 'fresh product rotation'. In the case of draught beer, the maxim 'the fresher the product, the better the taste' is especially true. Asahi's Marketing Department were also given strict orders to ensure that only fresh beer was sold. As a result, 'Koku-Kire Beer' won consistent and steadily growing popularity among consumers. *In its first year, the new Asahi Draft Beer enjoyed a 12 per cent increase in sales over the previous year's sales of the old beer, an increase three times the industry-wide average (i.e., 3·9 per cent).*

The Sale of 'Asahi Super Dry'

Based on the success of the new Asahi Draft Beer, the company took up the challenge of developing a beer with another new flavour. According to recent data, 10 per cent of Japanese of drinking age are heavy drinkers who consume 50 per cent of all beer sold in Japan; 10 per cent are medium beer drinkers who consume 25 per cent, and 50 per cent are light drinkers who account for the remaining 25 per cent. To further Asahi's growth, the management knew that it would have to offer a product that the heavy drinkers would drink every day. Asahi's answer was the development of 'Asahi Super Dry'. In the 5000-sample research which they had conducted an overwhelming number of consumers indicated a desire for a beer with a 'smoother' taste. Therefore, the target of the next development to follow Asahi Draft Beer was to place even further emphasis on the 'smoothness' factor while still retaining a balance with the 'richness' factor.

What does 'smoothness' mean in the beer industry? As mentioned earlier, it is 'the ability to satisfy the palate and leave a refreshing aftertaste'. Heavy drinkers wanted a taste which they would not soon tire of, of which they could drink glass after glass. They wanted a dry 'smooth' beer. With this goal in mind, the technical staff devoted their efforts toward realizing an entirely new 'dry' type of beer. They re-examined the basic raw materials and the manufacturing process, and they selected a particular kind of beer yeast, which is the key to the fermentation process. In other words, the technical staff examined the basics of brewing beer. To create the dry taste, a 'dry-type yeast' was chosen from among the hundreds of varieties developed by the company. The birth of 'Asahi Super Dry' draft beer was an achievement which resulted from the combined efforts of the marketing and production divisions.

'Asahi Super Dry', was introduced in March 1987, in Metropolitan Tokyo, and then released nation-wide in May. In 1987, 'Asahi Super Dry' set a sales record of 13·5 million cases (1 case = 20 large-size bottles). *Thanks to the impact of 'Asahi Super Dry', the company registered an overall increase in sales of 34 per cent, or about 4 times the industry-wide average of 7·4 per cent.* In the beer industry where a hit product achieves sales of 1 million cases in its first year, 'Asahi Super Dry' was a 'super' hit. As originally expected, the beer was very acceptable to the heavy and medium drinkers who account for 75 per cent of all beer consumed in Japan.

Advertising for 'Asahi Super Dry' was aggressively executed. The annual advertisement and publicity budget was increased from ¥5bn in 1986 to about ¥20bn in 1987. The following factors contributed to the huge success of 'Asahi Super Dry':

(1) Product development based on an accurate grasp of consumer needs and desires;

(2) Advertisement and publicity campaigns using a new media mix by which quality and quantity were both improved;

(3) Sales activities aimed at establishing and promoting fresh product rotation.

However, one more factor played an important part in Asahi's success: aggressive capital investment in plant and equipment. From 1986–1987, production capacity was increased by 50 per cent, and from 1987–1988, capital investment in plant and equipment was increased 50 per cent. By 1988, production capacity was 2·5 times the level in 1985. The company raised funds from the capital market and substantially increased the production capacity of its seven plants located throughout Japan. Thanks to these decisions and actions, the company was able to realize remarkable growth unprecedented in the industry. From 1989–1991, the company plans to invest ¥300bn with the aim of establishing a production capacity of 1,500,000 kilolitres by 1991.

Changes of Corporate Culture at the Top and Middle Management Level

'Management culture' refers to the shared value systems, decision making patterns and overt behaviour patterns of the top and middle management and other employees. The earlier changes in the presidency of Asahi have been mentioned. In order to revitalize the company, two presidents, Mr Murai and Mr Higuchi, promoted aggressive renovations and emphasized consumer-orientation, and they established the company policy that incorporated these changes.

Mr Higuchi is a 'hands-on' type of president who knows the importance of being on the scene. Once he became the president, he travelled around the nation visiting all wholesalers, both exclusive and affiliated, to ask for their cooperation.

Two important programs facilitated the decision-making process at Asahi: the TQC movement and long-range planning. The TQC movement (AQC in Asahi) which was mentioned earlier taught management the basic process of decision-making and resulted in the promotion of analytical decision-making. First, we will see how the TQC program was implemented and its results.

In order to infuse the company with drive and energy, revitalization at the section manager level was considered essential. Six hundred section managers were divided into six groups, Each group was taken on a 4-day retreat to discuss the ways and means of introducing TQC. In these sessions, communication gaps between the Production Division and the Marketing Division were removed, and mutual understanding deepened. During the period when Asahi's market share was on the decline, an adverse climate existed between these two divisions with each blaming the other for defeats suffered in the marketplace.

The TQC program emphasized three points: (1) dissemination of the corporate policy throughout the company, (2) improvement of the product quality, and (3) promotion and implementation of QC circle activities. Though QC circles were already being conducted at the plants to some degree, the problem was how to transform them to obtain practical results. However, the most significant outcome of the TQC program was an improved decision-making process.

The second program which contributed to the decision-making process was the formulation of long-range plans. In 1983, the first long-range plan included the introduction of the CI Project, the forementioned TQC program and changes in the corporate culture. In 1984, the second long-range plan was drawn up. These long range plans clarified the existence of strategic problems, particularly with respect to the means for changing the corporate culture, and contributed to their aggressive and analytical solution.

Improvements of Organizational Structure and Programs

The most effective factors in the revitalization of Asahi were the various programs rather than amendments to the organization and systems. However, one organizational change should be mentioned—the shift in emphasis to quality control rather than profit making by the respective divisions. At the plants, product quality was emphasized, and profit control was discontinued because an emphasis on a short-term profit led to a tendency to undervalue product quality.

One of the programs related to the CI Project and aimed at changing the corporate culture was the program under the basic concept 'Live Asahi for Live People'. In the past, Asahi's corporate climate had been internally oriented. Because such a climate does not permit adaptation to environmental changes, a marketing orientation was therefore stressed. As a concrete measure to express this change in orientation, changes of the corporate name and symbol were contemplated in order to renovate the company image. The decision was made to change the symbol. The name would remain the same but it would be expressed in English rather than Japanese lettering.

Figure 1. New labels for new beers

Figure 2. More than 700 employees were mobilized for the trial drinking campaign of new beers addressed towards 1 million consumers on the street

In his 1986 New Year's message, Mr Murai stated his committment to customer orientation and his intention to meet new challenges. In addition, Mr Higuchi, after he assumed the office of president, broadcast his video taped monthly speeches at morning meetings to deepen employee understanding of the top management views and philosphy.

The organizational structure was changed (see Figures 3 and 4). The change has aimed at the enhancement of strategic capability. The three changes were important (a) reinforcement of staff departments, (b) enhancement of development and research capabilities, (c) product divisions were introduced (except for beer and wine products) so that the new products would become successful products.

Changes in Employee Culture

In the past, Asahi was a loser, and its employees were preoccupied with internal matters. The only efforts which they put forward to increase sales were to pressurize the wholesalers into buying their products. However, as a result of the various measures mentioned above, the employees themselves underwent change; they became more concerned about their clients and approached their jobs with new confidence. Particularly, the rapid expansion of market share owing to the success of the new products as well as the rapid increase of profits contributed to revitalizing the corporate culture. The result was the creation of a beneficial cycle of change in the corporate culture→the marketing orientation→success of new products→revitalization of the corporate culture.

The summary of the various processes of change is shown in Table 3.

As one of the steps to realize a consumer orientation, a 5000-sample market research study was conducted to define what a tasty beer is. The research revealed that a 'rich and smooth' beer was what the consumers wanted. After the development of the first sample of 'Koku-Kire Beer', the sales campaign to distribute the samples to the 1 million consumers to try the drinking was carried out on the streets in front of liquor stores. For these trials, about 700 employees from the marketing and production divisions were recruited. But prior to their selection, trial drinking by all employees was arranged within the company because it was considered imperative that employees themselves should be confident of the taste. This operation not only contributed to sales promotion but also persuaded employees to take part in the sales activities and become more customer-oriented.

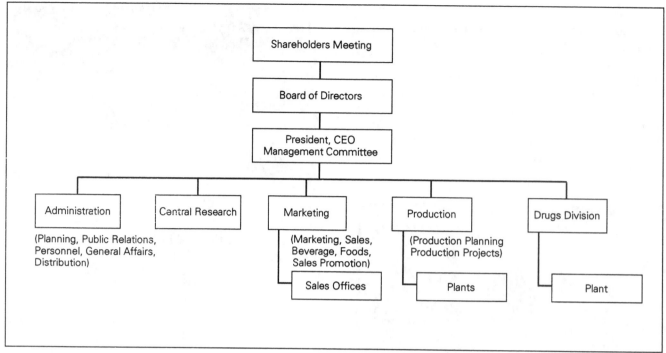

Figure 3. Asahi Organization 1984

Unfreeze, Change and Refreeze: Principles for Changes in the Corporate Culture

The transformation of Asahi can be explained by using the following principle. Change in the corporate culture takes the form of the process of 'unfreeze', 'change', and 'refreeze'. Let us compare this process to the process of 'brainwashing' applied to the war prisoners held by the communist bloc during the Second World War.

First, the prisoners' preconceptions were destroyed by pointing out the 'contradictions and errors' of capitalism (unfreeze). Next, they were taught the 'correctness' of communism. For those who did not change their minds, food rations were reduced, and for those who accepted this change in thinking, rations were increased (change). The change was then fixed and reinforced by the peer pressure exerted by fellow prisoners, etc., (refreeze).

(A) Unfreeze
To unfreeze is to destroy the conventional values. To achieve this, people are taught that their conventional values or ways of thinking are erroneous. In the case of an individual, each person is taught to reflect inwardly and confess the error of his ways. In the case of Asahi, the process of 'evoking a crisis mentality' corresponds to 'unfreezing'. In Asahi, despite the steady loss in share, there had always been profits due to the overall expansion of the beer market; therefore, the employees did not feel that the situation was critical. A feeling of a crisis was evoked by educating them about the declining market share and the deterioration of the company image in the minds of consumers. Also, a consulting

company was employed in order to diagnose and criticize the company management.

(B) Change
There are three ways to effect a cultural change:

(a) *The Information Approach* teaches a new way of thinking. In the case of Asahi, a new management philosophy was established, and the top management, including the president, promoted the new philosophy among employees at morning meetings and other occasions. The new CI Campaign emphasized consumer and market orientation. External views were collected through the 'Live People' campaign so as to sharpen employees' sensitivity to the outside environment. Moreover, the CI Campaign encouraged the formation of new ideas by encouraging new proposals. In addition, employees were taught analytical decision-making by the TQC program.

(b) *The Experience Approach* consists of having employees solve problems by themselves: go through new experiences; and it forces them to take new measures. This is most effective for creating changes in the corporate culture. Essentially, this amounts to a change in strategy, particularly with regard to the development of new products and their subsequent success. For Asahi, it was the development and success of the new draught beer (Koku-Kire Beer) in 1986. This deepened the understanding of the importance of a customer orientation, and the company emerged from having an 'underdog' corporate culture and acquired a new culture filled with confidence. The mobilization of the employees in the 1-million subject trial sam-

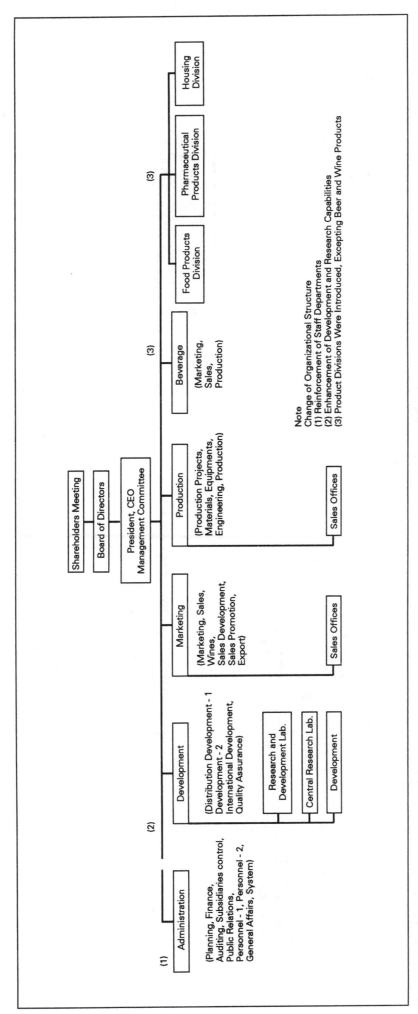

Figure 4. Asahi Organization 1989

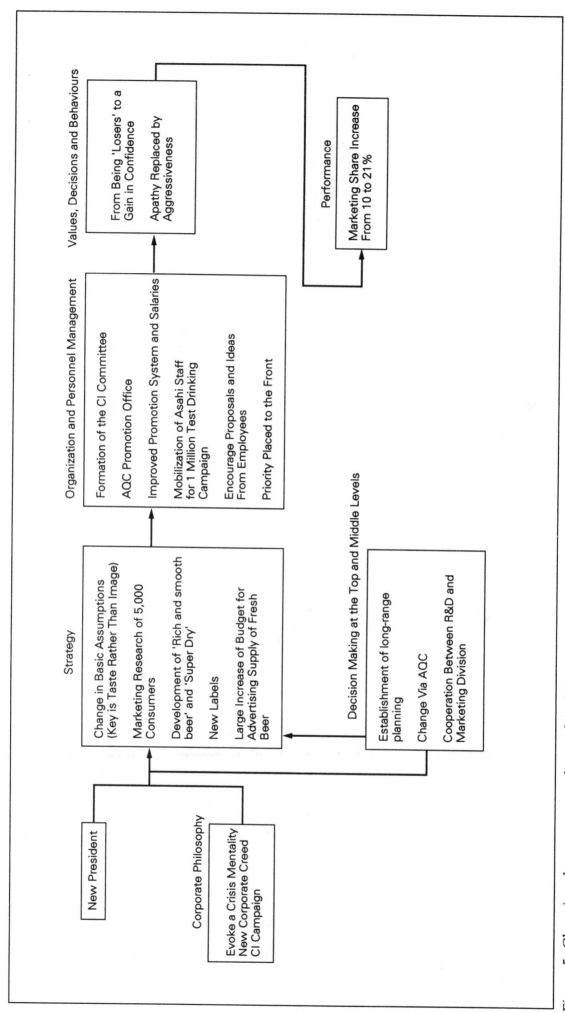

Figure 5. Changing the corporate culture of Asahi Breweries

pling provides an example of the Approach through Action. The phenomenal success of Super Dry in 1987 put new energy into the corporate culture.

(c) *The Approach through Reward and Punishment* involves rewarding preferable actions and punishing undesirable ones and is mainly achieved by changes in personnel management. The execution of various campaigns and corresponding performance commendations awarded to participating employees fall under this category. Mobilization of the employees for the 1-million subject trial sampling and commendations for the 'Live People Campaign' were also conducted. Also salaries were increased. Improvements in labour conditions which were triggered by the success of new products provided rewards for those who helped with the corporate culture.

(d) *Finally there is the 'Comprehensive Approach'*. This includes all three appoaches, and requires a replacement of the top management. Asahi used this method i.e. Information, Experience, Reward and Punishment.

(C) *Refreeze*
In order to 'refreeze' a change, it is necessary continuously to reward and punish, to teach new ways of thinking, and to provide new experiences which reinforce the correctness of the change in culture. In the case of Asahi, we followed the success of the first beer with the development of the second new product, 'Super Dry', thus refreezing the new way of thinking. To refreeze a change and maintain the impetus, a continuous revolution such as the continuous development of new products is required. Maintaining the momentum of the revolution by the continuous development of new products and business is essential to maintain a revitalized corporate culture.

References

Junya Ishikawa, *Asahi Beer no Chosen* (Challenge of Asahi Breweries, Ltd), Japan Management Association (1987).

Toyohiro Kono, *Henkaku no Kigyo Bunka* (Change of the Corporate Culture), Kodan-Sha (1988).

Tadashi Umezawa, *Kigyu bunka no Sohzoh* (Creation of the Corporate Culture), Yuhi Kaku (1986).

G. C. Morris, *Psychology, an Introduction,* Prentice-Hall (1982).

E. Shein, *Organization Culture & Leadership,* Jossey-Bass Publishers (1985)

R. H. Kilman, *Gaining Control of the Corporate Culture,* Jossey-Bass Publishers (1986).

The Transformation of Nissan— The Reform of Corporate Culture

Yasuhiro Ishizuna

This is the story of how a change in corporate culture affected corporate strategy and led to the turnaround of Nissan Motor. Nissan's domestic sales had slumped and there was discord between top management and the labour unions creating company malaise. A change in top management and a different union leader led to the inauguration of a new organization which transformed every area of the company.

Introduction

It has been said for many years now that the global automobile market is mature. Yet, there is a widely held view that automobile demand will continue to expand at an annual rate of around 2 per cent, supported by rapid growth in Asian markets and by stable growth in the markets of the industrial countries. Based on this assumption, it is projected that global demand in the year 2000 will be in the neighbourhood of 60 million units compared with the 1988 level of approximately 48 million vehicles.

Nissan's world-wide vehicle sales in fiscal 1988 totalled approximately 2·8 million units, representing roughly 6 per cent of global demand. By around the year 2000, Nissan wants to expand this sales figure to approximately 4·8 million units, corresponding to roughly 8 per cent of global automobile demand. The company's strategy for supplying this volume of vehicles is to build a production system for manufacturing 60 per cent of them in Japan and the remaining 40 per cent overseas. In round figures, that works out to a domestic production volume of 2·8 million units and an overseas volume of 2 million units.

The Early 1980s

In the early 1980s although Nissan was attracting much public attention for its enterprise abroad, its base in the domestic market was shaky. With the slow-down in demand that began in 1980, the company's sales in Japan went into a tailspin. Prior to that time, Nissan had consistently held around 30 per cent of the domestic market, but during the 1980s our share continued to slip every year until it finally dropped below 24 per cent in 1987. Instead of being admired for its bold international strategy, Nissan began to attract public attention as a large manufacturer that was in trouble. As a result, even the company's international strategy came under fire. Nissan was criticized for directing all of its attention overseas while measures for correcting the sales situation in the home market took a back seat. Because of successive investments made in large-scale projects overseas and slumping domestic sales, the company's profits during this period remained virtually flat.

Labour Problems

Nissan's poor business performance during the first half of the 1980s was the result of various interrelated factors. One of the biggest obstacles keeping the company from breaking out of the slump, was the conflict between the labour union and management. It was ironic that labour–management relations should serve as shackles in Nissan's case whereas they are generally recognized as one of the factors behind the success of Japanese-style management.

Relations between the labour union and management at Nissan had begun anew from the time of repeated labour disputes in the early 1950s. A new labour union was formed in 1953 out of a protracted dispute led by the then radical labour union organization. The aim of the new union was to improve the living standards of its members through a co-operative relationship with management and improvement of the company's performance. It also received the strong support of

Mr Yasuhiro Ishizuna is General Manager, Business Research Department, Nissan Motor Co. Ltd., Tokyo, Japan.

management, beginning with Mr Katsuji Kawamata, who later became Nissan president in 1957.

The years that followed marked the beginning of a honeymoon period for labour and management, and Nissan's growth during the 1960s and 1970s owed a great deal to labour–management co-operation. Unfortunately for Nissan, at some point that labour–management co-operation resulted in a blurring of the respective roles which each side was supposed to play. For example, the labour union gradually came to have a say in personnel matters and other issues which were the prerogative of management. In addition, union-related activities and meetings were openly held during working hours and were tacitly tolerated by the company.

Mr Ishihara's Appointment as President

The man chosen to fill the post of president in 1977 was Mr Ishihara, who had objected all along to the developing situation and had worked hard to change labour–management relations. As was expected, the labour union reacted strongly to his policy and labour–management relations rapidly deteriorated. This, then, was the situation at Nissan as it moved into the 1980s. Nissan was pushing ahead with an aggressive international strategy, but the company had problems in its home market.

The labour union opposed Nissan's international projects believing that they would 'export' jobs to overseas locations. It also stepped up its criticism of management over the slump in domestic sales. However, there were no constructive debates as to what steps labour and management should take to overcome the company's difficulties. Things eventually reached the point where labour and management could no longer carry on an effective dialogue.

Declining Public Image

The deterioration of labour–management relations were only an internal problem up to this point. However, the situation was exacerbated in August 1983, when the top labour union representative called a press conference to announce the union's opposition to a plan the company was studying for the construction of a manufacturing plant in the United Kingdom. The breach between labour and management was unmistakable.

Nissan's industrial relations problems were given extensive coverage in Japan's mass media. They were even publicized in major publications overseas as a scandalous situation for a leading representative of Japan's automobile industry. This seriously damaged Nissan's public image, and caused internal turmoil and delays in carrying out important projects.

Ultimately, ordinary employees, who were themselves members of the labour union, began to question the union's position in view of the worsening state of affairs. There was a ground swell of opinion among the employees in favour of normalizing labour–management relations to protect their own livelihoods and their future careers. As a result, of this pressure, the union leadership resigned and relations with management started to improve.

The 8 years from 1977–1985 in which Mr Ishihara served as the company's president were devoted primarily to the promotion of Nissan's international projects and the normalization of labour–management relations. However, these two contributions were extremely significant because they formed the basis for the company's subsequent transformation. The normalization of labour–management relations was especially important because it gave a large boost to the morale of the ordinary employees and younger managers, who became the nucleus of the drive to transform the company at the grass roots level. As Professor Toyohiro Kono states in his book *The Reform of Corporate Culture*, the section managers are the bearers of a company's culture and their energies are crucial to a successful culture change.

Changing the Corporate Culture

In 1985, Mr Ishihara assumed the position of chairman and a new organization was established under the leadership of the current Nissan president, Mr Yutaka Kume. As labour–management relations improved, Mr Kume directed his energies toward a reform of the company's systems and organization. The motto that he put forward was that 'management and the labour union should both discharge their respective duties properly'.

He appealed to everyone 'to change the traditional currents and create a new corporate culture'. He also pointed out the necessity of turning our attention to the outside world, i.e. the market-place and customers, without being restricted by the company's hierarchical structure or past customs.

Soon after Mr Kume took over as president, he visited the company's offices, dealers and affiliated firms throughout Japan and made a vigorous effort to improve direct communications with the employees and the other companies in the Nissan Group.

Moreover, he encouraged all employees to address each other as 'mister', regardless of the other person's rank in the company, and that included himself as well. While this reform did not go as far as the first name basis common in Western countries, it was a break from the previous practice of addressing other people by their titles.

Other measures that were taken to reform the company's systems and customs included stopping the wearing of uniforms by female employees and the introduction of flexible working hours.

Specific efforts were also directed toward changing the employees' traditional attitudes and ways of thinking, in order to firmly establish the practice of putting the customer first. For instance, the manner in which visitors were received by receptionists at the head office was reviewed and improved. The writing on vistior's badges was also changed and eventually the badges were discontinued altogether.

In the first year or so of his tenure as president, Mr Kume implemented one reform after another. Yet it was no easy task to turn around the company's performance, which continued to slide. The slow erosion of Nissan's domestic market share continued for another 2 years, until 1987.

The Appreciation of the Yen

Just as the internal reforms launched under Mr Kume's new leadership were beginning to move ahead, a dramatic change in the external environment dealt Nissan a further blow. This was the sharp appreciation of the yen following the Plaza Accord reached by the 'Group of Five' finance ministers in October 1985. In October 1985 the dollar was trading at around ¥240. In the next year the yen appreciated by more than 70 per cent to a rate of about ¥140 to the dollar late in 1986. In 1987 the yen continued to climb until the exchange rate reached a level of ¥120 to the dollar in 1988.

In overseas markets, Nissan had no choice but to raise prices. Needless to say, it was impossible to increase prices to the same extent as the yen's appreciation in value. Naturally higher prices translated directly into a decline in competitiveness.

Nissan's First Operating Loss

Beset by sluggish domestic sales and a drastic reduction in profits on exports to the U.S., Nissan posted an operating loss of ¥20bn for the first half of fiscal 1986. That was the first red ink the company had ever recorded since being listed on the Tokyo Stock Exchange in 1951. By registering an operating profit of ¥79bn for the second half of 1986, Nissan was able to offset the first-half loss and avoided ending the year in the red. Nonetheless, Nissan suffered the ignominy of being the only firm among Japan's 11 automobile manufacturers to show a loss during that year.

Looking back on it now, the sharp appreciation of the yen was a blessing in disguise for Nissan in the sense that it enabled us to mount an all-out effort to transform the entire company. The crisis suddenly brought into view a number of problems that had been lurking just below the surface and heightened the employees' consciousness of the need for change. Since the improvement of employee relations had already prepared a receptive environment within Nissan for change, the sense of crisis felt by the individual employee proved to be one of the strongest forces driving the company's transformation.

The Change Process

Both labour and management clearly understood that Nissan would go under unless something was done. The proposal advanced earlier by Mr Kume to 'change the traditional currents' in the company was thus taken up as a practical issue that had to be addressed. Already changes were under way at the grass-roots level throughout the company, and virtually overnight they were accelerated into a concerted drive to transform the corporate culture. What pulled all those efforts together was the new corporate philosophy adopted around the end of 1986.

Nissan's corporate philosophy states that, 'our first commitment is to customer satisfaction. Through diligent efforts to develop new customers and expand our customer base we are contributing to the ongoing progress and enrichment of society'. The drive to reform Nissan's corporate culture, which had begun with Mr Kume's call to 'change the traditional currents' following the improvement of labour–management relations, now had a clearly defined objective—customer satisfaction. The corporate philosophy was printed on a card and distributed to all the employees. After that it became the standard for all of Nissan's operations.

Table 1. Corporate philosophy and principles

Corporate philosophy
Our first commitment is to customer satisfaction. Through diligent efforts to develop new customers and expand our customer base we are contributing to the ongoing progress and enrichment of society
Corporate principles
(1) To create attractive products by capitalizing on the company's innovative and highly reliable technologies, staying in constant touch with the needs of the global market
(2) To be sensitive to customers' needs and offer them maximum satisfaction based on steadfast sincerity and ceaseless efforts to meet their requirements
(3) To focus on global trends, making the world the stage for our activities, and to nurture a strong company that will grow with the times
(4) To foster the development of an active and vital group of people who are ready and willing at all times to take on the challenge of achieving new goals

Be-1 Story

Gradually, the drive for reform began to achieve tangible results. One example was the development of the Be-1. This limited production model, of which 10,000 units were sold only in the domestic market in 1987, was a phenomenal hit among the public because of its unique 'retro-look' styling. It was so popular, in fact, that Nissan almost had to hold a lottery to select from the queue of buyers.

The Be-1 was born out of an attempt by Nissan's young designers to create a 1-litre class car with no restrictions or prior assumptions regarding its design. This was in 1984, when Nissan was being criticized in the mass media for its conservative styling. Competing in the project were three teams from the design and product development division. The teams used different approaches, some of which had never been tried before, such as inviting participation by outside designers at the stage where the basic concept was created. The name Be-1 came from the fact that clay model 1 created by the B team was selected as the prototype design. It also included the idea that the car would be worthy of being number one.

In the design evaluation process, the model received the overwhelming support of the young employees. Older employees did not give it such high marks, because to them it seemed old fashioned. In response to pressure from the young employees, a working prototype was hurriedly produced and the Be-1 was exhibited at the 1985 Tokyo Motor Show as a prototype.

The Be-1 proved to be a tremendous favourite at the motor show, and Nissan saw in its popularity an excellent opportunity to strike a chord among young people and trend-setters. The commercialization was carried out at an unpecedented pace and the model was ready for release by January 1987. Within 2 months advance orders had been received for the entire planned production volume of 10,000 units. Owing to the enormous popularity of the Be-1 the price of a used car soon exceeded that of a new one, and the Be-1 attracted a great deal of public attention both at home and abroad.

Just a few months earlier, Nissan had announced its embarrassing operating loss, and the encouraging response to the Be-1 quickened the drive to transform the company.

Reforms were beginning to be seen in various departments, but some of the most dramatic changes took place in the product development division. Hot on the heels of the Be-1, Nissan created a succession of hit cars that radically transformed the product line. Nissan began to pursue a market-driven approach to product development that focused on customers' true needs and wants. Existing models, which had been criticized for their lack of individuality and old-

Figure 1. Be-1

fashioned styling, were rapidly replaced by new cars which were distinctive in design and targeted at specific market segments. As a result, the new products played a very important part in forging closer ties between Nissan and its customers.

Every time a new model was unveiled Nissan launched an aggressive advertising campaign as well. Just as the company was being reformed internally, its public image was also changing. People outside the company said: 'Nissan has changed' and 'Nissan has taken on new life'.

The Cima Phenomenon

If the Be-1 was Nissan's star attraction at the 1985 Tokyo Motor Show, the Cima was the company's centrepiece at the 1987 show. Designed and engineered to be Japan's first personal luxury sedan, the Cima was unveiled at the motor show in late autumn and released in the domestic market the following January. Although this top-of-the-line model carried a recommended price of ¥5·5m, the Cima set an amazing, sales record for its class of 8000 units in 1 month, a trend which was supported by a strong surge in consumer spending. Its remarkable sales performance gave birth to a new expression, 'the Cima phenomenon', which typified the new desire of Japanese consumers for big-ticket items.

Expansion of Overseas Operations

The company's turnaround in the domestic market represented first results of improved industrial relations, and was driven by the employees' sense of crisis. During that same period, changes were also being implemented to expand the overseas operations that had been established while Mr Ishihara was president.

One example was Nissan's decision to build a manufacturing plant in the United Kingdom. In 1981, Nissan announced that it was beginning a feasibility study and, in 1984, the decision to construct a U.K. manufacturing facility was made public. The first phase of the project saw the start-up of a pilot plant with an annual output of around 24,000 units. In 1986, after Mr Kume had come in as president, Nissan drew up plans for the second phase, which called for the annual production capacity to be expanded to 200,000 units by 1992 and the local content ratio to be raised to 80 per cent by 1991.

Similar expansion plans were also implemented at Nissan's U.S. manufacturing plant, which had started building pick-up trucks earlier in 1983. A compact passenger car, Sentra, was added to the production mix in 1985 and a study was launched to add a third model in the early 1990s. The local content ratio has also been raised steadily from

Figure 2. Cima

40 per cent, the level when the plant came on stream. Local content has now passed 60 per cent and the next goal is to boost it to around 70–75 per cent.

Promotion of Localization

One of the biggest changes in Nissan's overseas operations can be seen in the persistent effort to promote 'localization'. The term localization often refers to 'hardware', such as the percentage of locally manufactured components which are used or the local production of engines and other major parts. In recent years, however, positive steps have also been taken to localize 'software' through the establishment of design and R & D facilities overseas and the hiring of local chief executives to manage the operations.

Nissan's U.S. plant was managed from the beginning by an American and the U.K. facility has had a British chief executive since 1988. In the United States, Nissan established a design studio, Nissan Design International, in 1979 and a research and development arm, Nissan Research and Development, Inc., in 1983. In the United Kingdom, Nissan set up Nissan European Technology Centre, Ltd. in 1988 as the nucleus of its R & D activities in Europe.

The localization programme that Nissan is pursuing is not an *ad hoc* policy designed to meet the demands of local governments. It is aimed at enabling Nissan to become a good corporate citizen in the communities where the company does business.

The decisions to build manufacturing plants in the United States and the United Kingdom, were originally taken with political factors in mind such as the trend towards protectionism. However, the enormous changes which have occurred in the global economy since then have completely altered the position of Nissan's overseas operations. In exchange rates for example, the outlook for the medium term suggests extreme volatility. Yet there is no possibility now of returning to an international strategy based on the export of finished vehicles. In this situation Nissan needs quickly to raise the level of its overseas operations to the point where they can function successfully on their own. That course of action represents the best way for Nissan to stabilize its entire business and make it invulnerable to external factors such as exchange rate swings.

It was reported some time ago that the French government had decided not to recognize Nissan Bluebird passenger cars manufactured at the U.K. plant and exported to the European Continent as being U.K.-built products. Nissan's efforts to achieve a higher level of localization are based on a belief that these measures are necessary to ensure the success of the operations. They are not being made because of local content requirements, imposed for political reasons or governmental guidelines.

Globalization

Another aspect of Nissan's transformation is the globalization of the company's operations. Nissan announced a Programme of International Co-operation in September 1989 which is aimed at expanding production volumes at overseas manufacturing plants and substantially reducing exports of finished vehicles from Japan.

By the end of the 1990s Nissan intends to build two out of every three vehicles which the company sells overseas, with the remaining one-third coming from Japan. That will be a complete reversal of the present ratio of 2:1 in favour of Japan-built vehicles. Another aim of this programme is to double the value of parts and vehicles that Nissan imports from other countries.

The most significant feature of this programme is the clear statement it presents of Nissan's corporate policy on globalization. With the adoption of this programme, Nissan has said farewell to the previous growth strategy of producing products in Japan and exporting them in large quantities. In its place Nissan has embraced a policy of globalization that will be implemented through continuous efforts to localize operations overseas.

The key to the success of this challenging programme, lies in the construction of a network linking Nissan's global operations, including small and medium-sized offshore bases. This is a strategic task that will have to be addressed over the medium term as Nissan enhances the level of localization at its major manufacturing bases overseas.

Maintaining the profitability of each global base as localization proceeds will require a minimum scale of operation. Nissan plans to achieve this by constructing an operations network that will provide maximum overall efficiency. The three poles of the network will be North America, Europe and Asia. The network will facilitate mutual exchange of vehicles and parts among these three regions as well as within each region. The network will also include working partnerships and joint ventures with other competing manufacturers.

Conclusion

Nissan experienced some severe ups and downs in the 1980s. During this decade, a continuous process of change was under way at two levels. One was the macro-level involving the global organization of Nissan's operations; the other was the micro-level concerning labour–management relations and the corporate culture.

The company's transformation has only just begun. A long road lies ahead that is crossed by many hurdles. Whether or not we can meet the challenges before us will be the true test of Nissan's transformation. We are vigorously channelling our energies toward the attainment of the specific goal of constructing a network linking the company's global operations. Once that network has been completed, then we will be able to celebrate the completion of Nissan's transformation.

Appendix

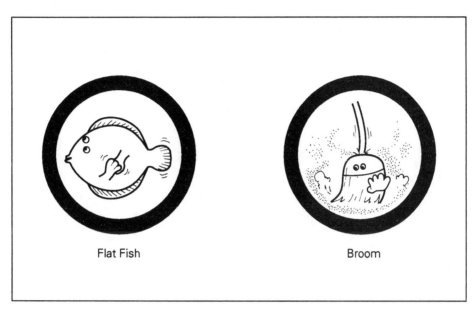

Figure 3. Stickers used to change the corporate culture

The flat fish has eyes looking up at only the upside. This symbolizes a person who only pays attention to the boss and looks up at him all the time.

The broom symbolizes a person who cleans only the spot on which he stands, moving the dust to others' spot, a bureaucratic person.

These stickers were invented by young managers in the development department, who were promoting the grass-root movement to change the corporate culture of Nissan. They wanted to visualize the new codes of behaviour.

These stickers were distributed to any person who wanted to have them, and they were put on tables, on cabinets and on walls for warning of undesirable behaviour.

PART FOUR

Managing Research and New Product Development

Planning Research and Development at Hitachi

Yutaka Kuwahara, Osami Okada and Hisashi Horikoshi

Research and development planning at the Central Research Laboratory at Hitachi Ltd. is reviewed and discussed, including its organization, resource allocation, interactions and collaborations, the cultivation of innovative ideas and the evaluation of R & D.
Emphasis is given to the synergistic effects which can be achieved through different kinds of interactions, through the co-existence of several research approaches such as independent and commissioned, basic and applied, main-line business and exploratory research, as well as through many kinds of collaborations. The authors also refer to the methods used to evaluate R & D, especially portfolio analysis and the assessment of cost-effectiveness.

Effective planning for R & D at an industrial research laboratory poses several strategic issues, such as resource allocation, technology transfer, relationships with outside organizations, e.g. government projects, co-operation with universities and international collaborations. The Central Research Laboratory (CRL) of Hitachi has been performing R & D in microelectronics and information technology for the last 20 years.

Now in a technology-driven industry, strategic planning for R & D virtually determines the future of the company.

Hitachi was established in 1910, at Hitachi city—about 150 km north of Tokyo. In the beginning, its main products were heavy electrical machinery such as motors and generators. Gradually the product types expanded and the business focus shifted to electronics, in line with the trends in world-wide business. The shift was accelerated some time after the founding of the Central Research Laboratory in 1942, when other corporate research laboratories were established and engaged in electronics research.

The authors are executives at the Central Research laboratory of Hitachi Ltd., Tokyo. Y. Kuwahara is Head of R & D Administration, O. Okada is Assistant Head of the Planning Office and H. Horikoshi is Deputy General Manager.

In 1987 sales of information and communication systems and electronics devices were the largest activity in the company. R & D expenditure in 1987 was $2bn, which was about 9 per cent of sales and employed 12,000 R & D people.

In Hitachi, there are now nine corporate level research laboratories which have about 4000 staff. These research laboratories report directly to the executive vice president in charge of research. In the business group, there are several research centres and many development or design departments, where about 8000 people are engaged in new product development. In the head office, there is a department in charge of co-ordination, promotion and assessment of large inter-divisional projects or large prototype development.

Among the nine corporate research laboratories, Hitachi Research Laboratory and the CRL are the two oldest and largest. The other seven laboratories are fairly new and most of them are offsprings of the CRL. The Advanced Research Laboratory is the newest and the smallest and it's mission is to sow the seeds for the 21st century. It is important that the other research laboratories are also engaged in basic or fundamental research in their own research area.

Figure 1 shows the R & D categories at Hitachi. There are three types of research at the corporate level—Independent Research, Commissioned (or Sponsored) Research, and Product Development. There are, of course, strong relationships among these three types of research. As Fig. 1 shows, independent research is done at the discretion of the general manager of the laboratory, targeting beyond 5 years of research results. Commissioned research aims at a shorter term target of 3 to 5 years. Product Development is done by the production plant. On average 70 per cent of the research conducted at the corporate laboratory level is commissioned research and the remaining 30 per cent is independent research. However, at the CRL, 50 per cent is independent research.

	Independent Research	Commissioned Research	Product Development
R & D Funding	Head Office	Sponsor (Works, Subsidiary Companies, etc.)	Works
Project Authorization	By General Manager of Laboratory	On Contract Basis (Sponsor–Laboratory)	By General Manager of Works
Target	Beyond 5 years (Risky and Callenging)	Within 5 years (High Percentage of Success)	1–2 years (Product Strategy)
Ratio — 9 Corporate Labs	30%	70%	
Ratio — Central Research Lab. (CRL)	50%	50%	
Ratio — Advanced Research Lab. (ARL)	100%	0%	
Ratio — Development Dept. at Works			100%

Figure 1. R & D categories

Basic Philosophy and Attitudes Towards Research at the CRL

The CRL was established in 1942 in the forest of the old Musashino plateau in Tokyo prefecture by Hitachi's founder, Mr Namihei Odaira, for the purpose of 'creating new technologies for 10 or 20 years hence, as well as pursuing development work for the present business'.

Figure 2 shows a bird's eye-view of the CRL with three main research buildings and other facilities scattered around in the 215,000 m² wooded precinct.

Figure 3 shows the basic R & D philosophy of Mr Namihei Odaira. This became Hitachi's basic R & D philosophy, and especially that of the CRL.

Historically, the first 5 years were a period of confusion, followed by the next 10 years until 1960 as a learning period. From 1960 to 1975 was the growth period when Hitachi gradually intensified its concentration on electronics. 1975 to 1985 can be called the 'shifting from quantity to quality' period, followed by the last 3 years of 'innovation age'.

The CRL has about 1300 employees—970 researchers and 330 in support and management. The CRL alone requires $150m dollars per year.

As to the areas of research at the CRL, right now about 40 per cent are engaged in information technology, 35 per cent in microelectronics and the remaining 25 per cent in fundamentals. Here, fundamentals mean basic component technologies for information technology and microelectronics.

The reason for limiting the scope of the research area is in order to deepen the research activity in these three areas, avoiding the shallow diversified research activity with limited personnel.

For the goal of creating new industry and business, there are two approaches to initiating the research.

(1) In the new systems research area, future 'latent' social needs must be converted into the actual technologies to be pursued.

(2) In the new materials or devices research area, 'a quantum jump' must be achieved in both quality and quantity.

International R & D collaboration has been especially promoted recently, including contract-based joint research, accepting foreign researchers to do research here at Kokubunji in Tokyo and the direct support of international conferences or seminars.

Figure 4 shows the yearly cycle of research planning at the CRL. Every year in early autumn, after the strategy discussion on important technological areas, the general manager gives guidelines for the next 5 years long range planning. Based upon the guidelines given, each research department makes up the departmental long range plan (5 years, usually) including those of the research units in the department. Through a strategic planning meeting, the CRL's long range plan is formed based upon the departmental long range plans, and it is submitted to the corporate R & D co-ordination department. Then the proposals for new research subjects and their preliminary evaluation starts, to be followed by the laboratory–sponsor meeting to determine commissioned research. At the final stage of planning, an overall research plan meeting is held to give the final 'go' or 'no-go'. Then the approved research starts. Special care is taken to make the

Figure 2. Bird's eye-view of the Central Research Laboratory

1 year cycle-based R & D planning effective, and to eliminate unnecessary overheads—like the duplication of documents. Flexibility is especially stressed so that, for example, any new commissioned research can start at any time of the year.

Resource Allocation

Co-existence of Different Kinds of Research
At the CRL, several kinds of research co-exist to allow individual researchers to be involved in their most suitable style of research. It is expected that discussions among different areas of research on related technology will produce something new and innovative.

Independent Research and Commissioned Research
Figure 5 shows the relationship, especially the migration among three kinds of research—North Star Research (NSR), Independent Research (IR) and Commissioned Research (CR)—at the CRL. NSR is new research pursued by an innovative

researcher as one of the future areas of development. NSR is funded and managed on a departmental level and is part of IR.

Also shown in Fig. 5 are exploratory, creating-new-business and trunk-line business types of research, which are explained in the next section.

The three kinds of research at the CRL are closely interrelated. Therefore, in the research discussions on a certain technology or product, there are participants from three kinds of related research. This will stimulate the discussion and lead to the birth of creative ideas.

Trunk-line Business Research, Creating-new-business Research, Exploratory Research, Three Types of Research
It is very important for the CRL to contribute to immediate and future business, because this will engender trust on the part of sponsors as well as the corporate management, and especially when the CRL challenges future innovations. Therefore,

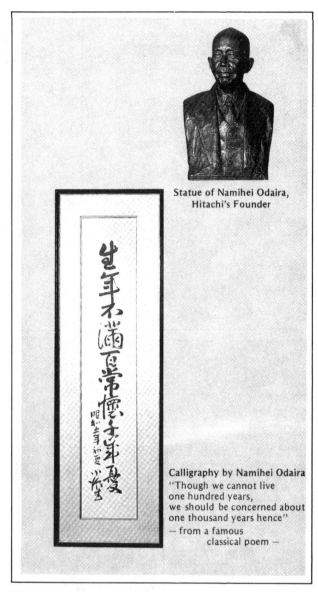

Statue of Namihei Odaira,
Hitachi's Founder

Calligraphy by Namihei Odaira
"Though we cannot live
one hundred years,
we should be concerned about
one thousand years hence"
— from a famous
classical poem —

Figure 3. Namihei Odaira and his R & D philosophy

R & D planning must be effectively applied to project-type team-based trunk-line product development, challenging new business creation research and individual high-risk future-oriented research for new frontier exploration.

Quite often, there are lively discussions among these different areas of research. Often something new comes out of the discussions, because it involves researchers with different but deeply-held ideas. Every year there is a thorough review to maintain the balance of these types of research in all departments, and some guidelines are laid down.

These are carefully formulated to allocate research personnel and funds to these different types of research, so that through the 'synergistic' interaction between them, the maximum innovative outcome will develop.

Interactions Outside the CRL

Technology Transfer
Technology transfer is shown in Fig. 6, where solid lines represent the transfer of technology and the blank lines show the transfer of personel. Here, (A) is the simplest case, i.e. just transferring technology alone. (B) represents the case where researchers are temporarily sent to the factory to transfer the developed technology, while in (C) factory engineers go to the laboratory to absorb the new technology. Case (D) is unique, it is where a branch of the laboratory plays the key role in transferring technology and sometimes researchers, too.

Relationship with Government/University
It is becoming increasingly important to maintain

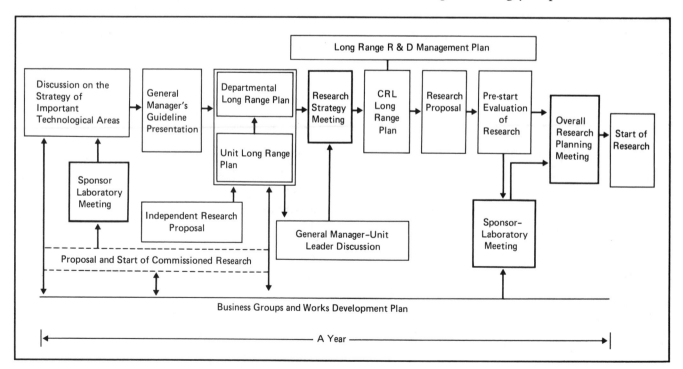

Figure 4. Yearly cycle of research planning

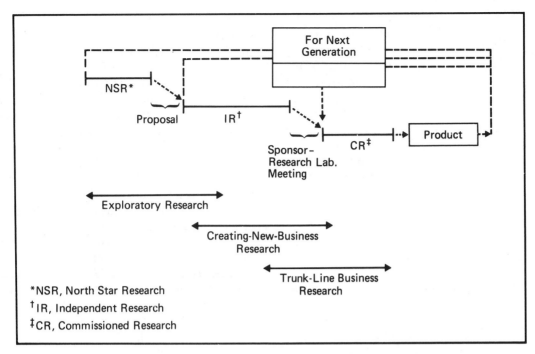

Figure 5. Three kinds of research

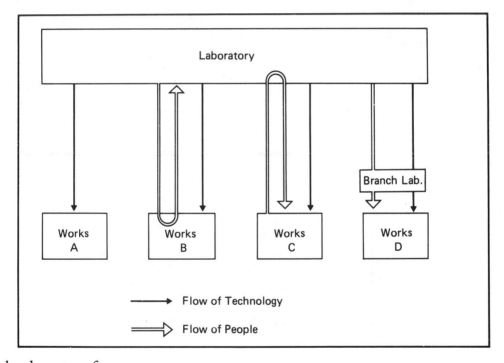

Figure 6. Technology transfer

good relationships with government and universities, as the globalization of the industry proceeds. Although government funding in the CRL is less than 5 per cent, this is used most effectively, for basic or fundamental research into future development. For example, the Fifth Generation Computer System project (ICOT) or Extended Definition TV advisory committee, significantly stimulated and encouraged concerned research areas within the CRL.

Two typical examples of the relationship with universities is the research on Quantum Flux Parametron (QFP) with Prof. Eiichi Goto of the University of Tokyo, and Universal Representation of Real Numbers (URR) with several other professors. In the former case, the CRL succeeded in the experimental realization of QFP which was invented by Prof. Goto. While in URR, professors helped to evaluate and refine the scheme proposed by a senior researcher of the CRL.

More than ten researchers and middle managers are now being sent from the CRL to participate in several ongoing governmental projects.

International Collaborations
The laboratory conducts collaborative research

with foreign institutes and foreign researchers. The fellowship programme is called HIVIPS (<u>Hi</u>tachi Research <u>Vi</u>sit <u>P</u>rogram<u>s</u>). The CRL directly supports the international symposium called ISQM (<u>I</u>nternational <u>S</u>ymposium on Foundations of <u>Q</u>uantum <u>M</u>echanics). The 1st and 2nd ISQM were held in 1983 and 1986 at the CRL and the 3rd will be held in August 1989. In order to contribute to the international science/engineering arena, the CRL sends about 200 researchers a year abroad to present technical papers at international conferences. Also, the CRL annually holds seminars at such universities as Stanford, MIT, UCB, etc. HIVIPS was established in 1984 and has become more and more popular. This year the CRL will accept about 30 foreign researchers to spend about a year on research work. Among the three types of sub-programs (VRP, EXP, TRP—<u>V</u>isiting <u>R</u>esearchers <u>P</u>rogram, <u>Ex</u>change Researchers <u>P</u>rogram, <u>Tr</u>ainees <u>P</u>rogram), VRP researchers always predominate. As was expected, the HIVIPS program succeeded in creating new innovation through the synergistic interaction of professionals with different professional and cultural backgrounds.

Cultivation of Innovation

Dynamic Research Organization

In order to achieve effective dynamic research, the research organization of the CRL is in two areas—static and dynamic—as shown in Figs 7 and 8. Static organization, including the key R & D

activities, is shown in Fig. 7. There are 11 research departments or equivalents, a few supporting and three staff offices. Dynamic organization is shown in Fig. 8. In a research department there are several research units. A research unit is the smallest organizational cluster of researchers with the same technology potential, consisting of a unit leader plus an average of ten researchers. Usually a few North Star, Independent and/or Commissioned research subjects are pursued in a unit, with some participants from other units, either inside or outside the department. Sometimes, instead of a unit, a branch laboratory is provided at the same level. A research unit includes researchers in a certain technology area, such as supercomputer architecture, optical disk, or superconducting device technology. Besides the research subjects, 'projects' or 'programs' are organized dynamically to achieve strategic research, as shown in Fig. 8. A project aims at achieving the goals, either for urgent business needs or for required technology, and involves researchers from different departments, but a programme is for the purpose of preliminary investigation of key technology before the actual start of such research. A project or programme belongs to a particular department. Researchers participating in a project or a programme, report to the project leader or programme manager who in turn reports to the departmental manager. Once a project or a programme is finished, researchers participating in it return to their original units to re-join the research in the units.

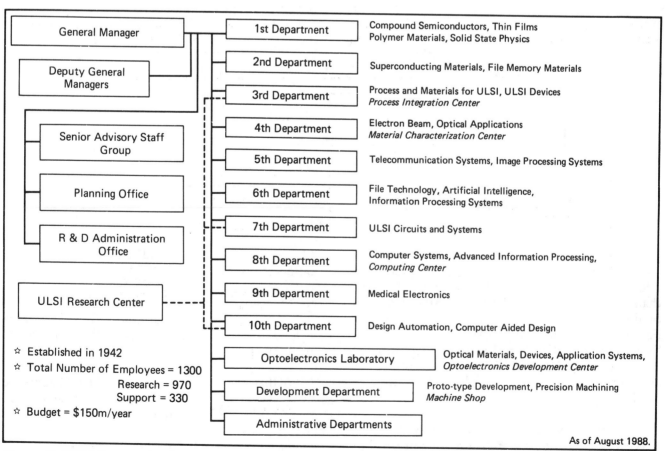

Figure 7. HCRL organization

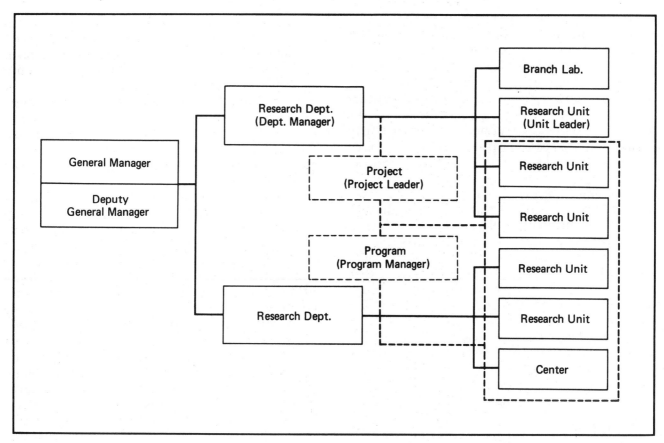

Figure 8. Research organization of CRL

Sometimes, an inter-divisional project called 'Tokken' is organized to achieve strategic R & D on an important product or technology. A 'Tokken' is proposed by corporate research laboratories, divisions, works or sales offices, and is organized and promoted by the R & D promotion centre of the corporate research and technology co-ordination department at the head office. Here, again, researchers participate in 'Tokken'.

Promoting New Proposals of Research
In order to encourage researchers to propose new innovative research, a 'research proposal system' is provided, as described in Fig. 9. A 'research pro-

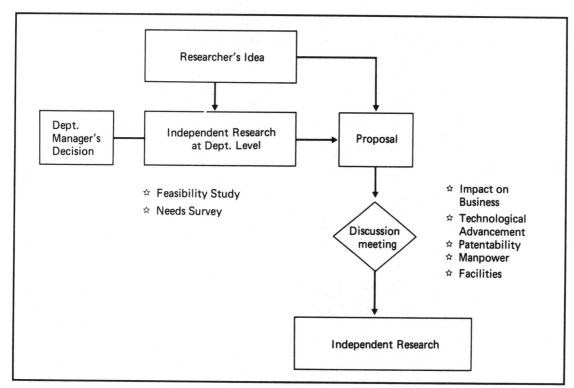

Figure 9. Research proposal system

posal' is sometimes an out-growth of a 'North Star Research' and may grow into an 'Independent Research'. When a proposal is submitted by a researcher, a meeting is held to discuss its impact on business, technological advantages, patentability, needed man-power, required facilities, etc. In order to promote the research proposal system, the 'proposal' without actual implementation plan may be approved, because sometimes research cannot be started immediately.

Three Ladders Promotion System
In order to encourage and promote technically and managerially talented people, a promotion system with three ladders was introduced. As Fig. 10 shows, a person is closely filtered when he or she is promoted to a senior researcher level, and is either assigned to a unit leader or becomes a senior researcher. There are even cases of such a researcher being assigned to a unit leader as a manager without being promoted to a senior researcher. However, at this level, the distinction is less rigid. When a senior researcher is promoted, it is a definite step up this ladder, either to chief researcher or to departmental manager. From this level upward, there are virtually no interchanges between the two ladders. There is another ladder linked directly to the income level. This third ladder is the common basis of both technical and managerial ladders. Levels of the third ladder are closely determined by the comprehensive evaluation of each individual.

By the effective functioning of this multi-ladder

system, all researchers, supporting personnel and managers are encouraged to exhibit the maximum performance. Of course, there is some competition for promotion. However, technical promotion is determined more by absolute ability than by relative superiority, and this encourages researchers.

Evaluation of R & D

Historical Efforts
Figure 11 shows the historical efforts of R & D evaluation at CRL. As the figure shows, although quite a few trials were made for this purpose, the portfolio method for evaluating Independent Research and the RCP (Research Contributed-to-Profit)-method cost-effectiveness evaluation for commissioned research are two means now being actually used.

Portfolio Method (Pre-start Evaluation)
Figure 12 shows the portfolio method used for the pre-start research theme evaluation. As the figure shows, every Independent Research theme falls into one of the nine areas on the two dimensional chart.

Cost Effectiveness Evaluation by RCP-method
In order to perform the overall evaluation of R & D cost-effectiveness, a figure-of-merit is calculated. The Research Contributed-to-Profit (RCP) is divided by the research cost. This shows the overall cost-effectiveness status of R & D in product-

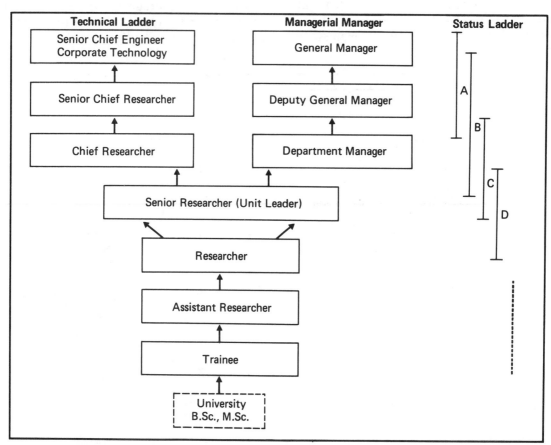

Figure 10. Three-ladders promotion system

	Activity	Methodology	Items to Evaluate
Investigation	~1969	Comparison and Some Trials	Quality of Researchers and Their Leaders Researcher's Motivation Research Cost Research Result Level of Research Innovativeness
Evaluation of Research Theme (Cross-impact Matrix)	~1974	Ranking all Research Themes by Cost and Result and Put Them Into Computer Simulation	Market Needs Innovativeness Side-effect Patent Timing of Start
	1976–1977		Simplify Items by Evaluating Independent Research, Commissioned Research
Evaluation of Research Theme (Intuition)	1974–1976	Intuitively Ranking Themes Into A,B,C, etc.	All Research Themes
	1977–1980	More closely Evaluate Newly Proposed Research Themes, Ranking Them Into A,B,C, etc.	Originality for Independent Research Superiority for Commissioned Research
Evaluation of Research Theme (Portfolio)	1980–1984	All Research Themes: Two-dimsional Evaluation of Research Result and Strategy	Market, Innovativeness, Academic Contribution, Impact, Cost, Technology Level, Patent
	1985–1988	Independent Research Only: Impact, Potential: Two-dimensional Evaluation	Market, Social and Technological Trend, Innovativeness, Long Range Planning, Patent, Level
Macroscopic Evaluation of The Result	1979–1988	Cost-effectiveness Using RCP Method	Overall Evaluation of R & D Activity in Labratories and Works

Figure 11. Historical efforts of R & D evaluation at CRL

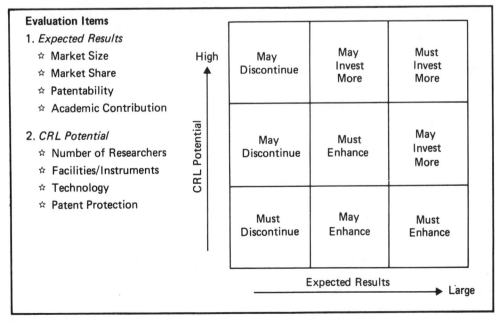

Figure 12. Research theme evaluation by portfolio method

oriented development (Commissioned Research plus related Independent Research). RCP is calculated by multiplying the profit of the product and R & D contribution factor given by the sponsor.

Usually the product will be in the market 1 year after the 'Commissioned Research' on development has been completed. By calculating in this way it is experimentally confirmed that about 70–80 per cent of results from the R & D cost are included in the calculated RCP. The cost-effectiveness of each research laboratory, each project, product group (such as computer system, communications), each product etc., can be graphically shown. Also it should be noted that this RCP cost-effectiveness not only shows the actual past results but also the future prospective curves. Therefore, the figure-of-merit can be used both for the preliminary and after-completion R & D evaluations.

R & D evaluation becomes more and more profit-oriented as the target is more closely related to the actual product. Here quantitative cost-effectiveness evaluation would be more suitable. However, it is hard to quantitatively evaluate the North Star Research or product-independent portion of Independent Research, although some portfolio guideline is set. These are for future studies.

Summary and Some Remaining Tasks

Increasing Importance of Market Information
As the impact of technology on society increases day by day, more and more market information is needed to maintain a close relationship with society, so that the new technology is acceptable. Also, this trend is accelerated as the software integration proceeds further. Keen matching with requirements is becoming far more important than just hardware performance.

Today's Busy Trunk-line Business Area Versus New Research
The mission of the CRL is to contribute to both today's trunk-line business and to future technology. However, it is sometimes dangerous to be too occupied by present profits and to disregard the tough challenges of the future. Actually, the CRL is now much involved in the development of such profitable areas as computer systems and semiconductors, but it must pay attention to long range future-oriented basic and fundamental research as well.

Future Prospects
Future areas of research as distinct from the present ones are summarized here. Nanoelectronics is crucial for future ULSI (ultra large system integration) devices. Superconducting devices can be categorized into wavefunction devices. B-ISDN and HIVISION/EDTV will perform the leading role in the future image-oriented communication society. Health care is the concern of every human being and therefore the CRL is devoting more research to this area.

Conclusion

In reviewing the R & D planning at the CRL, the following conclusions emerged.

(1) The co-existence of different types of research —such as North Star, Independent and Commissioned Research as well as basic/applied research—contributed to the interaction and stimulation which is necessary for innovation.

(2) A project or programme organized to achieve urgently needed technology or to assess crucial technology for future, can contribute to the dynamic operation of R & D planning in order to challenge the progress of high technology.

(3) International collaboration contributed considerably to the globalization of R & D, and encouraged research staff to improve the infrastructure of the CRL.

(4) A three-ladder promotion system is effective in encouraging all types of research staff to produce maximum performance.

(5) The RCP-method of overall cost-effectiveness, evaluation and portfolio analysis are a useful means of R & D strategic planning and result evaluation.

References

(1) Toyohiko Kono, *New Product Development Strategy* (in Japanese), Diamond Press (1987).

(2) Y. Kuwahara and Y. Takeda, A contribution to the managerial view on R & D cost-effectiveness evaluation at a large industrial organization, *Proceedings of the 1988 International Conference on Strategic R & D Management*, pp. E-1-1–E-1-9, May (1988).

(3) Y. Kuwahara and Y. Takeda, An empirical view over the managerial evaluation of overall R & D, *Proceedings of the 1988 IEEE Engineering Management Conference*, October (1988).

(4) Y. Kuwahara and Y. Takeda, Some experiences on HIVIPS, *Proceedings of the 1988 IEEE Engineering Management Conference*, October (1988).

(5) Nomura Research Institute, *Central Research Laboratory, Hitachi Ltd.* (in Japanese), pp. 34–39, NRI-Search, December (1987).

(6) Pelz and Andrews, *Scientists in Organization*, Wiley (1966).

(7) Thomas J. Allen, *Managing the Flow of Technology: Technology transfer and the Dissemination of Technological Information Within the R & D Organization*, MIT Press (1977).

(8) Industrial Research Institute, *R & D Strategy and Management* (in Japanese), IRI Press (1978).

(9) Industrial Research Institute, *R & D and its Management Innovation* (in Japanese), IRI Press (1978).

(10) Industrial Research Institute, *Technology Development Strategy and Management* (in Japanese), IRI Press (1983).

Creative and Innovative Research at RICOH

Akira Okamoto

'Research flourishes from People'—this is the fundamental concept of research management at RICOH. 'Creative and Innovative Research' is also the guiding principle for the researchers. To put these concepts into practice, research support, for both hardware and software, works effectively at RICOH R & D Center, Research support is relatively unique in Japan, and is one of the major factors contributing to successful research at RICOH R & D Center.

RICOH is a leading office automation equipment manufacturer, with the world's top-sales share for electronic copiers, facsimiles, and write-once optical discs. Other major RICOH products include office computers, Japanese word processors, printers, semi-conductors, software and cameras. The company was founded in 1936 and has grown to 13,000 employees. In 1990 fiscal year, net annual sales were $5bn and investment in R & D was $380m.

There are eight research laboratories at RICOH (see Figure 1)—the R & D Center, the Software Research Center, the LSI Technology R & D Laboratory, the Chemical Products R & D Center, the Production Technology Research Center, the Imaging Technology Research Center, the RICOH Research Institute of General Electronics and the RICOH California Research Center.

RICOH established the R & D Center in 1986, to commemorate the 50th anniversary. The RICOH R & D Center carries out basic research and development in advanced technology, particularly in Information Processing and Artificial Intelligence, New Materials, Optics and Mechatronics. A total of about 350 researchers work at the R & D Center.

The Research Laboratories Group Concept

Of the eight laboratories, the R & D Center comes under the direct control of RICOH's top management. The RICOH Research Institute of General Electronics and the California Research Center are subsidiary companies, and the other laboratories belong to their respective manufacturing divisions. The Executive Vice President in charge of Research (also the Director of the R & D Center) reviews projects from a research view point. Although each laboratory is managed by its own division, they are loosely combined as a Research Laboratories Group, which means that the RICOH Research Laboratories Group has the advantages of being in a group but respects the independence and autonomy of each of the laboratories. The Director's Meeting and the Research Planning Managers Meeting constitute official Group conferences. In these meetings, many topics—from long-range research strategy of the Group to small problems in one particular laboratory—are discussed. This concept is one of the features of RICOH's R & D management.

R & D Management and the Support System

'Research Flourishes from People'. RICOH believes that it is important to foster creative thinking. 'Creative and Innovative Research' is also very important in ensuring the technological future of RICOH, and is put forward as the guiding principle for all researchers.

The company strives to create the type of research environment which fosters creative thinking and communication beyond the confines of research fields.

Of course, success requires the very best in research facilities; but the core of any research effort is the people involved. The best R & D environment is that which brings out the creative abilities of each and every member of the research staff to the fullest.

The author is General Manager of the R & D Planning Department, R & D Center, RICOH Co. Ltd, Japan.

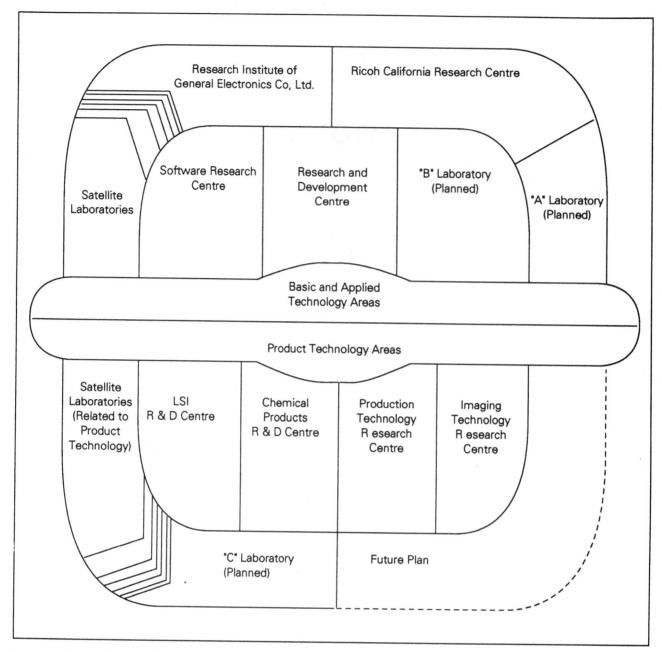

Figure 1. Ricoh Research Laboratories Group

The Support Systems
To foster good researchers and good research leaders, three factors are considered very important (see Figure 2). Researchers need both 'Hardware' and 'Software' support to pursue new and better research. 'Hardware' support, means a well designed space, conducive to bold, imaginative thinking and close interaction. 'Software' support means systems and rules which respect the individual. 'Incentive' is not a direct support, but it is an indispensable one. With this combination, RICOH R & D Center represents a completely new, people-oriented style of research. Some of the types of support provided are as follows:

Hardware Support
Open 24 hours. The doors are open 24 hours for the researchers and all entrances to the buildings are equipped with computerized card key systems. Researchers can enter the building without register-ing at the 'front desk'. The library is also open 24 hours, even during holidays. This leaves researchers free to use the facilities as if they were their own personal property.

Community Plaza—with a giant natural wood table. In the central research building, there is a giant table left in the natural shape of a tree. This is located in the centre of the building, surrounded by various laboratories. Researchers from different research fields are able to meet here freely, chat, drink coffee, and discuss research topics at any time. This promotes friendly interaction and communication and yields creative, innovative ideas for their research themes.

Software Support
Flexible work hour system. The R & D Center has adopted a flexible work hour system. This establishes a free, self-controlled working environment. The effectiveness of this system is apparent. The

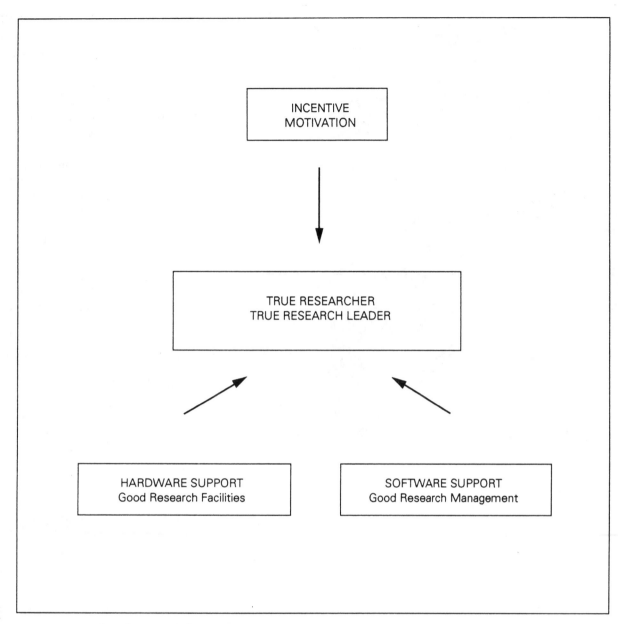

Figure 2. Support for the researchers

researchers welcome the flexible hours. They can avoid traffic jams, make time for private activities, work without concern about a fixed starting time . . . etc.

Absence of a dress code. Researchers do not wear company uniforms at the R & D Center. Wearing uniforms is considered effective for encouraging all employees to work together in the same direction, but at the R & D Center the opposite applies. Researchers may work in any clothing they choose. This encourages a freer working environment.

Total Fitness Plan. The treatment of physical and mental diseases is important, but it is more important to protect against these diseases. RICOH's 'Total Fitness Plan' targets disease prevention and, as part of the Total Fitness Plan, an experienced counsellor is invited to the centre twice a month. The counsellor is easy to talk to and researchers discuss many things, and talk to her freely.

Motivation
Appointing young research managers. Generally speaking, a section manager has passed a promotion examination. But in the RICOH Laboratory Group, there are many young research managers who have not taken the examination. They are given a section manager's full authority for pursuing creative and innovative research. Young people are considered to be crucial. The system gives young researchers a strong incentive to use their talent and ability.

Simplified research evaluation. When a researcher or a planner wishes to start a particular research programme, he/she has to submit his/her proposal to a 'review meeting' at which the director of the R & D Center, the chief scientists, the head of the research department, and planners will be present. Preparing the documents for this meeting requires a considerable amount of work, and takes a long time. It makes no sense to request extensive documen-

Figure 3. Community Plaza

tation from researchers when the proposed theme is a piece of fundamental research which researchers just wish to 'try out' in a short time. It was decided to allow such a theme to begin without making an official proposal to the top management. They need only present a one-page proposal to their research manager. Research managers, though they are relatively young, are given the authority to approve these themes.

Research strategy planned by all staff. In the R & D Center, research strategy involves everyone—the members of the planning section as well as researchers. The procedure for developing a research strategy is explained in the next section. The system allows researchers to think deeply about their own research strategy so that they can judge the direction of their theme when they arrive at a point of decision.

Research symposium. Once a year, usually in December, the R & D Center holds its annual research symposium. The style is the same as that for a general scientific society symposium. A call for papers is sent to all researchers at the R & D Center and the proposed papers are checked by a referee committee, consisting of the Director of the R & D Center, Chief scientists, and several research heads. Papers presented to the symposium must be completely new: if the same thesis has been presented at

another symposium, it cannot be presented again. The symposium serves as a rehearsal for presentations to symposia for other scientific societies.

The audience is mainly researchers and engineers from other laboratories, the manufacturing divisions, RICOH's subsidiary companies and top management, including the president.

RICOH's other laboratories also hold their own research symposia. Researchers from different laboratories support each other by attending one another's laboratory's research symposium.

Special lecture meeting. Every 2 months, the R & D Center invites a well-known person to give a special lecture, such as in November 1990, when a world-famous American chemist, a 1983 Nobel Prize winner presented an excellent paper. In this way, researchers are able to hear famous pioneers and are able to speak to them directly, providing real incentive for young researchers.

Award system. Researchers whose work results in outstanding patents and are successful in transferring useful technology to the manufacturing division, etc. are recognized at the R & D Center Openhouse held every year in April. Researchers who receive a PhD, or pass a state examination, etc. are given a special bonus.

Deciding upon Research Subjects

'Once a research subject is decided upon the research is 80 per cent accomplished.' In the research process, selection of the subject is the central concern.

In determining the research theme, there are two main considerations—'Picking out the candidates' and 'Evaluating them'. In 'Picking out the candidates', both 'need' and 'seed' oriented searches are necessary, and here, imagination and creativity are essential. These are innate abilities, and recent research shows that these abilities can be improved by training such as brain-storming methods, checklists scenario-writing etc. The RICOH R & D Center has tried several of these and found none is useful on its own. A combination of the brainstorming method and scenario writing is the most effective.

'Needs'-oriented Selection
Generally, 'needs-oriented' subjects are broken down into three phases—(1) Investigation and analysis of social and technical trends; (2) Shaping, evaluating and selecting ideas about the targets (hypothetical future products); (3) Breaking down the target into technical subparts, i.e. the research subjects. (1) and (2) are done mainly by the planners. Researchers are in charge of (3).

Investigation and analysis of social and technical trends. To begin with, the planners investigate general trends in fields of interest. These include office equipment, communication networks and computers. The important thing here is not just to prepare a good report on trends, but to understand clearly and to reach a consensus on what the trends indicate.

Shaping, evaluating and selecting ideas about the targets.
After planners grasp global trends, they shape ideas about targets i.e. hypothetical future products. Ideas are shaped in several ways. RICOH uses the scenario-writing method, whereby planners write scenarios of the future, i.e. 'The office in the year 2001', using knowledge of the future gained in (1). Unlike a forecast which uses just numbers, this method can create an unrestricted future image. An original, daring idea can be incorporated into the scenario.

One of these scenarios, 'Mr R's morning in 2001', begins like this . . .

> 'One fine morning, Mr R got up at 8 a.m. as usual. He sat down on the sofa in front of the wide flat-panel screen. His home-computer, connected with his office, . . .'

The planners extract the images of future products which appear in the scenario as candidates for RICOH's future products. Then they think out the concepts and specifications for each product.

Finally these candidates are evaluated, and 10–15 hypothetical future products are decided upon as research targets.

Breaking targets down into research themes. During this phase, researchers join the project. Planners, together with researchers, investigate hypothetical future products, and break them down into components, sub-modules and individual technical subjects. These technical subjects are evaluated, and candidates for research themes are chosen.

'Seeds'-oriented Subjects
Alternatively, researchers may propose 'Seeds'-oriented research subjects based on their own inclinations and interests. This process is important because a needs-oriented process does not cover unexpected technical innovation. Researchers, with planners, are expected to be strong gate-keepers.

Devising the Research Strategy
The total process of developing the research strategy is shown in Figure 4. Planners and researchers together discuss the two types of research subjects described in order to choose research themes, and compile a 'Mid-range Strategic Research Plan'. After approval from the Director of the R & D Center, this plan is further broken down into 'Short-range Research Plans'. Generally, individual research themes are proposed according to this plan. Any research theme proposal resulting from a new idea is welcomed. These themes are then managed as described above.

Assessment of the Subjects
Once in a while, all of the themes at the R & D Center, including the themes in the planning stage, are assessed using various methods. Mapping all the themes is one such method. The assessment was done subjectively, and enables the themes to be seen from a 'bird's-eye' view.

Classification of Research Subjects
At the R & D Center, research themes are classified as shown in Figure 5. As explained, 'Fundamental Research' is seeds-oriented, guided by researchers' interests, and the researcher need only present a one-page proposal to his/her manager. 'Applied Research' is the next category in fundamental research, and requires a fixed budget, and more manpower. Researchers must submit these proposals to their department head for approval. 'Joint Research' is an 'Applied Research' which involves two or more research departments or research laboratories. The final research stage at the R & D Center is 'Practical Research'. The output of this research is targeted for transfer to other laboratories, manufacturing divisions, etc. A 'Special Project' is one ordered by the Director of the R & D Center. 'Requested Research' is a theme carried out by request from the other laboratories, from manufacturing and other divisions. Research themes in the last three categories must be approved by the Director of the R & D Center since the R & D Center has responsibility towards other laboratories, manufacturing divisions, etc. with regard to the research output of these themes.

Carrying Out the Research Subject
The basic concept behind the assessment of research themes is that emphasis is put on originality, creativity, and innovation in Fundamental and Applied Research, and on the guarantee of the quality of the research output to the next stage for Practical Research and Requested Research.

(1) *Proposal assessment.* As necessary, theme proposal assessment meetings are held. The participants vary according to the types of theme as follows.

☆ Fundamental Research: Research manager, Researchers (informal)

☆ Applied Research: Head of the research department, Research manager, Researchers, (Planners, member of the patent division)

☆ Practical Research, Special Project, Requested Research: Director of the R & D Center, Director of the other laboratories, manufacturing divisions, etc., Chief scientists, Heads of the research departments, Research managers, Researchers, General manager and managers of research planning department, Planners, member of the patent division, etc.

Main points for evaluation are:

(i) The plan's originality, creativity, innovation.

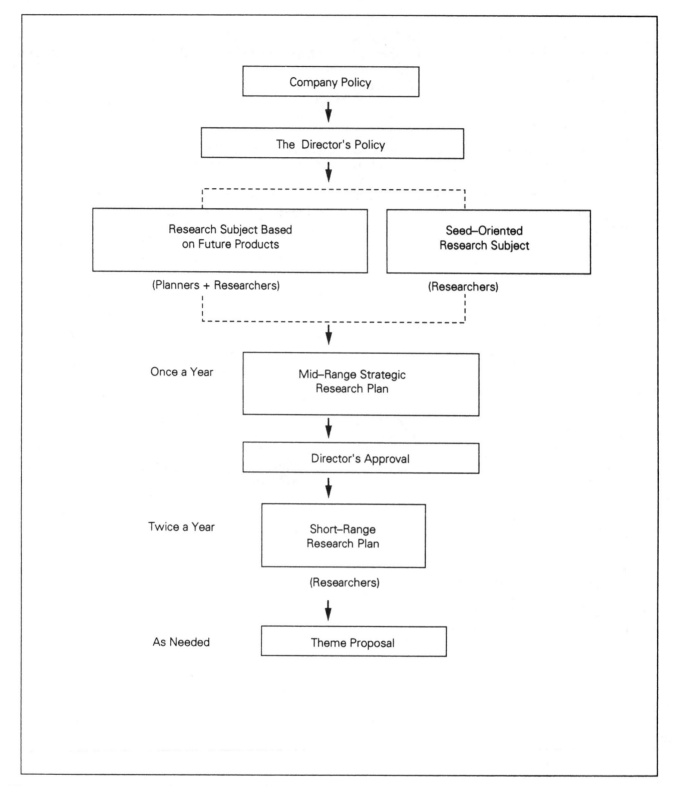

Figure 4. Devising research strategy

(ii) Clarity of the research purpose.

(iii) Suitability of the research specification.

(iv) Suitability of the approach method.

(v) Suitability of the schedule, manpower, budget etc.

(2) *Intermediate reviewing.* When the research reaches a decision point, researchers can request an intermediate review, Researchers must make clear the points of discussion and required decisions. The participants are the same as for the proposal assessment meeting.

(3) *Completion evaluation.* A completion evaluation meeting is held immediately following completion of the theme. The participants are again the same as in the theme proposal assessment meeting.

Main points of assessment are,

(i) Originality, creativity, innovation.

Classification	Description	Approved by
Fundamental Research	• Seeds–oriented • Unnecessary Clear Target Products Business Plan	Research Manager
Applied Research	• Stage Following Fundamental Research and Before Practical Research • Requires Clear Research Purpose, Image, Results • Can be Accomplished by one Laboratory or Research Department	Research Department Head
Joint Research	• Applied Research Involving two or more Research Departments or Laboratories	R & D Center Director
Practical Research	• Requires Clear Research Purpose, Image, Results • Output Targeted for Transfer to Other Laboratories, Manufacturing Divisions	
Special Project	• High Priority due to Emergency, Extreme Importance, etc. • Special Order of Director of R & D Center	
Requested Research	• Special Request from other Laboratories, Manufacturing Divisions, etc.	

Figure 5. Classification of research project

(ii) Applicability and practicality.

(iii) Level of completion of the research specifications.

(iv) Definition of the problems to be solved in the next process.

(v) Quality of patents and technical papers.

(vi) Avoidance of conflict with patents belonging to other companies.

(vii) Adherence to the schedule, manpower, budget etc.

Technology Transfer
The smooth transfer of research results to the next stage (other laboratories or manufacturing divisions) is very important but not so easily accomplished. Results from laboratory research may be only partial and not ready for transfer to the manufacturing stage. This could lead to misunder-

standing of the technology itself or even mutual distrust between the R & D Center and the receiving organization. To avoid this, the R & D Center has a Technology Transfer Center whose task is to effect the transfer of the research results to the next process. The research results then proceed to the pre-manufacturing level in the Technology Transfer Center, so that the group receiving the technology can make use of it. Of course, not all research results are transferred through the Technology Transfer Center. Advanced results are transferred directly from individual research departments. Even preliminary results can be transferred directly by mutual agreement and in these cases, some of the researchers are also transferred in order to carry on the investigation.

Another system employed to insure a smooth transfer is a 'Task force' or a 'Project team'. When the technology matures, the organization itself is transferred along with the technology.

The Task Ahead for R & D Management

RICOH's R & D Center pursues creative and innovative research. To foster this, it has provided 'Hardware' support and 'Software' support for the past 5 years. For the most part, the 'support' has been successful, but some problems remain. How to provide incentives to, and to motivate the researchers is one of the biggest problems. To obtain good research results, we must provide incentive and motivation as well as good support. Another problem is measuring the effectiveness of these supports. It is not enough to say simply that 'These wonderful research results were produced by a good support system.'

There are many other tasks ahead of the R & D management in RICOH, and we are trying to create the ideal research environment to pursue them.

How the Japanese Accelerated New Car Development

Toru Sasaki

New car development is a key factor for success in car manufacturing companies. It absorbs a huge amount of money and requires the co-operation of a large number of specialists. The technical quality and the design are two important areas in development, and design has become more important in recent years. The shortening of the time taken to develop a new car is one of the competitive advantages of Japanese car manufacturers. It is achieved by close co-operation between research, market testing, product design, production and marketing.

Introduction

New car development is a highly visible part of the activities of an automobile manufacturer. It is also a part of the daily operations which go on for many years. There are a number of pitfalls a car manufacturer can fall into in new car development despite the experience which has been accumulated. Sometimes it takes longer and the costs are higher than was expected. Immediately after the launch of a new car, a rival company may release a new model which is better in performance and lower in price, or a new model introduced into the market with pride and confidence may not be accepted by consumers for reasons which are not clear and this results in a painful failure. In the early days, Japanese automobile manufacturers believed that success in new car development was very much dependent on luck. Even today, companies take care by announcing their new models on days that are believed to be 'lucky days'.

Today, however, the dominant thinking is that the success of a new car depends not upon luck but on how the new car development activities are operated by the company. Reducing the time needed for developing a new model is thought to be the key to success. Recent articles in American journals focus less on quality, cost, or Toyota-style production methods, and are more concerned with the differ-

ence between U.S.A. and Japanese companies in the time taken for new car development, suggesting, for example, that Japanese car manufacturers take 3 years to develop new models whereas U.S.A. manufacturers take 5 years.

In this article, I will describe the efforts which Japanese automobile manufacturers are making to reduce the time taken for new car development.

The Position of New Car Development

First I would like to take a look at the importance of new car development in the corporate strategies of car manufacturers and the difficulties they are facing, from three view points.

The commitment of top management is indispensable for the automobile business. The automobile industry is the kind of business in which tens of thousands of components are developed and assembled to form a product which aims to satisfy the changing needs of customers. The range of the development required is extensive and time-consuming, and the process requires decision making on crucial issues. Unlike the management of diversified companies, who only have to check the progress of their businesses periodically, the top management of automobile companies have to continuously monitor the activities of their competitors and the market trends, by visiting manufacturing sites, and the headquarters of component manufacturers, distributors and car dealers all over the world.

A huge amount of money is at risk. Just for one new model, it costs tens of billions of yen to produce a new engine and other components. Setting up a new plant and a new distribution channel for this new car would mean placing orders worth hundreds of billions of yen. Of course, a typical car manufacturer has many product lines so this investment has to be

Mr. Toru Saskaki is General Manager of the Business Development Division at Toyota Motor Corporation, 1-4-18 Koraku, Bunkyo-ku, Tokyo 112, Japan.

multiplied several times. To manage this process—a portfolio of products and markets—we prepare a matrix of technology needed for each product, and the market that product is aiming at, so that the optimum combination can be assessed. This inevitably means that we sometimes get out of step with the changing tastes of consumers. During the oil crises, for example, some companies failed to adapt to the market situation when sales of large cars declined and sales of compact cars increased because consumers were looking for cars with higher fuel efficiency. In this case not even the most sophisticated analysis anticipated this huge shift in customer demand.

New car development takes several years and involves dozens of departments in the company. Automobile manufacturers organize themselves by functions such as product concept development, research and development, product development, production and sales. Each group of people is highly specialized. For example, a research and development department tends to be indifferent to the fate of individual products because they are committed to managing good R & D activities. Each department tends to take a narrower view of its function. With this problem of 'sectionalism', the fate of a product, from concept to sales, is placed in the hands of organizations with different ideas, just like a child being handed on from one step-mother to another.

The Process of New Car Development

Next, I would like to touch briefly upon the process of new car development which is to be shortened. It is difficult to generalize about the new car development process because it differs among companies and products. Also, some parts of the process are now tending to take more time not less time. The stages of the product development process, the work content, and a typical time allocation for a 5 year programme, are shown below:

(1) *Designing the product concept. (12 months)*
Where will the product fit in the company's product line? Is it going to be a completely new product, or will it be a model change? If it is to be a new product it can affect the company's future, and it is necessary to analyse the company's production system and the distribution channels for it. This will take more time.

(2) *Research and development. (12 months)*
This is research and development on new materials and new processes to generate a new product. This part of the process has been emphasized in recent years. With the increased activity in this area, it would now be more feasible to create a breakthrough product, and the research period would be shorter than previously.

(3) *Analysis of market and profit potential. (6 months)*
A survey of the target consumer group for the product and the profile of those consumers is in order to assess the product against its competitors. Also, an investigation is made to see whether it is possible to use existing technology, components, plant and distribution channels or if new investments will be necessary. In this part of the process, a mistake might be made if the management are too concerned with short-term profits.

(4) *Product design. (18 months)*
The product concept is then converted into detailed specifications and performance goals, drawings are prepared, components are developed, trial vehicles are made and test runs are conducted. This part of the development process has been throughly standardized and studied to improve its efficiency and as a result, the time needed here has been progressively shortened.

(5) *Production planning. (6 months)*
Commercial production lines are designed and component suppliers are evaluated. The key to time reduction in this part of the process are the day-to-day developments in production technology and the improved relationship with subcontractors, starting with the preliminary work.

(6) *Planning the marketing strategies and the product launch. (6 months)*
The marketing decisions on the sales volumes, prices, distribution channels, public relations advertising, product name, etc. have to be taken. Here again, the key to time reduction is to make on early start.

The Focus on New Situations

In new car development, the production planning and marketing departments are deeply involved. In the profitability study, the accounting department plays an important role. The personnel department is also involved in recruiting, selecting and training the employees concerned with development. Acquiring facilities for research activities and experiments including, test-run tracks is part of the work of the general administration and property departments.

However, the product concept, research and development and product design for the new car are discussed in detail to focus on *new situations,* since new activities need more time than other areas of new car development work.

Another reason for selecting them for scrutiny is that these parts of the process are a kind of *preliminary process* of new car development which has gone through major changes recently in terms of work contents and procedures.

Product concept

Many companies have become more aware of the importance of the product concept in generating sales. As a result, they invest more time and manpower to develop and assess product ideas. The background to this trend is that customers are demanding more original products. The following are three examples of changes.

(i) The product concept, which is expressed in the specifications and dimensions of the finished product or in the concise characterization of the product, e.g. as 'a sporty compact car', has been recognized in recent years as a world created by designers.

T. S. Eliot, made a comment on Shakespeare's plays which is applicable to automobiles. Adapting his comment we would say: 'Excellent cars have different levels of meaning for different customers. For simple customers, prices and passenger capacity are important; for the more prudent customers specifications and equipment which are better than the competition; for the enthusiasts acceleration and steering; for those with sensitivity design and finish; and for those with the highest sensitivity and the deepest understanding, they offer a meaning that becomes clear with time.'

The product concept, on the face of it, seems to be nothing but an abstract idea conceived by designers. It is, in reality, the result of a vast amount of creative work which takes time to mature.

(ii) Companies are now giving increased support to their designers. An excellent product concept is generated where designers and consumers share a 'contemporary atmosphere' and interact with each other. This contemporary atmosphere is found not only just in companies but is felt by designers in their exchanges with other people who are working creatively and in a pioneering way in different parts of society.

As they have more opportunities for contact with mature cultures and their history by visiting museums of fine art and historic sites at home and abroad, they can be more imaginative than their predecessors. Companies cannot control the minds of their employees but they can give them more opportunities to travel overseas and provide them with a better working environment. Companies must also recognize that designers need to make these visits in their working time.

(iii) The development of global product concepts has begun, and it has been promoted by development agreements between corporations.

American cars, since the emergence of Chevrolet, have aimed to provide a comfortable means of transportation, whereas West German cars have been sold as 'express trains' which transport people safely in high speed on the country's autobahn highway system. Japanese compact cars have enjoyed a reputation for quality, reliability and 'value for money'.

The excellence of the product concept, considered against this geographical and cultural background and reflecting technological innovation and the globalization of world markets, has become the key to survival in a highly competitive environment.

Research and development

Now the automobile industry is in the middle of a technological revolution which has increased the speed of competition in research and development, and the crucial importance of this part of the new car development process is increasing. It is vital that the fruits of these research and development activities are commercialized in the form of successful new products. The result of this increase in competition is a progressive *growth of investment in R & D*. As a result of increased investment on basic research in fields such as new power sources, new materials, electronic and communication technology, the automobile industry which at one time used the technologies of the nineteenth century, is being restructured as a high technology industry. In this environment, the gap between companies which can invest tens of billions of yen every year and those which cannot, is getting wider. Corporations which continue to spend vast amounts on electronics technology can win in the competition to converting automobiles into electronic products. How much investment should be made on electronics technology in new car development is one of the most important items in corporate decision making.

Another key factor is the improvement which has occurred in the *methods for controlling research and development*. The fields available for research have been continuously expanding, and now all of them cannot be covered even by the largest corporations. Therefore, it is not just the individual research projects that have to be controlled but the broad areas for research from which promising research themes will be chosen for intensive investment. A concrete example of this is that, in the general field of converting automobiles into electronic products, choice for focus has to be made between the development of electronic fuel injection systems and that of electronically controlled suspension.

It is also important to reflect in R & D priorities the viewpoints of customers in domestic and overseas markets, and evaluate the marketing implications. For example, it would be a waste of resources if technologists and engineers made strenuous efforts in the development of electronically controlled air conditioning systems for the West German market and ignored the fact that air conditioners are not normally used there. Contingency planning to cope with the environmental changes which affect long-term research projects such as an oil crisis, is also important. In the case of an oil shock, higher sales would be expected if a rapid shift could be made to research and development of fuel efficient engines rather than continuing to sell high-fuel-consumption engines.

The use of computers in research and development, is a third important factor. In the 1990s our automobile company's success will depend very much on the introduction of computers and telecommunication technologies into research and development work. For example, a fully equipped data bank will make it possible for a company to obtain, instantaneously, vast amounts of technological information from all over the world, which will help the management to improve their efficiency in research. The exchange of data within a company and among affiliated companies will also be possible, which will help to promote a dialogue among the engineers.

Computer simulation which increases the frequency of experiment and improves accuracy is proving useful especially in the use of experimental data: so, attempts are being made to expand the application of *LA (laboratory automation)* to reduce the time required for new car development.

Product Design
New car design today is required not only to deliver the expected performance, quality and cost specifications but also to shorten the time it takes so that a new product can be put into the market quicker. This is partly because new product design usually takes several years. Therefore it is considered to have a good potential for reducing the time taken for the entire new car development process. The time for product design had been reduced, but there may be a danger of inferior products unless the following points are considered:

(i) *Passenger car design requires a huge amount of work.* 'Fast and comfortable' is not the sole criteria for purchase of passenger cars. Other characteristics are demanded such as high fuel efficiency, especially after the oil crises. Also, it has become necessary to improve the car in many ways such as car-body structure, material, components, etc. as a result of tighter government regulations on exhaust gases, safety standards, and noise reduction.

The work required to adapt the cars to the restrictions imposed by different countries is sharply increasing as automobile manufacturers move from exports to local production.

(ii) *The widely different tastes of consumers.* In order to satisfy the demands of different customers, car manufacturers have to produce an increasing range of body variations, and differences in styling, interior design and equipment for different types of cars. For example, young users are high-technology oriented and will not be satisfied if a car is not filled with new technology or new equipment. Model changes or styling changes are indispensable because these users are very keen on staying in fashion.

(iii) *How to deal with computerization.* It requires a huge amount of work to continuously revise the drawings of tens of thousands of car components. Computers are used to handle this tremendous amount of work, but in the initial stages of computer introduction, the work involved in introducing the computer is *added* to the manual work which is being automated.

Japanese automobile manufacturers started to introduce computers in the late 1960s choosing the field of styling design which is easily computerized. In this field, the computers convert rough sketches into design drawings and then into clay models. There was some resistance from designers, who are proud of their craftsmanship, to working with computer displays, but they gradually accepted it.

Then, more complicated interior designs and the design of important components including engines followed, with the application of *CAD (Computer Aided Design)*.

Some manufacturers have now arrived at the stage when they can expect to achieve a reduction in the development period as a result of using CAD.

Now, companies are aiming at *CAM (Computer Aided Manufacturing)* as the next stage. When computers become part of normal daily work in a manufacturing process such as component fabrication, then the next part of the new car design process, namely production, may also take less time.

New Car Development by Major Automobile Manufacturers

New car development demands a massive commitment of manpower and capital. The process requires a large amount of communication between departments, between individuals, between men and machines, and between different kinds of machines. In this process trouble can occur at any time. What can control this complex process is ultimately common sense, and good judgement and it is these same human capabilities which are enabling companies to shorten the development period.

The following section describes the evolution of new car development activities by three Japanese car maufacturers in terms of product concept generation, research and development, and product design.

(i) *Nissan Motor Company*

Nissan is a typically Japanese automobile manufacturer which merged with Prince Motor in 1966 and then had the largest product range of all Japanese car manufacturers. After the merger, the company fought against the growing diversification of products, which had led to an increase in development costs, by developing common components for its different products. This, however, produced a range of products which were too homogeneous, and this led to a decline in Nissan's market share.

In the latter half of the 1980s, Nissan started a drastic reform of its new car development process. The management decided to review the process from the very beginning and they completely re-structured their approach to product concept generation.

The product concept, as was mentioned earlier, is a message to contemporary society and is the area in which the creativity of designers is tested. New product concepts wither in a company which imposes too much bureaucracy on designers and restricts their creativity.

The top management of Nissan were determined to change this situation and to provide a better corporate environment for designers. They decided to revitalize not only the departments and groups concerned with new car development, but the entire company, by making the company more open to society and by making Nissan the kind of company which the public would identify with. The top management knew that their designers, even though they belong to technological departments, feel the enthusiasm of the entire company for new car development through their colleagues and superiors and they hear about the company's reputation through their dealers and component manufacturers.

In 1986, Nissan revised it corporate philosophy to put the first priority on 'customer satisfaction', and to provide people with a comfortable attractive and well equipped means of transportation. The management saw their business as: 'the production of a mobile life stage' and 'the presentation of new life space'. With this kind of corporate philosophy, their product concepts have become new and free. The confusion and complexity have disappeared. The design concepts have improved, and, at the same time, the frequency of reworking product concepts has been reduced which has led to the shortening of the new car development period.

In research and development, even though the company has always been called 'Nissan of technology' which indicates the investment it has made in human resources and facilities it was not too successful in producing new products. To remedy this, the management set clear development targets and established programmes to eliminate the duplication among research projects and to overcome the

problem of conflict between departments. After considering various candidates for development, engine body design, etc., they narrowed down their goal to 'the development of the world's best suspension' in order to focus their investment in this area. As a result, the company succeeded in speeding up the development process in product design, the company introduced three divisions for the three markets of full size cars, compact cars and subcompact cars so that one manager in charge of development can co-ordinate the activities at all stages from product design to setting the price, designing the advertisement and even providing after-sales services. Before this change, new car development was controlled by departments which related to different parts of the car such as engines and chassis. Under the new system it has been possible to develop new cars with distinctive characteristics which are more market oriented.

Nissan also revised its personnel evaluation system which was based on seniority of its employees on a company wide scale. The management appointed young workers to important positions and transferred employees across departmental boundaries. This merit system is also used in departments concerned with new car development. This has dramatically strengthened the authority of the persons responsible for development-related activities within the divisions. This has reduced the number of negotiations between different departments and it has made it easier to get co-operation between relevant parts of the company in making the best products. This has also had the effect of shortening the development period.

(ii) *Toyota Motor Coporation*

Since the merger, in 1985, of Toyota Motor Co., and Toyota Motor Sales Co., Toyota Motor Corporation has launched a number of successful products. This is in line with the company motto which is 'to develop attractive products'.

Building on its competitive strengths, its large-variety small-lot production process, known as the Toyota production system, and its powerful marketing capability, Toyota has increased its market share and consolidated its position as the leading car manufacturer in the Japanese market.

To prepare for further expansion, the company inaugurated the development of a prestige car which was intended for an international market. In 1989, the car was launched in the North-American market under the name LS 400 through a new chain of dealers called Lexus and in the Japanese market with the brand name Celsior. The car has established a good reputation. The section which follows describes the development of this car from product concept, to research and development, and product design.

In the product concept stage, the target customer,

was selected, based upon the result of a survey conducted in North America, the typical consumer would be: a 43-year-old male with $100,000 income residing in Los Angeles. To satisfy this target customer, three design goals were set in concrete terms:

☆ A Maximum speed of 250 km per hour.

☆ Mileage per gallon of more than 22.5 mpg.

☆ Quietness in running which is equal to the best cars in the world.

At a glance, these goals may seem easy to reach but an engine with high horse power and a low fuel consumption is a contradiction in terms, so is the reduction of weight and quietness.

In the area of research and development the company attempted a number of breakthroughs.

For the engine, aluminum blocks, and composite materials were used to obtain high horse power, low fuel consumption and low noise. Electronic control of the air intake and the exhaust mechanism were also introduced. So the technological know-how for low fuel consumption, developed after the oil crises, was exploited in this new model design.

In the area of product design, the company had traditionally adopted a 'chief examiner' system to concentrate authority for new car development in one person, but, with the increase in the number of organizations concerned with new car development inside the company, and with the chief examiner's decision that the principal components would be newly designed, a new committee was organized to keep an eye on the development work.

For the first time in the company, a design engineer was nominated to be the committee chairman in the initial stage, and then a production engineer was nominated as the chairman for the production preparation stage. This overlapping system improved the morale of employees in the production technology area, and also provided them with a opportunity to use the production technology at its highest level of sophistication to produce the new car with the understanding of the concept which they acquired from an early participation in the development activities. This also allowed a lead time for turning the product concept into actual materials. In concrete terms, the accuracy of component production was dramatically improved, and the quietness achieved exceeded the initial design target.

This quietness, combined with the advanced audio equipment fitted in the car, exceeded the designers' expectations and was acclaimed as a 'running audio room'. The organization of the production preparation process produced a new product concept.

(iii) *Honda Motor Company*
Honda is the world leader in the motorcycle industry. Their move into four-wheel vehicles was based upon the technological advances which were developed in 'running experiment chambers', i.e. through participation in severe motor races and motorcycle races.

The company has a corporate culture in which the young employees are encouraged to take on new ventures. This has become the driving force behind successive generations of hit products.

One of the hit products that helped Honda become an international corporation in a short period is the first-generation CIVIC, the FF 2 BOX which was launched in 1972. The following section describes Honda's approach to new car development, taking this CIVIC model as an example to explain the product concept development, research and development, and product design.

In product concept, the CIVIC is a car in which the idea, 'man maximum, mechanism minimum' was thoroughly carried through. This concept means that the mechanical parts, including the engine, should be small and the space for passengers should be large. Supported by their 'high-densifying' engine technology fostered through their experience of car races and with the decision to adopt a front-wheel drive system, they proceeded to 'materialize' this concept. As a result, the tunnel for the shaft under the floor was eliminated and the floor became flat. This had already been done in Japan in 1966 by Fuji Heavy Industries, with its SUBARU 1000 but Honda went further by deciding to adopt not the traditional 3 BOX style but a 2 BOX style for the CIVIC's body. The station-wagon-like 2 BOX has a large interior space, but it had been avoided by other Japanese car manufacturers because it is a popular style for business vehicles. Honda worked on the body design to make the car acceptable to young customers.

In research and development, the CIVIC engine was developed. While the other car manufacturers in the world were troubled by exhaust gas regulations, Honda took the lead in developing a clean engine for the CIVIC. With this innovation, Honda became famous for its technological capability.

This break through was achieved in Honda's research centre which was established in 1960. The secret of their success lies in the company's 'parallel heterogeneity competition principle'. Using this approach the company's researchers compete with each other by submitting different approaches to the same research problem.

Their success also owes much to the desire by the top management and the engineers to accept the people's demand for cleaner air and to use it for the company's advancement. Other manufacturers at the time were committed only to short-term measures which would meet the standards demanded by the government.

The company has a system which allows employees to attack difficult problems without restrictions and they are even rewarded if they fail because the management knows that research and development involves the risk of failure. This is what made their technological breakthrough possible.

In product design, the challenge was how to complete this large amount of work without mistakes. Honda's solution was to prepare a good system in which each employee was given a wide responsibility and was expected to work well in harmony with his colleagues. Honda's project management system is well developed and the members' attitude to each other, their co-operation with the top management, and their evaluation programme are well tried and tested.

Honda also has a guest-engineer system. In the Japanese automobile industry the engineers of affiliated component manufacturers are often invited to provide help to car manufacturers at peak periods. In Honda's case, these engineers participate in development work from the initial stages. The company's idea of having them is not just to meet a manpower shortage but to have new ideas from engineers who live in a different company culture.

Honda was the first of the Japanese automobile manufacturers to set up a factory in North America and to have the local product development centre there, which enabled them to use American designers and engineers from a different social background. The manufacture of cars has become highly systematized but also diversified, and the participation of a large body of people from different backgrounds at the design stage enhances product quality and shortens the development period.

Reducing the Time for New Car Development

So far this has been a description of the general situation in new car development with specific case histories from three leading Japanese car manufacturers. This section examines the measures taken to accelerate new product development.

Traditionally, the problem of reducing the time taken for new car development, was worked on by management only in the time they could spare from the new car development work itself which the company's future depends on. So one of the measures taken, was, to use the same components for different products. This reduced the development time required but it also gave the companies a reputation for having stereotyped products. Com-

pany wide aproaches have been adopted in recent years, but there are still many short-sighted managers who believe that the introduction of a larger number of employees and machines or introduction of a new technology such as automation will suffice.

At this time automation has been adopted only in some parts of the new car development process, and it has not had an overall effect. For example, using the CAD system for style design has improved the quality of design drawings and shortened time necessary for the work, but CAD does not contribute to the creativity in the original drawing; it is only good for improving the finished drawings.

We need a combination of measures that will:

☆ improve product quality

☆ shorten the development period

☆ cover the entire process of new car development.

In the following section the results of these measures are shown not in the form of tables but in charts in accordance with Toyota's approach to production through 'visual control'.

In Figure 1, the horizontal axis shows the new car development period, and the numbers 0 to 5 are the years required. If the 5 year period, which is normal, is shortened to 3 years, it will be shown on this axis.

The vertical axis shows the degree of uncertainty to demonstrate the need to achieve product quality in new car development. If the degree of uncertainty appears in the form of quality problems then the level of quality trouble will appear on this axis. As the development progresses, efforts will be made to reduce the problems with quality, so the initial 100 per cent should become close to zero. Cost reduction is another important task in new car development which can be used as an indicator shown on this axis. In the same manner, fuel efficiency in terms of performance can be visualized and controlled on this chart which shows the reduction in fuel consumption as the development work progresses. In this way, degrees of different kinds of uncertainties in new car development are shown on the vertical axis in order to visualize the problems associated with the new car development activities of different car manufacturers and then to find solutions. Figure 1 shows a case in which 5 years are needed from defining the product concept to formulating the marketing strategies with a straight line A on the plane between the two axes. And as a reference, the standard time periods needed for different parts of the development process in this case are shown by the numbers (1) to (6).

Against this, a straight line B shows a case in which only 3 years are needed for new car development.

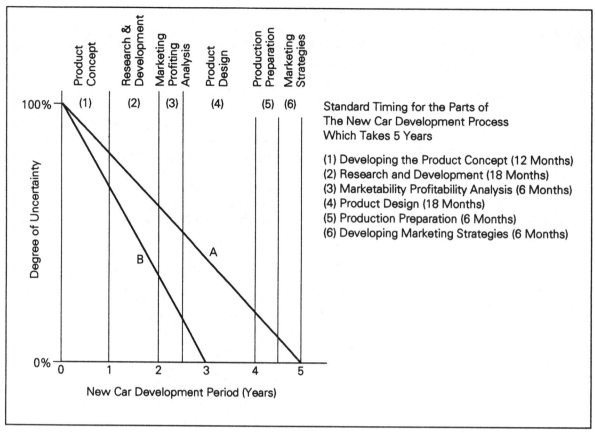

Figure 1. New car development in 3 and 5 years

The reference periods (1) to (6) are omitted to avoid making the diagram too complicated. The following six cases of C through H are compared with the 3 year and 5 year development cases. This is only to examine the length of development periods. The number of years do not have to be 3 and 5. Four and 6, for example, can be used. But here, 3 and 5 are used because it is said that it takes 3 years for the development of a new Japanese car and 5 years for a new American car.

There are various kinds of problems which occur at different stages of the new car development process, and the following cases C to H demonstrate the kinds of problems which hamper development and provide opportunities to shorten the time taken.

☆ Case C: the second half of development process falls behind schedule. (See Figure 2)

In this case, the development process proceeds as is shown by line B in the first half so that the development should be finished in 3 years, but the process slows down in the second half as is shown by the dotted line C and as a result it takes 5 years. In other words, production preparation and marketing strategy formulation in this case are taking more time than they should. Often new car development is kept confidential even within the company and the departments which are concerned in the second half of the development process are not informed about it until the time when they are involved. It is necessary for the personnel in the production and

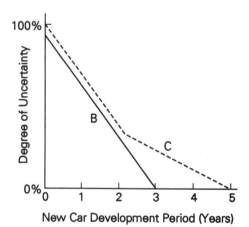

Figure 2. The second half of the development process falls behind schedule

marketing departments to participate in a project team or a committe from the initial stage of the development to enable them to start preliminary work and so avoid delays.

☆ Case D: the first half of the development process falls behind schedule. (See Figure 3)

The second half of the development process in this case has the same angle as line B so that development should be completed within 3 years, but the identification of the product concept and research and development in the first half take too much time as is shown by the dotted line D and the overall development takes 5 years.

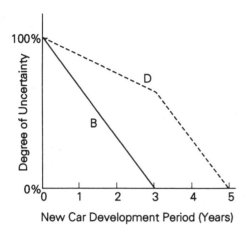

Figure 3. The first half of the development process falls behind schedule

People tend to have the illusion in the initial stages of development that the time given to them is unlimited. Designers also want to take as much time as possible to elaborate the concept. Also, controlling time in R & D is rather difficult.

The problem of this case should be solved by measures such as motivating management to become more customer-oriented, increasing the intensity of work on basic and applied research, the development of an R & D evaluation system and the introduction of the PERT technique to control the project process.

☆ *Case E: the middle parts of the development process falls behind schedule.* (See Figure 4)

In this case, the middle parts of the new car development process, such as marketability–profitability analysis and product design, have problems and this prolongs the development period as is shown with the dotted line E.

Marketability–profitability analysis has both a traditional and a new problem, that is, a company dealing with the designers' proposal for the development of a new and challenging product. With a management who are not fully aware of the real state of the market and put priority on short-term

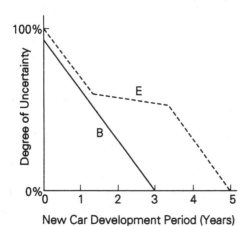

Figure 4. The middle part of the development process falls behind schedule

profit, this part of the process constantly stagnates. Also, the entire market research period causes delays in development.

In product design, a large number of people can be brought in to complete the job within the time allotted. Having excellent help from outside in the guest engineering system is also effective. However, improving efficiency or standardizing the work, together with the automation of design work, are the key to shortening the development period. The automation of design is particularly effective in improving existing products where the available data should facilitate smooth and rapid design work.

In developing innovative products, however, it is necessary to choose carefully the person to take charge of development and to provide them with the authority and responsibility necessary to co-ordinate the relevant departments. In the marketability–profitability analysis, if this person who is in charge of development has strong voice, a more precise evaluation of marketability and profitability is possible.

☆ *Case F: a part of the development process falls behind schedule.* (See Figure 5)

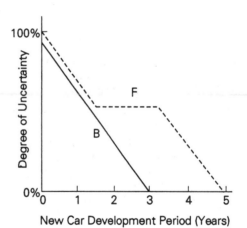

Figure 5. A part of the development process falls behind schedule

In this case, it is not a period such as the first or second halves or the middle part of the development process but a smaller part of it e.g. the new car design may have a problem and this may extend the development process. As is shown by the dotted line F, the process comes to a stalemate. In some cases, hidden problems remain unsolved even though they are concerned with only a small part of the development process.

For example, in product design, the procedure is, first, to confirm the required specifications and performance levels, next to make the drawings, and then, to design the moulds for the components at which stage a situation such as a slow improvement in accuracy or a variation in quality might occur. The moulds for the components tend to be hidden behind the good work on specification design or performance design. Therefore, it tends not to be handled as a company-wide problem. But it is an important factor in shortening the development period if we can reduce the amount of reworking which is needed on a large number of component moulds before they satisfy our requirements.

However, even when this problem is noticed in the process of development, it tends to be ignored because our staff are too busy. Therefore, it becomes important to keep separate records for each of these phases and solve their problems before the activities for the next development start.

☆ *Case C: the transfer of work between parts of the development process is poor and causes a delay.* (See Figure 6)

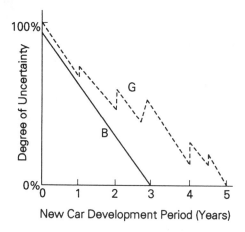

Figure 6. Transfer of work between parts of the development process is poor and causes a delay

In this case as the transfer of development work between departments is poor, trouble occurs whenever work is transferred and the level of uncertainty remaining increases as is shown by the dotted line G despite the efforts made prior to each transfer.

The cause is partly the conflict between departments, but also the poor communication in the company as a whole.

The difficulty in dealing with this problem is that it occurs all over the company. Its origins are found in conflicts among directors, middle management and staff in the departments concerned. Even though a solution is worked out for a specific situation, at the next stage we might have another problem, and so, the problems continue to occur.

In this case, it is necessary not just to treat the symptoms but to cure the diseases. Top management must insist on clear all-out company-wide co-operation for the development and successful introduction of the new car which may be critical for the future of the company. The improvement of communications is also important. For this purpose, it is necessary to hold meetings to build trust inside the company.

☆ *Case H: failing to cope with external risks results in delay.* (See Figure 7)

In this case environmental changes or the emergence of competing products during the new car development forces the company to go back to the development process and redo the work. Although the management wish to launch the new car as soon as possible, the development process falls behind schedule.

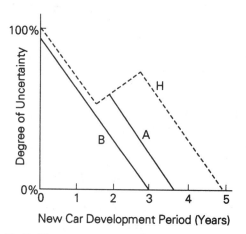

Figure 7. Failing to cope with external risks results in delay

In order to shorten the period of new car development, it is necessary to prepare an alternative plan in case this kind of situation arises. Otherwise as is shown by the dotted line, uncertainty increases in the face of external risks and this extends the development period.

In research and development, for example, the priority might shift suddenly from energy conservation to discovering a countermeasure for a chloro-fluoro carbon (CFC) problem. In this case, an enterprise which has anticipated the fact that the chloro-fluoro carbon problem could appear and prepared for it would have an alternative plan, but a company which had not foreseen the problem would have to start by studying this substance and would suffer delays in development.

This kind of delay can happen at every stage of the development process. Therefore, an alternative plan must be prepared for each part of the process in order to reduce the time period for development.

When this is possible, the development will proceed on a course which is very close to the straight line and will be completed in a period just a little longer than 3 years.

Conclusion

The first part of this article provides an overview of the situation in the Japanese automobile industry, focusing upon the shortening of new car development. This is followed by the description of the product development process in three Japanese car manufacturers, Nissan, Honda, and Toyota. The next part of the article analyses the nature of problems we meet in our efforts to shorten the new car development period, by breaking down the development process into its key activities, and discussing the appropriate solutions to apply at particular parts of the process.

One way of shortening the development time is to analyse the parts of the new car development process. But there are other approaches as well.

For example, one approach is to seek solutions by categorizing the nature of the problem by their type i.e. organization vs organization, man vs man, man vs machine and machine vs machine.

CIM (Computer Integrated Manufacturing) for example, is a clear case for attempting to solve problems by using this approach.

CIM is a new, highly efficient and flexible production system which integrates information from R & D, design, production and sales by the use of computers, networks, databases, etc. based upon the established CAD/CAM technology. As the work processes are standardized, human errors will be reduced, the speed of transmitting information will be increased, and, as a result, the new car development period will be shortened. Also, the market information which is acquired by the sales departments, and which is at the end of the entire process, will be transmitted more quickly to the technology and engineering departments. This will help to reduce the lead time in product planning. Also the time needed to move from product development to production may be shortened with CAM. Also, the time from production to sales and the lead time from receiving orders to product delivery may be reduced.

In these ways CIM seems likely to be a very effective technique for saving time at almost all stages of new car development process. U.S. automobile manufacturers pioneered the approach and Japanese manufacturers are now actively trying to introduce it.

CIM, however, is not a panacea. It can offer some major benefits, but it could be risky to place too much dependence on it. For example, using the CAD for designing car styles might only improve the quality of detail finish on computer displays whilst neglecting the creativity in original design drawings which is most essential. Customers tastes, also, might be ignored by introducing CAM if products are designed largely to meet the requirements for the automation of production.

A more serious concern is that the illusion might be generated that success in shortening the development period will solve all other problems.

Shortening the new car development period certainly reduces the possibility of being affected by environmental changes or the emergence of competition. In some cases, however, a delay of several years might turn out to be only a minor problem. This was the case with Toyota Motor's LS 400. The product took 6 years to develop but it has been established in the market for a very long time. The real driving force for the development of the industry and the establishment of a sustained competitive advantage can be found only by formulating a product concept that pioneers a new age or through effective research and development to cope with problems in resources and energy, environment, transportation, etc.

It is necessary therefore, to consider the measures for shortening the new car development period as one of the productivity improvement measures in a range of corporate strategies which make more effective use of human and other resources which are found inside and outside the company.

One objective of this article was to make it clear that improvement is possible when both time and the degree of uncertainty are used as achievement indicators for reviewing each part of the development process. In order to achieve this improvement, it is not simply a matter of reducing the time taken, but sometimes, on the contrary, acquiring time is important.

An old Japanese proverb says, 'A fool and scissors are useful only when used correctly.' 'A fool' is man, 'scissors' are tools, and the proverb teaches the importance of skill in utilizing man and tools.

When the relationships between organizations, men and machines becomes progressively more complicated as is the case in new car development, it is even more important that man makes full use of organizations, and machines.

Breakthrough: The Development of the Canon Personal Copier

Teruo Yamanouchi

This paper describes the development of a breakthrough product in the copier industry. This new product was Canon's cartridge-loaded, personal copier—the PC-10 and PC-20. This case study makes clear the special character of the new product development process in a Japanese corporation. The managerial environment, the copier business environment and the development process and system are discussed. In conclusion, the psychological and behavioural process is assessed and the key factors for success in this case are explained.

Introduction

This paper describes an innovative new product development in the copier industry. The new products are Canon's PC-10 and PC-20 maintenance-free cartridge type personal copiers. These were introduced in 1982 and were regarded as revolutionary new products which became trend-setters in the world copier market. Given their significance, it is important to review the process of their development during the 3 years from October 1979. The case study also describes the special character of new product development in a Japanese corporation.

There are very few papers in American and European academic journals on management concerning the research and development activities of Japanese corporations. Imai, Nonaka and Takeuchi presented a case study of Japanese companies (Canon, NEC, Honda, Fuji–Xerox, Brother) to a Harvard research colloquium[1] which was later published.[2] Yamanouchi described Canon's R & D system[3] and Teramoto discussed Japanese experiences in technology management and innovation.[4] In 1984, Kono describes it in *Strategy and Structure of Japanese Enterprises*.[5]

Teruo Yamanouchi is Professor in the Faculty of Business Administration, Yokohama National University, Japan. He worked with Canon Inc. until June 1988 and his final job was Director of the Corporate Technical Planning and Operation Centre.

Managerial Environment for New Product Development

The new product development is affected by the corporate mission, management philosophy, corporate vision and organizational culture which strongly influence the process of new product development.

Business Diversification of Canon
The late Dr Takeshi Mitarai (then president of Canon) indicated, in his new year address for 1967 (Canon's 30th anniversary), the direction of business diversification that Canon had to follow: 'cameras on the right hand and business machines on the left hand'.

Canon entered the copier business in 1965; 15 years later in 1979, copier sales accounted for about a quarter of Canon's total sales. The tremendous success of Canon's AE-1 camera (an LSI controlled single lens reflector) meant that corporate profits were heavily reliant on this new product. This acted as a challenge and a spur to the Canon's copier division to do as well as, if not better than, Canon's camera division which had been the traditional base of the company.

Canon's Basic Business Philosophy
One of Canon's corporate objectives states 'We will create the best and most unique products based on leading edge technologies. We have a responsibility to create the best products possible. To achieve this goal, we will concentrate our efforts in the areas of R & D, product planning and marketing, adopting an enterprising attitude.'

This philosophy permeates throughout the whole company. R & D drives Canon's strategic thinking and is central to Canon's behaviour and management style. As an example, the medium range management plan of each product division is drawn up by the development centre of the product group.

Table 1. Canon sales by product

1979[1]	%	1987	%
Camera	46	Camera	18
Copier	24	Copier	35
Calculator		Laser beam printer	20
Micrographics	23	Electronic office machines	20
Industrial optical equipment	7	Industrial optical equipment	7
Total	100	Total	100

[1]1979 is the starting year of personal cartridge copier development.

This 3 year product and development plan is then presented for discussion to the international meeting for product strategy held every autumn. Canon's R & D staff therefore believe that their work is essential to the growth of Canon.

Type of Organization

Since its foundation in 1937, Canon's functional management system remained unchanged for the 40 years up to 1977, when, under the strong leadership of its president Ryuzaburo Kaku, Canon adopted the product group management system. Canon's management system has therefore been based on a matrix structure since 1978 (Figure 1).

For instance, the project team approach is used in many areas of managerial problem-solving throughout the whole of Canon and not just in the area of new product development. The integration by the project team of business operational activities and functional management activities has been well accepted. This means that efficiency in business operations and effectiveness in innovation are able to co-exist in Canon. The close co-operation that occurs between the functional organization and the divisional organization is very important in promoting Canon's ability to innovate.

Organizational Culture of Canon

Since its foundation, Canon has emphasized a corporate tradition of respect for the individual. The company has made every effort to recognize and reward individual merit. To foster individual enthusiasm, integrity and creativity, they have tried to provide a motivating work environment at every level of the organization.

Canon's personnel policies are based on the '3 J Policy' as follows.

☆ self-motivation (*ji-hatsu* in Japanese)

☆ self-awareness (*ji-kaku*)

☆ self-reliance (*ji-chi*)

This is not to say that the 3 J Policy is paternalistic in the usual sense of that term. Rather, the stress is on work responsibility with an awareness of the organization's basic goal. Canon people believe that self-awareness, enthusiasm and responsible behaviour are the three keys to good results.

For example, people will see six Chinese characters, corresponding to the 3 Js (*ji-hatsu*, *ji-kaku*, *ji-chi*) on three large columns at the main entrance of Canon's central research centre. This means that Canon's R & D people challenge themselves to dream of new technology and new products in the light of the '3 J Policy'.

The Copier Business in the Late 1970s

The Notice to the Niche Market

During the 1960s and 1970s the plain paper copier was widely used in large scale offices such as those of the government, big companies, etc. The senior management of Canon (i.e. the Director of Canon Inc.'s Reprographic Products Division and the President of Canon's Sales Co.) however, wished to develop a new market for the plain paper copier. Canon's market survey data given in Table 2 shows the distribution of offices in Japan in 1979 according to size. The conventional copier business corresponds to segments A–D. Segment E, offices with less than five employees, were outside the conventional copier business. In the late 1970s it was considered too difficult to develop a new copier market in segment E for the following reasons.

(1) *Market price*. The price of the lowest copier at the time was more than 500,000 yen ($2300). This was considered too expensive for the small office.

(2) *Maintenance services*. Conventional copiers had to be serviced by professional service engineers, which again for reasons of cost limited the copiers to larger offices.

(3) *Sales channels*. The main sales channels for conventional copiers were the manufacturer's own direct sales force and the dealer's sales force. It was felt that in addition to these, new sales channels such as shops and mail order would be necessary for the small offices in segment E.

In terms of product concept, the conventional copier market was seen as being divided as in Table 3.

These concepts would have to be transformed if the new copier market was to be developed. At the start

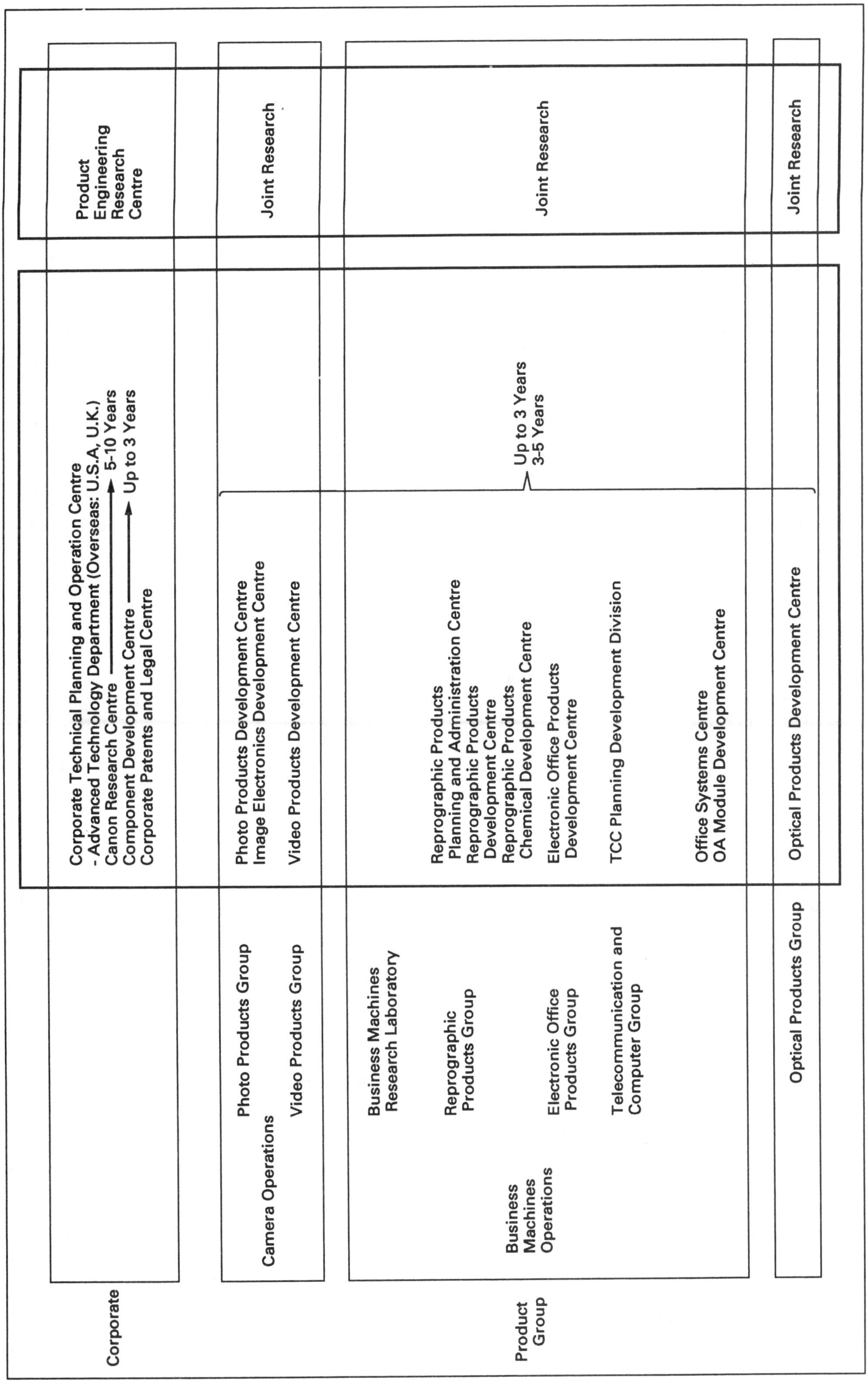

Figure 1. Canon R & D organization

Table 2. Office-size distribution in Japan (1979)

Copier market segment[1]	Number of office workers	Number of offices	Working population
A	300+	200,000	9,300,000
B	100–299	30,000	4,800,000
C	30– 99	170,000	8,300,000
D	5– 29	1,820,000	15,400,000
E	1– 4	4,110,000	8,700,000
			36,500,000

[1]A–D: conventional copier market; E: new market.

Table 3. Conventional product concepts

Product concept	Copier speed
High volume copier	High speed (50–150 copies/min)
Medium volume copier	Standard speed (10–50 copies/min)
Low volume copier	Low speed (0–10 copies/min)

of the 1980s therefore, new concepts such as the personal copier, colour copier, and digital copier were introduced by Canon which in effect became the market trend setter.

The Internal Environment of Canon's Copier Business
After a careful analysis of the copier market environment in the late 1970s, Dr Keizo Yamaji, Vice President of Canon Inc. (then Director of the Reprographic Products Division), and Mr Seiichi Takigawa, President of Canon Sales Co., were very keen to develop a new copier market and to create a unique product for this market. They determined that the new market would cover:

(1) Small offices with less than five employees (segment E, Table 2),

(2) Personal side desk copiers, (segments A–D, Table 2), and

(3) The home-use copier market.

These were further discussed by Dr Yamaji and Mr Takigawa with Mr Hiroshi Tanaka, Managing Director of Office Products Operations (then Director of the Reprographic Products Development Centre).

Canon's copier division was already in a state of excitement as another division, the Camera Division, had introduced the AE-1 camera which was having a major impact on the world camera markets. The Copier Division had not had a success like the AE-1, which acted as a stimulus for them to produce a similar success. The AE-1 was the world's first electronically controlled totally automatic single lense reflex (SLR) camera with a built-in microprocessor unit. This new camera was the world trend-leader as the LSI controlled SLR camera. Because of the AE-1 boom in the world market, they produced from April 1976 to October 1977 over 1 million cameras. In 1980, the produc-

tion of AE-1 series reached 72 per cent of all Japanese 35 mm SLR cameras.

The Development of the Personal Copier

Standard Process for New Product Development in Canon
Canon has a basic procedure for new product development which applies to every product area. This is outlined in Table 4. This standard procedure is the phased planning process and its purposes are as follows.

(1) Because of the review which occurs after each stage, the 'Go or No Go' decision to move to the next stage is very clear.

(2) In each of Canon's development centres, the design-review, patent-review, cost-review and quality assurance of the trial model are led by the product champion.

(3) The market requirements are discussed thoroughly during the product concept stage.

Discussion and Outline of the Product Concept
After considering both the external and internal environment of the copier business, the senior management were eager to realize their 'dream' of a unique, innovative copier that would cost $1000. They communicated this wish to the director of the Reprographic Products Development Centre, Mr H. Tanaka. The stimulus given by senior management then acted as a trigger for the development of the $1000 copier development. Mr Tanaka by nature is always seeking new challenges in innovation. In accepting this particular challenge he became the new copier's champion. The process of stimulation whereby energy is transferred from top management to the product champion has been

Table 4. Standard procedure for new product development

Classification of stage	Development stage	Remarks
DA	Product concept stage	The distinctive features of the product with respect to market and technological factors are determined and the originality of the new product is investigated.
DB	Elemental key device stage	Factors (key devices, components, processes and materials) which influence product functions, are investigated.
DC	Feasibility model stage	From the results of stage DB, the feasibility of the product is investigated through studying the machine-unit function.
DD	Prototype model stage	The first trial model of the product is designed and made in the trial production plant. The functioning, cost, industrial design and serviceability of the model is investigated.
DE	Engineering model stage	A second trial model is designed, made and evaluated in the trial production plant with mass production in mind.
MT	Trial mass production stage	A few hundred units are made using mass production facilities and the problems of mass production are solved.

called 'catalytic stimulation' by the author.[3,6] Mr Tanaka called an informal meeting of a few of his most reliable subordinates and initiated a free discussion about a hypothetical $1000 copier. The discussion in particular centred on the following items:

(1) The target market segment (Table 2)

(2) The quality level required for personal use

(3) Maintenance

(4) Expected market price and target cost

(5) Size and weight of the machine

(6) New functions additional to the conventional copier

These discussions generated an organizational commitment to accept the challenge of innovation in the $1000 copier.

The product concept of the personal copier can be summarized as follows:

☆ The most compact and the lightest in the world (under 20 kg).

☆ A market price in the Japanese market of less than 200,000 yen (less than $1000 in the U.S. market).

☆ Maintenance—exchange of disposable parts from time to time.

☆ New functions—functions to ensure that the machine is easy and enjoyable to use.

This informal discussion, led by the product champion, encouraged the team and promoted acceptance of the challenge.

Feasibility Study and Design
After defining the product concepts, a feasibility team was organized in October 1979 to study the

realization of these concepts. The team studied the feasibility of disposable photoreceptors, disposable development apparatus, an instant toner fuser and a target cost of 50,000 yen.

At the same time feasibility studies in the field of materials technology and components technology were also carried out (stage DB in Canon's standard development process, Table 4). In parallel with the feasibility studies, the first stage design team was organized in December 1979. They discussed the general design of the copier, working initially with the design of the feasibility model from January to late February 1980.

In stage DB (the elemental key device stage) and DC (the feasibility model stage), technical staff met to confront the issue of cost vs reliability. In the development of the personal copier, the cost target was less than a half of the conventional copier and the product reliability target was increased 10-fold. So, technical staff were required to produce new concepts and new approaches.

Mr Hiroshi Nitanda, the group leader for mechanical design, said that in the feasibility stage, they had discussions in groups every day and learned many new ideas from electronic consumer products such as TV receivers and electric fans in relation to cost vs reliability. At this stage various ideas to achieve compactness were proposed and built into the design model, for example,

☆ An outer structural design using foam plastics

☆ A piston motion mechanism using a mechanical clutch

☆ A small diameter (60 mm) photoreceptor drum.

Organization and Start-up of Task Force 'X'
Running parallel with the feasibility model, prep-

arations for the prototype model and engineering model were already underway in the selection and organization of the company-wide task force for the development of the Personal Copier, called the Task Force X. The planning of the Personal Copier project was the responsibility of Strategic Corporate Planning supported by the relevant departments. On 1 September 1980, Canon's president, Mr Ryuzaburo Kaku formally inaugurated the Task Force X in the Shimomaruko Plant, Tokyo. In Canon the Task Force is an independent group whose members are appointed by the company president. Task Force X was the second largest horizontal development team in the history of Canon, the largest being the AE-1 camera team. When Team X was established, the AE-1 camera was the star of the organization and was constantly cited as an example of success. It was clear from the beginning that, the personal copier would need the co-operation of many departments. To mobilize the company behind the copier project, Mr Tanaka invented the slogan 'Let's make the AE-1 of copiers!' This slogan had two meanings: first, to demonstrate the synergy between Camera and Copier divisions in sharing the 'Experience of Success'; second, to encourage the transfer of know-how within the company-wide large scale task force. As in the case of the AE-1, the organizational unit for the development of the personal copier was the task force.

The Development System for the Personal Copier

Organization of Task Force X

The organization of Task Force X at the prototype, engineering model and production model stages, is shown in Figure 2. Task Force X had two development groups. The first, Group A was responsible for technological development and design. The second, Group B was responsible for production engineering. Group A was further subdivided into seven subgroups and B into 10 subgroups (Figure 2). In addition the following six staff groups were incorporated into the Task Force:

☆ Task force steering committee

☆ Cost assessment group

☆ Quality assessment group

☆ Patents application group

☆ Marketing group

☆ User application software group

The task force members were selected from the relevant departments as follows.

(1) reprographic products development centre,

(2) production engineering research centre,

(3) corporate technical planning and operation centre,

(4) corporate patents and legal centre,

(5) reprographic products planning and administration centre, and

(6) copier sales planning department.

As shown in Figure 2, the integration of the parallel team activities by 17 subgroups and six staff groups was very difficult.

The total number of members in the task force was about 200, which made it a very large team. From time to time membership of the steering committee was expanded, if it would facilitate more rapid policy decision making and smoother team operation. The following factors were important to the efficient running of the steering committee: making sure all the relevant departments and members were at the same level of understanding about the project, managing the timetable of the task force, controlling its budget, and ensuring frank and thorough debate particularly with respect to cost and reliability.

The mutual transfer of the technological information and know-how created day by day in each group in the task force was the key factor for success. So, the role of the liaison staff of task force was very important.

The Relationship Between the Reprographic Products Development Centre and the Production Engineering Centre

During Canon's history the Production Engineering Centre had acquired important know-how in the mass production of cameras. Since this know-how was felt to be important for the personal copier, co-operation between the Reprographic Products Development Centre and the Production Engineering Centre was vital for the success of the project. Mr K. Naito, Director of the Production Engineering Centre (now Managing Director) was responsible for redesigning the copier production line for the manufacture of the personal copier. He planned the rationalization of the production process with two main aims, (a) 'nonadjust' and automated assembly and (b) automatic inspection. Production Engineering staff participated in the copier project from its earliest stages (e.g. DA and DB in Table 4). The exchange of information was frequent and useful and influenced to good effect the direction of the task force afterwards.

Generally in Canon, from stage DE (engineering model) the production engineering staff participated in the new product development.

On the other hand, from stage DC (feasibility model) to DE (engineering model), the production engineering staff worked together in the design phase with mass production in mind.

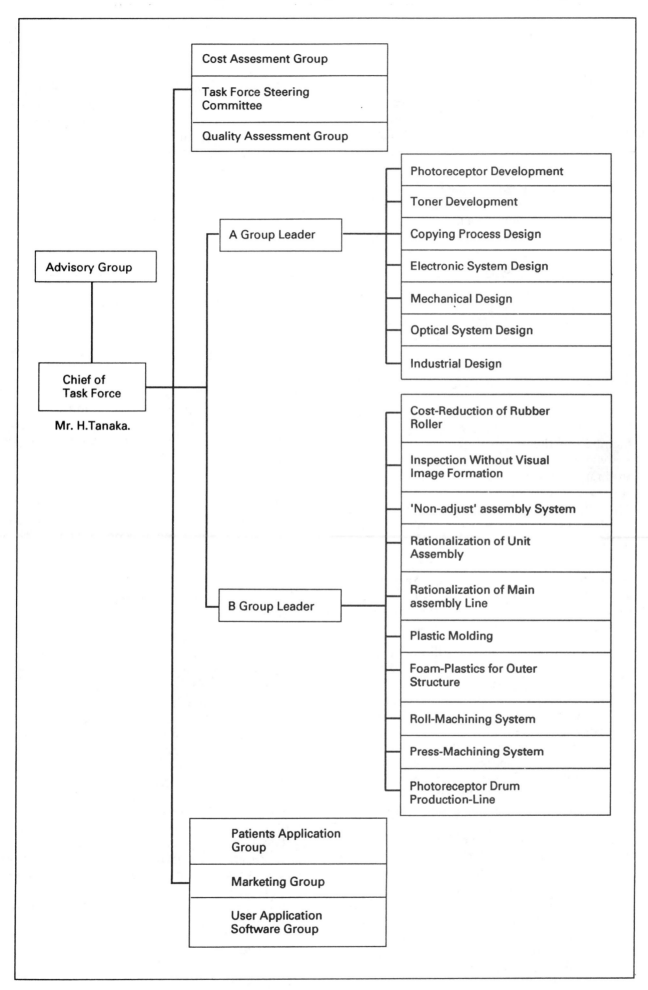

Figure 2. The organization of Task Force X

The Psychological Process of Innovative New Product Development

A summary of the development process of the personal copier and other successful new products is shown in Figure 3. From a psychological and scientific behavioural view, there are 10 stages to the process:

(1) Innovative new product development starts with stimulation from senior management. The necessity for the new development is strongly influenced by the market environment and by the inner management environment occurring at the time (Figure 3—A).

(2) The next part of the process is an honest self-evaluation as to deficiencies in technology, products and business (Figure 3—B). For this self-evaluation, informal meetings are very important.

(3) Through frank and thorough discussion, the members of the development team can discover those aspects related to technology and the market which are lacking (Figure 3—C). The members of the informal meeting should have an awareness of the market and technology. For any range of products or services there are always products or services that are missing. The unfulfilled needs or desires of the consumer for these products or services is what sets the goals for innovation.

(4) Awareness of the market and business environment also stimulates the challenge to achieve the goals set for innovation (Figure 3—D). Stages A to D comprise the first phase in which the product 'dream' is honestly designed.

(5) At stage D a tangible goal is still not clear and technological solutions are still not in sight. Utilizing the imagination and dynamism of young engineers and the assistance of other experts a wide range of ideas and options are created (Figure 3—E). It was in this stage that the cartridge technology of the personal copier was created. The opposing constraints of 'cost' vs 'reliability' were discussed in free and thorough debate, eventually giving rise to the unusual idea of the cartridge technology.

(6) In the next step, which involves narrowing the options, the team leader plays a key role (Figure 3—F). Through his leadership the motivation of the team members is enhanced. Stage G is where formulation and recognition of the team mission, (rather than assignation of team responsibility) takes place. Phases D to G comprise the second phase, that of divergence of options and then their contraction.

(7) The third and final phase, going ahead to the creative goal, occurs after phase G. The task force goes ahead to the creative goal though, on the way, the team members meet with various obstacles. For the realization of the product concept, the task force team members had to find the solution to many technical difficulties in four technology fields, material technology, functional component technology, design technology and production engineering technology. The solutions encountered to these obstacles are given in Table 5.

The correspondence between the standard process (Table 4) and the psychological and behavioural scientific process (Figure 3) is shown in (Table 6).

Key Factors for Success in the Development of the Personal Copier

On reflection the key factors for success were as follows:

(1) Senior management stimulated the staff of the reprographic products development centre with their dream of a $1000 copier. This dream which was both highly innovative and challenging, consisted of two main factors. The first was the development of a new market which was not covered by the conventional copier business. The second factor was the invention of a maintenance-free copier, which was regarded as impossible since the invention of the Xerox system. The idea of creating the new personal copier was very attractive for the Copier Development Centre. The result was a climate of enthusiasm and co-operation in the organization.

(2) In the belief that the realization of a $1000 copier was possible, a key factor in its development was the establishment of a company-wide system of co-operation. In particular co-operation was promoted between Canon Inc. and Canon Sales Co. Inc., sales subsidiaries and between the Reprographic Products Development Centre and the Production Engineering Centre. The operation of the company-wide Task Force X was particularly successful.

(3) The utilization of the energies and resourcefulness of young engineers was very important. The average age of the engineers in the early stages of development (e.g. the feasibility studies) was about 27. They have innovative ideas and it was they who created the technology for the cartridge which was such a breakthrough.

(4) The character of the Product Champion, Mr Hiroshi Tanaka was critical, particularly in respect to points (2) and (3) above. He was important and effective as a bridge between top management and the younger engineers.

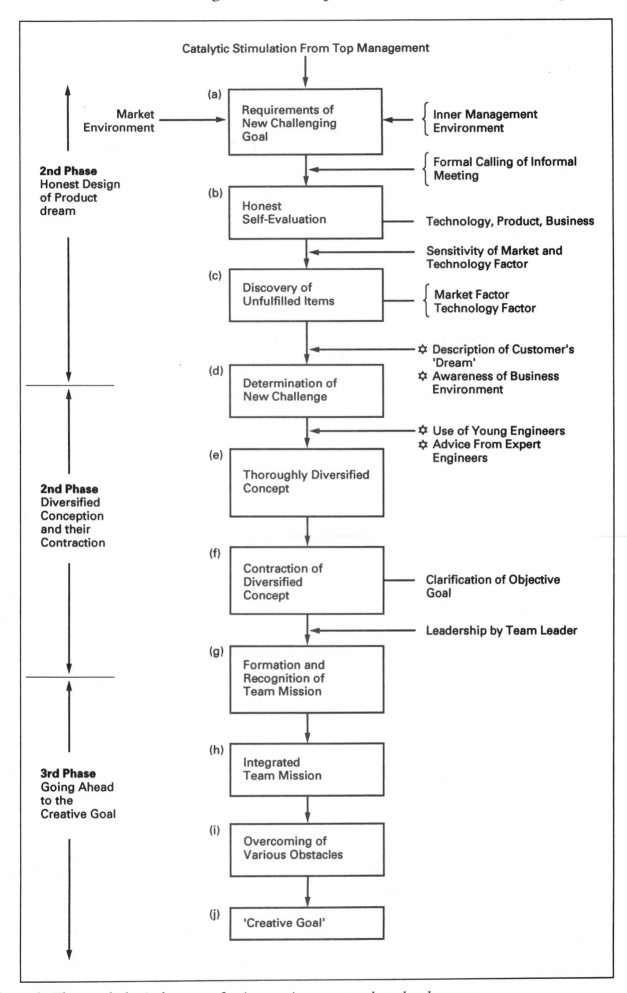

Figure 3. The psychological process for innovative new product development

Table 5. New technological system in personal cartridge-type copier

Material technology	Photoreceptor	(1) Non-pollution type photoreceptor composed of organic photoconductive material (2) Manufacturing technology of aluminium impact cylinder (3) Precision dip-coating technology of organic photoconductive material
	Toner	(1) One-component magnetic colour developer (2) Colour toners for jumping development process
Functional components technology	Development	(1) Development magnetic roll composed of plastic magnet (2) Small diameter aluminium sleeve cylinder for developing (3) Colour toner jumping development system by developing-blade
	Fusing	(1) Instant fusion by low-pressure thermal roller
	Cleaning	(1) Non-adjust precision installation of cleaning blade
	Charging	(1) Non-adjust installation of charging wire
Design technology	Mechanical and structural design	(1) Outer structural design using foam-plastic (2) Piston-motion mechanism using mechanical clutch
	Production design	(1) Basic design concept based on non-adjust assemblage (2) Rack–pinion style driving mechanism of original document table for easier assemblage
Production engineering technology	Automatic assemblage	(1) Establishment of automatic assembly line (2) Non-adjust assembly line (3) One-way assembly line (4) Parts drop assembly line
	Automatic inspection	(1) Dust inspection by laser scanning (2) Automatic precision measurement of cleaning blade (3) Automatic inspection of paper carriage

Table 6. The relationship between standard process and psychological process

Figure 3	Table 4
1st phase (A–D)	Product concept stage (DA)
2nd phase (D–G)	Feasibility study (DB–DC)
3rd phase (G–J)	Trial product stage (DD–DE)

(5) The need to balance cost against reliability gave rise to the invention of cartridge-based technologies for the personal copier. A total of 594 patents were applied for, and granted, to protect these technologies.

(6) From the product concept to the sales launch, it took 3 years to develop the personal copier. The enthusiasm of the task force members to achieve the goal, the close company-wide co-operation, and the well-structured development process all helped to accelerate the process.

The Significance of the Development

The effects of the development of the copier were far reaching:

(1) *The creation of a new market.* The new cartridge technology created a market for a maintenance-free copier that did not require maintenance by service engineers. This was totally different from the Xerox system which up to then had dominated the world copier business.

(2) *The development of a family copier.* In 1986 Canon launched a *family copier* that was not simply an extension of the personal copier product line. It was two-thirds of the weight of the personal copier and was half the price.

(3) *The foundation of Canon Bretagne.* After the development of the personal copier in 1982, Canon founded in 1983 Canon Bretagne, a French subsidiary based at Rennes. This subsidiary has made an important contribution to the globalization of Canon and is the largest business machine factory in Europe.

(4) *The technological effect on the laser beam printer business.* The synergy between the personal copier cartridge and the semiconductor laser technology used in the LBP-10 laser beam printer led to the development of the maintenance-free laser beam printer.

Acknowledgement—I want to thank Dr Mattew O'Callaghan heartily for constructive criticism and comment.

References

(1) K. Imai, I. Nonaka and H. Takeuchi, *Managing the New Product Development Process,* 75th Anniversary Colloquium of Productivity and Technology, Harvard Business School, March (1984).

(2) H. Takeuchi and I. Nonaka, The new product development game, *Harvard Business Review,* January/February 1986).

(3) T. Yamanouchi, Research and development systems and corporate culture of Canon Inc., *Gestion 2000,* No. 4 (1987).

(4) Y. Teramoto, Japanese experiences in technology management and innovation, *Gestion 2000,* No. 4 (1987).

(5) T. Kono, *Strategy and Structure of Japanese Enterprises,* Macmillan Press (1984).

(6) T. Yamanouchi, *Management of Technology for Business Innovation,* Japanese edn, Nippon Keizai Shinbunsha (1986).

PART FIVE

Harnessing Information Technology

CIM at Nippon Seiko Co.

Masakatsu Hosoda

This article describes a case study of a successful CIM application. The company is applying a computerized total information system to achieve better customer service with lower costs. There are two core systems. FENICS deals with engineering product design and the specification of components and materials for each order. ASPACS links the marketing to production and relates the customer's order to production and inventory control. The NSK case is about the construction of a vertical information system, from customer to production. Another system is the horizontal information system which is an information network e.g. with retailers. NSK uses a top-down approach. First, the total system is planned and then the parts are constructed. The other approach is a bottom-up approach which means the construction of an information system by a piecemeal, step-by-step approach.

Nippon Seiko K.K. (NSK) is one of the world's leading manufacturers of bearings and automobile components. The company also produces a wide range of equipment incorporating precision motion technology. Its operations span the globe, with nine domestic plants and seven overseas manufacturing facilities. On a consolidated basis, NSK has $2285m sales. Their computer integrated manufacturing system is called MAGMA (MArketing desiGn and MAnufacturing) and it integrates aspects of production, marketing and technology. MAGMA has been a major success, improving customer services and aiding management decision-making.

The Implementation of CIM at NSK

(1) *The Development of the Third Generation Computer and the Database Data Communication System*

In the latter half of the 1960s, the third generation computer and the Database Data Communication System (DB/DC System) were developed. The database system was enthusiastically received by many data-processing technicians because the system improved upon the previous batch processing system which handled the application program and the data as one integrated item. The new system separated the application program and the data and created a database which organization members could have access to and which could be referenced and updated at will.

System engineers and data processing technicians realized that an integrated system which employs the DB/DC system would be the key to enhancing the company's competitiveness. This enthusiastic reception triggered a boom in the use of the Management Information System (MIS).

However, many enterprises, particularly in the manufacturing sector, have failed to successfully adopt the DB/DC system or MIS and have returned to the batch processing system again. Such failures dampened the enthusiasm for MIS in manufacturing.

(2) *Why Japanese Manufacturers Failed to Meet the Challenge of MIS*

The reasons manufacturers failed to meet the challenge of MIS can be summed up in the following points:

☆ The general design of the system was not able to achieve management goals.

☆ Defects in design due to a lack of experience in business practices on the part of the system engineer and the data-processing technician.

☆ Failure to set up an organization-wide database which would replace the filing systems employed by each division of the organization. Moreover, even if the system had such a database, it failed to provide timely maintenance and updating.

☆ In parallel with the creation of the new software, there should have been a wholesale revamping of the previous job classification and span of responsibility with regard to the operation of database, and changes too, in work methods and batch-processing. This was not done.

☆ No recognition of the need for capital investment in information technology.

Mr Masakatsu Hosoda is Executive Vice President of Nippon Seiko Co. in Tokyo.

☆ System-design failed to overcome inefficient input/output devices, and as a result the system was not able to carry out real-time data-processing, which was absolutely essential for such a database.

Reviewing the above points, one cannot help but notice that management's lack of understanding of computer data-processing, their misguided decision-making and ineffective leadership were the major causes for the failure of MIS.

(3) The Decision to Introduce a Total System at NSK

In 1967, Mr Arata, currently president of NSK, was director of business planning. He realized that it was time to take aggressive action to prepare the company for the technological and competitive challenges of the decades ahead, and decided to develop a total system by computerizing as many functions as possible. A total system, then, was set up at NSK as an essential part of its business strategy.

(4) Challenges Posed by a Total System at NSK

We decided that a completely new approach was necessary for the future development of the company. The goal was a highly integrated organization and database system, but this was not easily achieved. NSK was established 70 years ago, and many long-standing regulations that were, in effect, barriers had to be swept away.

It was essential to replace the batch-processing system with the DB/DC system in order to respond dynamically to changing customer demands. It was also important to change the employees' way of thinking and to introduce training programs in order to minimize the impact of job changes and broadened spans of responsibility. The president appointed members of the staff as system designers and system promoters; these members were heads of the sales department, the production department, the design department and various plants.

Since 1970 NSK has continuously developed information processing technology, taking into account cost-performance. Over the subsequent years, computer and communication technology has advanced rapidly, and cost-performance has improved dramatically, giving us an opportunity to use computers in areas that previously could not be cost-justified.

LSI produced high-density, sophisticated compact computers that could be used on the shop-floor or in the field by salesmen and engineers. A wide variety of input/output devices were developed, permitting us to collect data with sensors and scanners, and to present computational results in a multitude of ways. Such remarkable changes took place not only in hardware, but in operating systems and other software as well. Moreover, in parallel with the computer revolution, communications technology also made significant advances.

This rapid progress in computers and communications also changed the way businesses operate. Computer and communications technology allowed business to adopt an entirely new approach to the marketplace. Because of competitive pressures, companies focused on producing unique products and reducing life cycles. Above all, business became multinational and it was necessary to adjust to this new borderless world.

With this computer and communications revolution and our president's directive in mind, we at NSK invested in new technology, and developed our own advanced flexible manufacturing system, with the objective of supplying products to our customers with guaranteed quality, cost and delivery, and at the same time enhancing our information processing and analysis capability by a continual improvement of this man-machine interface system.

CIM System at NSK—MAGMA

Our flexible manufacturing system is called MAGMA. MAGMA derives its name from the <u>MA</u>rketing desi<u>G</u>n <u>MA</u>nufacturing functions. MAGMA means that marketing and manufacturing are linked by a design which combines customers' ever changing needs and NSK's technology.

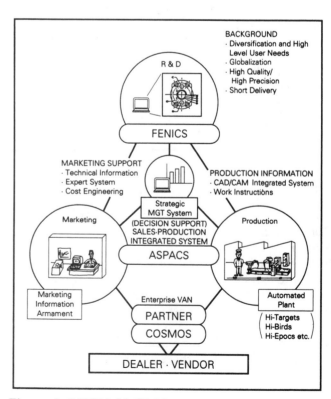

Figure 1. NSK MAGMA system

(1) *The Composition of MAGMA*
MAGMA is composed of two basic functional areas:

(a) Headquarters functions which include marketing and design, database maintenance and general control.

(b) Plant functions which produce the product and guarantee its quality, cost and delivery.

Each of these functional areas is composed of several sub-systems and all of these sub-systems are tied together by a high-speed communication network called NICE-II (NSK Integrated Communication Exchange-II).

The headquarters functions include ASPACS (Automated Sales and Production Adjustment Control System), an on-line system executing order entry, inventory allocation, production orders, order planning and shipment; and FENICS (Flexible ENgineering Information Control System), an on-line CAD/CAM system which implements design specifications and work instructions for quality-control.

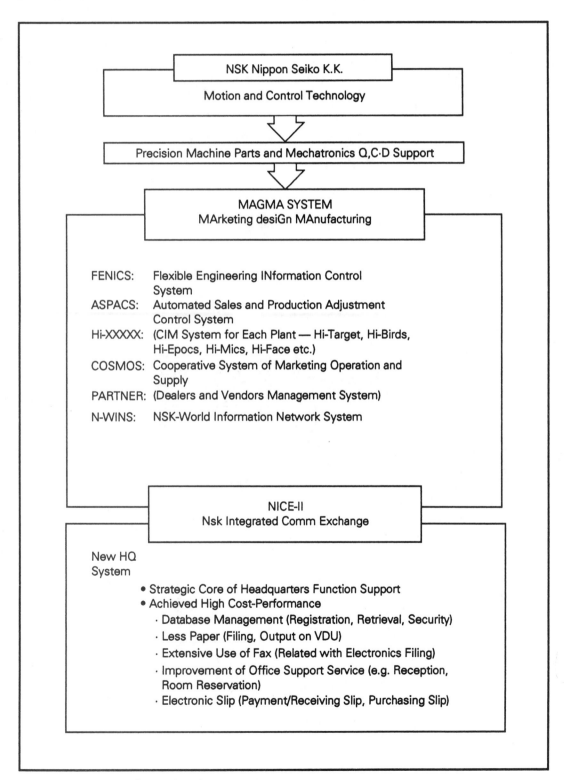

Figure 2. The composition of MAGMA

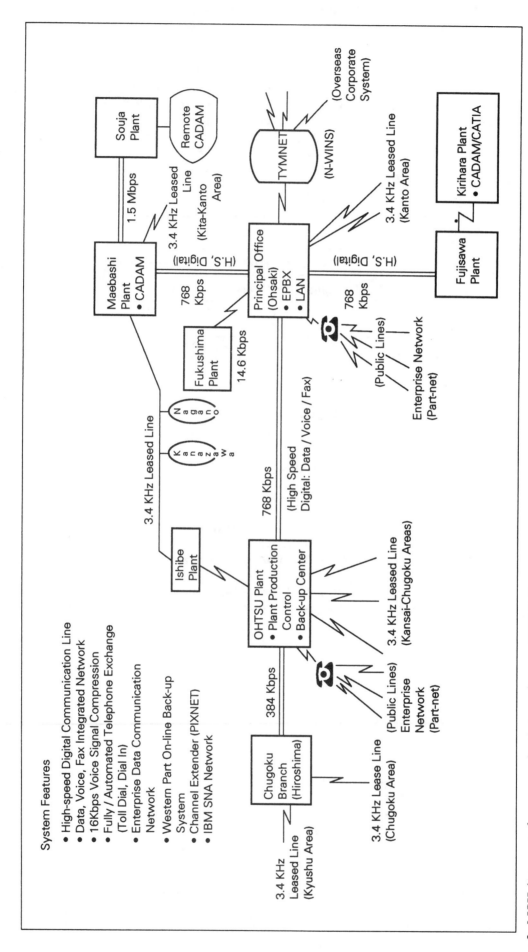

Figure 3. NSK integrated communication exchange, NICE-II

Plants functions include unique on-line systems, usually with a 'HI' (Highly Integrated) prefix, developed for order-dispatch and quality-control. Several other sub-systems (COSMOS PARTNER and N-WIN) support ASPACS and FENICS.

With each of these sub-systems on-line and with the high-speed network NICE-II in place, we have a total system, supporting quality, cost and delivery, tracking and monitoring the movement of the resources of the enterprise (men, machines and materials).

(2) FENICS and ASPACS

FENICS is the first major sub-system of MAGMA, and comprises many databases, simulation programs and expert systems. Our design engineering and production-engineering staff utilize it for simulations, analysis and the design of components. It also indicates the work process and work instructions to be followed for each shop order. At our sales department, by entering specifications received from a customer, salesmen can select the bearing that best fits those specifications, and can receive a drawing of the part from a fax machine connected with the expert system.

ASPACS is also a major sub-system of MAGMA.

ASPACS is an on-line system, supporting forecasting, and directing order entry, inventory allocation, production orders, order sequencing, and shipping. ASPACS controls the entire cycle from forecast to customer order to plant production order and finally the actual delivery of the products to the customer. ASPACS also provides input into MRP (Material Requirement Planning), which is a 'push' system, and into a KANBAN, which is a 'pull' system. Here ASPACS is adjusting conflicting factors—push and pull—to minimize the volume of components in an inventory. All elements of this system are on-line, real-time and available to anyone 'with a need to know'.

(3) Fukushima Plant as a Typical Example of MAGMA

Figure 6 shows the production control system of our Fukushima plant in modular format. This system is connected with FENICS and ASPACS through the NICE-II network, and the communications channels in the plant are supported by a Local Area Network (LAN) which uses noise-resistant fibre optics. We have installed a real-time system for data collection, analysis and feedback which utilizes automatic inspection machines and measuring instruments, and provides a high-level quality-control system.

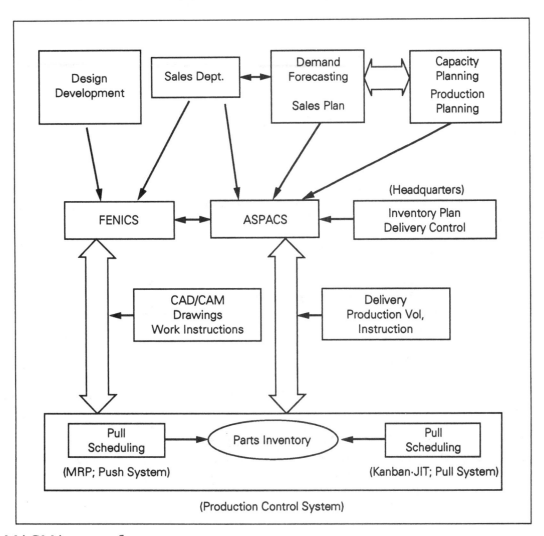

Figure 4. MAGMA system flow

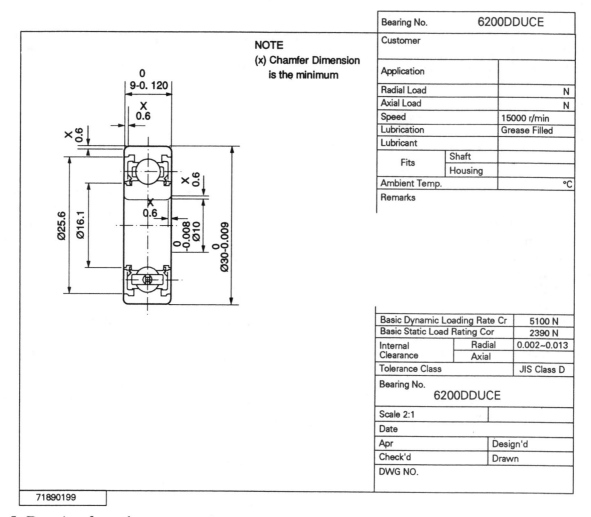

Figure 5. Drawing from the expert system

We have engineering workstations in the Fukushima plant which are connected to the FENICS system of the design department in the head office, and can access to the design specification database. These workstations are low-cost terminals; they display work instructions and monitor the status of each machine tool in a coloured format. This coloured panel shows the status of each machine; for example, when the red-coloured symbol blinks, urgent action is required from the workers. If this action is not taken within the allotted time and the problem status is not redressed, the computer system alerts the foremen or the production engineers by an electronic pager. The Fukushima plant system (HI-TARGETS) had developed not only an automated production control system but also a man-machine interface system which promotes continual improvement.

Progress control on the plant floor is a key application of a production control system. Briefly speaking, the purpose of the system is to work out an optimum production schedule and to collect data for progress and quality control; product costing and quality assurance are done automatically by a sensing system that is interfaced with the machine tool.

The quality-control information system operates in the following way. Shop order data from the scheduling system of ASPACS and corresponding work instructions from FENICS are directed to each workstation on a real-time basis. Quality data is collected by a sensing system and displayed on portable terminals with conventional video displays. When we have to analyse the quality of parts produced some years before, archival data can be retrieved.

Usually the number of workers increases in proportion to the volume of goods stored in the warehouse, but at the Fukushima plant, only a single worker mans the warehouse, thanks to a combination of a rotary-rack automated warehouse and the issue/receipt control system of ASPACS. Under the control of ASPACS and FENICS, when the products are finished and boxed, labels with bar codes are attached and the cartons are automatically transferred to the warehouse by the conveyer. In terms of data-processing, the item status has been changed from work-in-process to completion through a shop order control process. With regard to shipping, when the destination codes are indicated by database, pre-stored cartons are automatically transferred to the shipping station.

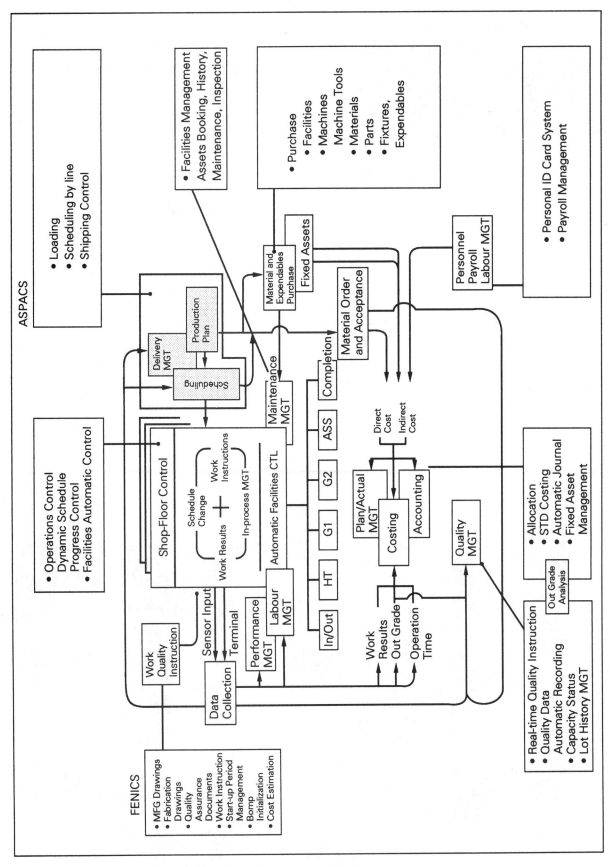

Figure 6. MAGMA system and production system functional outline

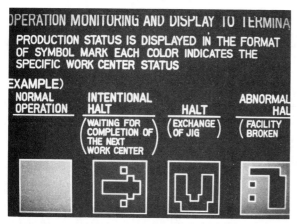

Figure 7. Workstation monitoring the status of a machine-tool

All the sub-systems are tied into a budget control system. The basic idea of this system is that the transaction data, collected on real-time, is sorted out and edited as accounting data.

The benefits of the total plant control system can be summed up as follows: (i) The reduction of personnel, which enabled us to attain not only high productivity but flexibility of production. (ii) The improvement of quality and the realization of quality assurance. (iii) A shortening of production lead time. Physical cycle time required for the process can be reduced. (iv) The improvement of the inventory turnover ratio by ASPACS supported by an expert system and a tracking system.

(4) *Headquarters*

NSK celebrated its 70th anniversary in 1986. In Janaury 1987, we built a new headquarters building, which now functions as the heart of our total system. We developed a decision-making system which ensures maximum cost-performance of headquarters functions. Even during meetings of the board of directors, board members can access the decision-making system by using on-line terminals, and study the information they require. Managers can also log into this system with a password.

At NSK, ASPACS directs order entry, inventory allocation, production orders and shipment, so headquarters functions are primarily restricted to strategic and staff-control activities.

So, instead of the old span of responsibility, a much wider span of responsibility was established by using a multi-window display terminal.

(5) *The Features of MAGMA*

☆ MAGMA is an advanced flexible manufacturing system with the objective of supplying products to our customers with guaranteed quality, cost and delivery.

☆ MAGMA is a total system, encompassing the NSK industrial group and its core is the DB/DC system.

☆ Taking into consideration the fact that human input would promote progress, a man-machine interface was built into MAGMA.

☆ MAGMA is an expert system that directs operations.

☆ MAGMA is a tracking system of management resources.

Figure 8. Engineering workstation displays shop order and work instruction

Figure 9. Engineering workstation displays shop order and work instruction

☆ MAGMA is a system making estimates and managing the execution process.

☆ MAGMA is a system that continually improves cost-performance.

(6) *Benefits Brought by MAGMA*

As shown in Figure 13, MAGMA effectively reduced personnel, for in proportion to our growth in sales the increase in personnel was relatively small.

Perhaps the principal benefit of MAGMA was that every department of the company can now have its data displayed and used by all for analysis, planning, projection and execution; data that was once restricted to the department is now part of a common pool accessible to all.

Furthermore, by using the newest and most sophisticated 'expert system', the pace of operation has changed from human speed to computer speed, and prompt and collective action can be taken to deal with necessary change.

Along with these changes in the computer system, the production orientation of the old organization has been superseded by an orientation towards the market and the customer.

A graphic representation of the results of introducing MAGMA in 1980 can be seen in Figure 13.

Figure 10. Rotary-rack type automated warehouse

Figure 11. Pre-stored cartons are automatically transferred to the shipping station by the conveyer

Figure 12. The board of directors. By using on-line terminals, board members can access the database

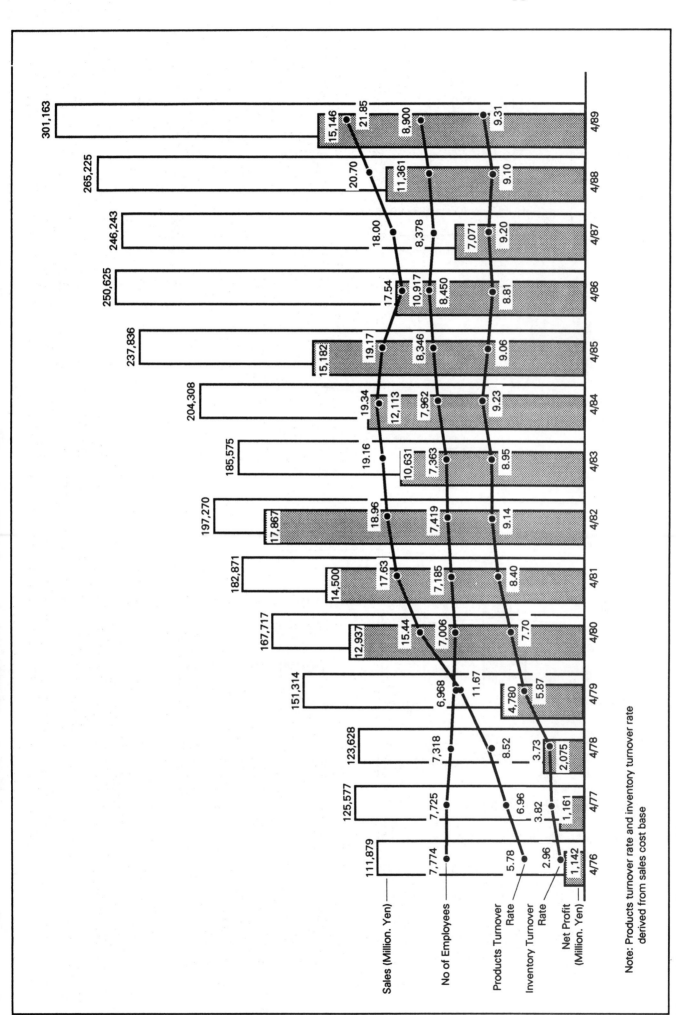

Figure 13. Major business index

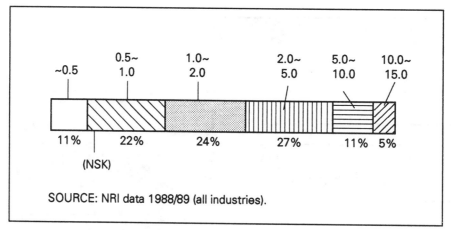

Figure 14. Computer equipment expense against sales amount

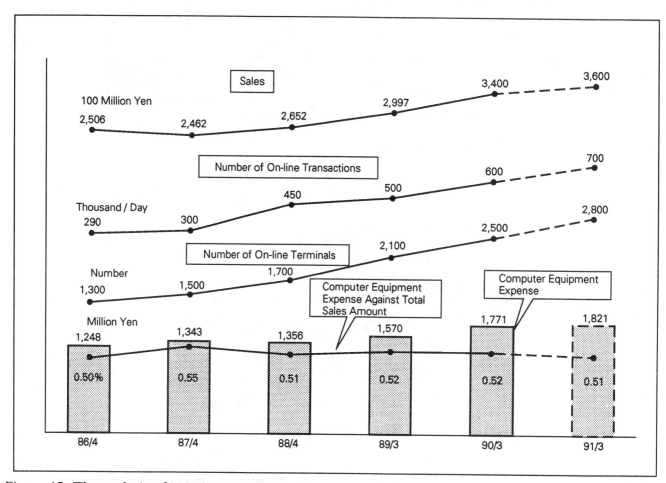

Figure 15. The analysis of NSK's computer equipment expense

As can be seen, the 1976 finished products turnover rate* was 5·78 per year, while the 1980 finished products turnover rate came to 15·44 per year. At present the rate is levelling off at 20 per year. The slump shown in 1986 was due to the fact that NSK undertook certain products from outside the NSK organization. Yet once they were placed under MAGMA's control, the products turnover rate was rapidly improved.

(7) *Computer Equipment Expense against Total Sales Amount at NSK*
The effectiveness of our investment in CIM can be appreciated when it is realized that our investment in the computer equipment amounted to only a mere 0·52 per cent of the total sales amount.

*Sales ÷ finished products average inventory.

Value Added Distribution of Parcels in Japan

Takashi Sekita

Yamato Transport Corporation recently entered the parcels business and has been very successful, taking the largest share of the market, in competition with the Japanese Post Office. By the use of a computerized information system, the company provides a rapid high quality service. Yamoto offers a pick up and delivery service. It uses retail stores for receiving the parcels and every driver has a small 'point of sale' terminal. The company has built its transportation network systematically, one step at a time.

Construction and Usage of Yamato's Strategic Information System

1989 was the company's 70th anniversary. In 1919, Yamato was the first firm to start operating a regular road freight service between Tokyo and Yokohama. It was called the Yamato Bin. In 1926, we expanded the network within the Kanto area which enabled us to offer a small parcel service including the transportation of goods for department stores. After the war, in 1950 Yamato obtained a licence to handle railway freight, expanded into air and sea freight, established an air passenger service, art packing, etc., and grew into a nationwide firm offering a total transportation service to industry and commerce. The oil crisis of 1973 was a turning point. The company launched its 'Takkyubin' service—a parcel service for the domestic consumer, and this is its main business today.

'Takkyubin' triggered a boom in the door-to-door service. The company diversified and went into the leisure market (Golf and Ski Takkyubin), the international parcels market (UPS Takkyubin), mail order sales (Collect, Book service). Recently a refrigerated delivery service 'Cool Takkyubin' with three ranges of temperature control, became a great success, reflecting the increasing consumer interest in gourmet food.

Mr Takashi Sekita is Director, Applications Improvement Department, Yamato Transport Corporation, Tokyo.

Table 1. Yamato Transport Corporation

Head office:	Ginza, Chuo-ku, Tokyo
Established:	December 1919
Capital:	31.6 Billion Yen
Revenue:	269.2 Billion Yen
Employees:	31 Thousand
Vehicles:	17 Thousand
Offices:	1.3 Thousand

1. The History of Computerization

Table 2 shows the history of computerization. Takkyubin's system was integrated in 1980 as the NEKO-II system.

Step 1. The invoicing and accounting system was established. The aim was to rationalize the operation by automating the complicated transportation fare calculations, systematizing the accounts and bookkeeping, etc., and as a result, to provide a better service to the customers and to save staff in the accounting department.

In 1973, EDP division became an independent company as Yamato System Development Co., Ltd.

Step 2. The company introduced a nationwide online system for freight transport. The automatic transmission of the data for each parcel enabled us to stop manual recording and to develop an integrated data processing system. In October 1974, Yamato received the Transportation Minister's Prize as an 'Excellent company in developing information systems'.

Step 3. The existing 'trucking' system was totally redesigned to fit the new Takkyubin service. Point of Sale (POS) outlets were introduced, the host computer and circuit networks were strengthened, and hand-held computers were introduced. As a result the company was nominated as one of the 'Hundred Pioneer Enterprises' by *Nippon Keizai*

Table 2. The steps in computerization

Steps	Introduction date	Main system	Main operation	Network	Input
Step 1	September 1969	Total transportation	Railway freight	Offline	Punch cards
Step 2	February 1974	NEKO-I	Yamato Bin	Online	Perforated paper tapes
Step 3	October 1980	NEKO-II	Takkyubin (unitary)	Online	NEKO POS
Step 4	October 1986	NEKO-III	Takkyubin (various)	Online	P POS

Shinbunsha (Japan's Business Newspaper) in September 1983. The package tracking system is especially popular with customers. The introduction of POS outlets speeded up the information processing and this was further improved when each individual could use a bar code input.

Step 4. The company handed portable POS terminals (PPs) to each 'sales driver' and installed workstations (personal computers) in each sales office in order to cope with the wide range of new services: Takkyubin [Golf Ski, Collect (COD), Cool (refrigerated), UPS] service in various fields of leisure, trading and international distribution, and to prepare for the development of new businesses in the future.

Table 3. The present equipment

Host computers:	M780, 760, 380, 180, IBM4381	5
Clusters:	M730, 340, K280	34
Work stations:	F9450 II,	573
Portable POS's:		17,683

2. The Takkyubin Information System (NEKO)

NEKO means New Economical Kindly On-Line, Neko is the Japanese word for cat and it also refers to the company symbol which is a black cat.

(1) Package Tracking System
Each sales driver inputs, by bar code, the information for each parcel from shipping to delivery using a portable POS terminal. Then the PP is connected by jack to the workstation and the data are transmitted to the central processing unit through the public telephone system. Also the information goes through a high-speed private circuit and is collected in the host computer. In this way, the data for all the parcels are tightly controlled, and by using the invoice number, it is possible to obtain the history of the parcel, and its status.

(2) Quality Control System
'To meet our customers' demands'—this phrase describes the aim of the Takkyubin service, and the Takkyubin's information system should suggest this objective. The Package Tracking System and the

Pick Up Command System which will be explained later, provide examples of the support which is provided. Also we must check if we are fulfilling the promises we make to our customers, which means 'quality control'.

Days for delivery—How many days will it take from pickup to delivery? This is the basic transportation measure. Ninety-one per cent of the Takkyubin parcels are supposed to be delivered on the next day after pickup, and the rest on the second day, but is this achieved? We group parcel data according to their distribution areas and calculate the quality of service rates, so that they can be improved. The parcel records are sorted by colour into red, blue and yellow, according to the quality of service which has been achieved.

Data input—The information system plays an important part in the door-to-door delivery service. A major issue on the information system is to have prompt input. In order to make the staff concerned with the timely-input, we record the time when the information is inputted for each bill, and we classify the results according to the sales offices, and congratulate the best sales office.

(3) Stock Control System
We had no systems for stock control because a transportation service has no shape, but as we started to sell coupon tickets and packing materials, such as golf covers, packages of drinks, boxes, etc., it became necessary to take care of the stock.

Transportation vouchers—We have a prepaid system of transportation fees. For example, 11 1000YEN vouchers cost only 10,000YEN and at the point of shipping, they are stuck on the bill like stamps. There are several kinds of vouchers and such large amounts are sold that it is important to control the stocks and sales accounts or it can lead to trouble.

At present, the sales drivers, as part of their daily work, make the inputs for the vouchers and the sales accounts.

Packing materials—Sales of golf covers, drinks packages and boxes, etc., used for the Takkyubin service are going well. This job again is done by the SDs (Sales Drivers) along with pick up and delivery.

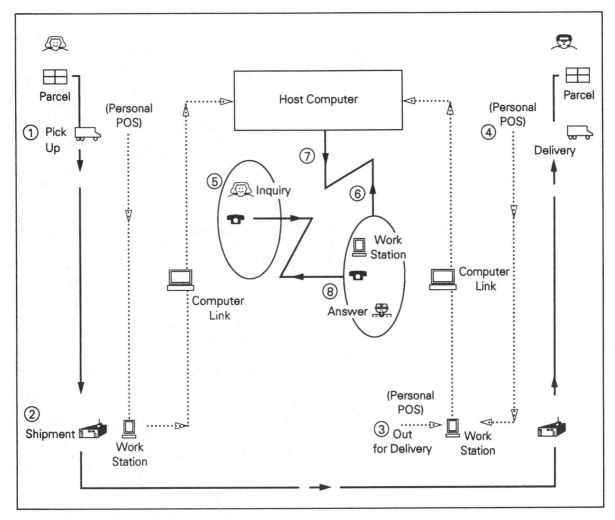

Figure 1. Package and information flow

The variety and volume of the packages has increased and it is important to take care of the stocks and accounts. This is also done using the PP.

(4) Transportation Fees

Formerly the automatic calculation of transportation fees was a very difficult area. But in the case of Takkyubin we do not need the automatic calculation, because we have a simple and clear Takyubin-fee-system, that is to say, the fee depends on the size and destination alone. The collection of debt has also been simplified because our main targets are personal consumers who pay cash.

So these days, our main purpose is the management of cash, and the 'Accounts Receivable Searching System' is one of the examples of cash control.

Accounts receivable—As the packages we handle increase, the problem is to check that the fees are being paid. Once we pick up a package, no matter whether it is paid for or not, we do our best to get it delivered. After it has been delivered, we check on each parcel by the computer and find out from our accounts receivable who is responsible for the payment and get it collected.

Allocation of revenues—How should we allocate the

revenues? The past results are allocated according to three operating steps; pickup, transportation and delivery. Since it has a great effect on revenue and expenditure management in each office it is a matter of primary concern. However, the value on each bill is small and the number of bills is very big so we must rely on the computer. (We will not describe the calculation of accounts, the pricing, credit control, etc., for they are well known.)

(5) Operating Statistics

PP information is batched in the host computer and is made into flash reports, daily reports and monthly reports, which are used in sales, operations and accounting. The 'Past Result of Each Sales Office Data Base' enables us to record the numbers of packages handled, and days required from pick up to delivery, etc., for any office. From the flow chart, we can see the number of Takkyubin packages that moved from one specific area to another.

(6) Operation Tie-up

The computer network was 'closed' and limited strictly within the company but it has been expanded to include international businesses and also customers within Japan, suppliers, and agents.

Tie-ups with customers—Usually, the Takkyubin

bills (address, name, phone number, etc.) are filled out by the customers, but when the customer has lots of packages to ship, as with catalogue sales, sometimes we are handed the delivery address list from them and we fill out the bills. The address lists come in various forms; bills, invoices, and diskettes, but the latest way is by the online system. No matter how the information comes in, all the bills are filled out not by hand but by PCs or on-line printers.

For the package tracing data, our regular customers inquire about their shipment using letters, diskettes, or online enquiries, etc., whatever media suits them, and we are working continuously to improve their service.

Domestic communication—Since we are aiming at a uniform pickup and delivery service for each customer, almost all the sales offices are operated directly by the company. However, we offer the service in Shikoku (the whole region), and in a part of Hokuriku and Sanin through outside contractors or agents. In this case, the information processing is done by PPs, and the information is connected online, just as the system operates within the company.

International communication—Takkyubin is becoming international. We are linked with the biggest small package company in the U.S., UPS (United Parcel Service) and we have established UPS Takkyubin, which handle packages sent to 175 countries. Our information systems are connected through International VAN. We exchange export pre-alerts (shipment information sent in advance) and point of delivery information to use them for customs clearance and customer service.

(7) *Characteristics of the NEKO System*
The characteristics of the NEKO system are summarized below:

① Network: 900 offices nationwide are connected by workstations.

② Data: In December 1989 at the busiest time 2·56m parcels were processed in one day.

③ Operations done by drivers: All 20,000 sales drivers input data using the PP.

④ 'Fresh, Fast Information': We can get information on packages sent 30 minutes before, anywhere, anytime, in 3 seconds.

⑤ Usage of Information: The information is used for package, quality, and stock control and for invoicing customers.

⑥ Equiping the Workstations with Spread Sheets: Work stations and PPs were designed to work together, but outside the busy hours for input in the morning and the evening, workstations can be used to do other jobs for we equipped them with EPO-CALC, and EPO-ACE enabling them to operate as 'stand alone' terminals.

⑦ Flexible Correspondence: Programs and tables are downloaded from the host computers. Workstations and PPs must be able to cope with changes in delivery area tables because of newly organized offices, new products being sold and changes of application programs. New programs are transmitted online to the local area and then downloaded to workstations. Just by connecting the PP to the workstation in the morning, the information will automatically be downloaded onto the PP.

(3) The Communication System

The basis of the technical system is the computer and tele-communication. Our technology has been developed using public and private telephone circuits, facsimile, and computer data. However, the use of the radio has also been expanded to speed up communications with drivers.

(1) *Communications Between Sales Offices (Wired)*
We use our exclusive wire (the NEKO-net) for telephone, computer, and facsimile and this brings benefits in cost speed and convenience.

Telegraphic message network—The telegraphic message network was established in 1972, when we started the nationwide online system, to enable us to send messages in 'Katakana' (one of the two kinds of Kana script used for writing Japanese) to any office within the country. Messages are punched in at the offices, transmitted through the NEKO-net, and communicated by the work station requesting the message. However, the frequency of use is falling because messages in Katakana are difficult to read and facsimiles are tending to replace them.

Fax-net (F NEKO MAIL)—In November 1988, we set up eight transmitters, linked them to the NEKO-net and established a '1000 offices in 30 minutes for 40 thousand yen' 'simultaneous reporting system'. Addressing is easily done using a marking sheet. 'F' stands for 'facsimile'.

Toll dial (long distance office telephone)—We have established a private telephone system by combining the EPBX and NEKO-net, and extending the line, which is 50% cheaper than using the public line. However, its use is limited to offices which need to make many phone calls, and most of the offices still depend on the public line.

Communication between personal computers (file forwarding)—The stand alone type of computer has become very popular for using spread sheets. Now the use of standard formats, collecting diskettes prepared by various offices and processing data has increased. This is one example of rationalization which saves processing time. But on the other hand, there have been such problems in transporting the diskettes that today, we prefer to transmit information online using the public lines. Although we still have the trouble of having to check with the addressee before and after the transmission.

(2) The Radio Pick-up Command System

The problems of small pickup and delivery trucks—Telecommunications can be classified roughly into two types; wire and radio. We must use radio if we are in the vehicles. The work of the small pickup and delivery trucks is fast pickup and delivery. If we do not go for a pickup right away, we know that our competitors will take the business. The customers' pickup requests are notified to the sales drivers at once, by radio. However, in the cities, the government allows us to use only a few frequencies and they are often busy. We sometimes cannot contact the drivers because they keep on using the radio, or they are away from the vehicles. We found that 50 per cent of the pickup requests were being reported to the drivers after a delay of 1 hour. Therefore, we have introduced a 'pickup command system' using computers. This is intended to speed up communication and should help us to win the pickup war.

The system in outline—When the customer calls for pickup, we ask for the phone number, which will be punched into the personal computer. Then we check to confirm that there is no input mistake, press the O.K. key, and then the information is transmitted automatically by radio. The digital signal goes through the radio and is transmitted and printed out by the printer which each truck carries. In this way, the driver will know the pickup command when he comes back to the driver's seat and he is able to go for pickup at once. (If the phone number is not registered, the information is shown on the computer screen and it will be hand written on the card by the operator. Then the operator will call the driver by the radio. Registration is done on the same day, and from the next day on, the computer command system will be used to arrange the pick up.)

Effects—The efficiency of pickup has improved 20 times and 100 per cent of pickup requests are now completed within 10 minutes. The system is popular among our customers because they do not have to give their name and address each time they ask for pickup. If the telephone number is not registered, the message, which indicates the first use by that consumer, is shown on the computer display. In this case the operator fills in the registration card which contains the consumer's name, address, phone-number and so on. The registration is done on the same day, and the next day the computer command system will be available for that consumer.

An unexpected bonus is that the female operators in the offices prefer this method of working.

(3) Trucking Management Radio System
The problems of large trucks—The task of trucks that run on arterial roads and connect cities is to be punctual. If they arrive at the base behind schedule, it has a bad effect on later operations, and leads to delayed deliveries. Where are the trucks running during the night? If they are behind schedule, the relevant offices must be informed. We must not sit and wait for the arrival of late trucks in the morning. That is why the arterial road trucks carry radios. When they pass check points, the information is submitted to the computer at the nearest base office. The trucking manager in Tokyo will collect all the information and make assurance doubly sure.

The system in outline—There are check points at every 50–100 km on the main arterial roads. Our main offices are placed near these points, which continually send out a certain radio wave. When our trucks, carrying their radios, pass by, they are caught by this wave and they will automatically send back the truck number in digital signals. Then the computer at the base will give additional information of 'checkpoint name' and 'passing time', and will be sent to the host computer in Tokyo automatically, using the ground personal computer system. In this way the check point information from all over the country is collected in the host computer. The host computer will check the information sent against the registered schedule and will automatically notify the offices. Analogue vocal communication is also possible. For example, if a driver sees a traffic jam, he can give the information to other drivers who need it via the nearest base office.

Effects—We had not been able to catch arterial road truck information, but now the problem has been solved. Now we can be prepared for delays and reduce the impact on other parcels. The drivers are less isolated and they can exchange information more frequently. For example they are supplied with information on traffic jams at once so that they can make a detour and still arrive on time.

4. New Businesses

What business should we launch after the Takkyubin? This is our primary concern. If we are to start selling goods, in most cases we will be competing with our customers, for Takkyubin is used by customers of all kinds of businesses. Knowing that *we handle 1m packages a day*, companies mainly in the mail order business use our service, and the numbers are growing.

(1) Cash on Delivery Service (Collect Service)
One of the problems which mail order companies face is collecting the money. Getting the money from each customer is very troublesome. So we have established a 'payment on delivery' company called 'Yamato Collect Service Co., Ltd'. The payment will be made by them to the suppliers whether the goods are delivered or not on the

Thursday of the week following the handling. The system is very popular for the mail order company manages all its payments through Yamato. We are able to trace if the payment has been made or not, also we can always trace the packages. However, the main attraction is Takkyubin's next day (or in a few cases second day) delivery service.

(2) *Information Processing (Joint)*

An information strategy is indispensable for a mail order service and for telemarketing. 'Joint' is a branch of our affiliated company 'Yamato System Development Co., Ltd', which does research for potential customers, takes orders by the phone, controls shipments, goods in stock, bonds, researches goods that will sell well in the future, likely customers and agents, etc., on behalf of mail order companies. If it is used together with the Collect Service, the company can concentrate on purchasing planning and promoting its goods. We would like our customers to make a full use of our nationwide NEKO-net.

(3) *The Book Service Company*

At present, we do not sell goods directly. The only exception is that we sell books by mail order. This business was started because we were unable to get the books we wanted right away because there are not enough stocks at the local book stores in Japan. Our new Book Service Company will take orders, and get the books. Transportation will be arranged by the Takkyubin service, and payment collection by 'Yamato Collect Service'. Orders are taken by telephone facsimile, postcards or by personal computer—in any way the customer wants, and just by giving the author's name or the title, we can search for the book using the computer. The order will be transmitted to the relevant publisher or to the nearest office, and the books will be collected at once. Then the parcel will be sent through Takkyubin with the COD bill on it, and will be delivered within a week anywhere in Japan just for the book price plus a 300 yen handling charge per box. The book service is popular because of its speed and cheapness.

5. Conclusion

(1) *Continuous Development*

The development and contruction of our inform-

ation system is a continuous process. Timely systems like package tracking, radio control, the fax network, etc. have been developed one by one while computer networks with affiliated companies, customers, and banks have been actively expanded.

(2) *The Aim of the Information Systems*

Our priorities are clear: first comes customer service, then comes quality control and the third is rationalization. Strengthening the connection between information and sales means putting our hearts and souls into customer service. We intend to keep improving the service and developing new information systems. Then we need to watch constantly the quality we promised our customers, that is to say improving our control of the process—the time from pickup to delivery, and Cool Takkyubin's temperature, etc. Finally comes rationalization. We must assume that we have efficient work and cost reduction, though when that becomes the priority and service-quality control is ignored, information and sales will be sacrificed.

(3) *What Should We Work On in the Future?*

As our service becomes more unique and differentiated from the services offered by our competitors, it will require more information and more flexible systems. The usage of our data base will increase and the quality of the information should improve in proportion to the progress of the information network. Our target is the construction and exploitation of an outlet-customer information network. Then, the rationalization of the transport operations and office work will progress simultaneously. For instance, transmitting information from PPs to an automatic sorter which will lead to the saving of operating time, it will also prevent miss-sorting, and will improve the package tracking system.

As a part of an information environment improvement program, the launching of a private 'communication satellite' is close at hand. There are many problems to investigate: a mobile communications centre to make the best use of radios, simultaneous broadcast communication to make better use of radio waves, data transmission high volume, etc. Last but not least, new business development should be seen from an international point of view, and the progress of the international network is an important subject.

Critical Success Factors in Factory Automation

Hideo Takanaka

The development of factory automation in Japan over the past 20 years.

Development of Factory Automation

The first stage of development of modern factory automation in Japan started about 20 years ago through the extensive introduction of unmanned operations of individual machine tools and unit operating machines. Today, Japanese factories using these techniques are the most advanced factories in the world.

Progress of Japanese factory production systems can be considered to have taken place in three stages:

(1) The period from the 1960s and 1970s used the automated production system with the production line of special purpose processing machines. The target of factory automation in this stage was the efficiency of mass production with a small number of product models too high in demand; this assisted in reducing the labour cost during a period of rapidly increasing wages. As a result the new machine systems were efficient special purpose processing machines, or continuous production machines, or a larger plant in the plant industry. However, production systems of this period lacked the flexibility to accommodate product model changes. But since the aim of system design was the efficiency of mass production, such limitations did not affect overall factory efficiency.

(2) In the latter half of the 1970s and the first half of the 1980s the second stage of factory automation —Flexible Manufacturing System (FMS)—was introduced. The macro economy had shifted from high growth to more stable growth, the consumer needs were becoming more diversified and the life cycle of the product was getting shorter. The conventional production system could not adapt efficiently to a variety of product types in small volume. As a result, the FMS concept was introduced. The early stage of FMS was again, to automate the machine and save the labour costs. The Numerical Control (NC) machine tools became widely used, including NC lathes, NC milling machines, NC drilling machines, etc. Once processing information was entered into the NC tape, various tasks of processing became possible with one set of machines and this substantially increased operational flexibility.

Next the Flexible Manufacturing Cell (FMC) was introduced. Here several hundreds of tools could be provided as a tool magazine for one set of processing machines; it was then equipped with automatic tool selection and exchange systems; as well as loading, unloading and transfer systems. Industrial robots were also introduced. Several FMC's were operated together with unmanned vehicles which ran between them, and they were integrated into an overall FMS both mechanically and electronically.

This stage, however, essentially automated the production workshop; it did not automate the whole factory. As the number of these systems increased, automated warehouses were built and the automated transportation system for parts and processed products between the various FMS units reached a stage that could be called Factory Automation (FA).

The aim of this factory automation was to achieve efficient small volume production of numerous product types using flexible automation of assembly and processing. As automation began to affect the research and development department, as well as accumulating past experiences and general information, the FA moved into Computer Aided Design (CAD) and Computer Aided Manufacturing (CAM), where computers were directly connected to the production line to exploit the advantages of the new systems.

Mr Hideo Takanaka is General Manager, Regional Project Development Department at Toyo Engineering Corporation, Tokyo. He was formerly Manager, Planning Department.

(3) The next stage of the factory automation in the latter half of the 1980s and taking us into the 1990s is the age of integrating production and marketing using Computer Integrated Manufacturing (CIM). It would be more appropriate to call this development a production activity information system rather than simply factory automation.

In the 1980s consumer behaviour reflecting the more abundant materialistic level, became more individualistic and rapidly changing. Consumption patterns became more common. New materials were developed and the variety of products rapidly increased. As a result today, it is increasingly difficult to predict long term demand for consumer products. Consequently, it is even more essential for a manufacturer to obtain good consumer information from the market quickly so that it can be fed into the product development and/or production changes. This is pressurizing enterprises to attempt to automate the entire enterprise, through the greater integration of the marketing, design and production functions.

The objective of a CIM system is to construct an efficient management system in relation to the unified information and servicing activities, ranging from assessing user needs to the delivery of a product that reflects those needs, as well as establishing unmanned production systems for small volumes with diversified types of products.

The machine system which is becoming the core of CIM is a system of information processing equipment that integrates the computer and intelligent robots. Non-machine systems are also information systems which transfer marketing information to the research and development departments as well as design and manufacturing through Local Area Networks (LAN), which in turn activates fully automated production lines.

From a different point of view, the purpose of the CIM introduction was to reduce the factory indirect costs, (design, procurement, process control, etc.). To take a specific example, when Hitachi Limited introduced CIM in 1987, their production line had already reached an advanced level of automation and there was little room to reduce its production costs through rationalization of direct manufacturing activities. Direct manufacturing labour costs had already been reduced to 7 per cent of total manufacturing cost, while the ratio of manufacturing indirect labour cost increased year by year and was now up to 22 per cent of total cost. In order to run the production system efficiently for a small volume with numerous types of products and accommodate ever changing marketing needs, an ever increasing number of indirect workers appeared to be required.

In order to answer the simple question of 'How many of what products shall be made by when?',

real time manufacturing coupled with information on the movement of the market can be achieved with a small number of people through the construction of an information system, in which manufacturing and marketing activities are integrated.

Even in Japan, there do not appear to be examples of perfectly built CIMs. However, pressure to build CIM is increasing among industries due to a combination of rapid changes in the market, the very tight labour situation and ever increasing competition. It is expected that one half of Japanese major industries will build some form of CIM system within the next 5 years. Below is a summary of the stages of factory automation:

(4) Development of factory automation by stages. Factory automation started from automated operation of individual machines, progressed to the automated factory (FA) and then to automated manufacturing (CIM). In each of these stages, there was a particular activity that promoted the automated manufacturing system and provided the basis of the changes and this was combined with the development of elemental technology which supported these changes. The flow of the development is expressed in Table 1.

Cases of CIM Introduction by Japanese Major Corporations

In Japan, very few cases of comprehensive CIM systems have been observed and most of the cases are in the stage of either partial introduction or still under construction. Hence the following examples are from those under construction.

Kao Corporation (Housewares and chemicals)

Kao has operated an information communication network in its marketing department since the 1970s. Everyday orders from large retailers are sent to the sales company via a Value Added Network (VAN) using a Point of Sales (POS) terminal. Sales personnel call medium size and small retailers and send order information to the sales company through telephone lines. or by car radio using portable terminals. The computer processes the data sent to the sales company, who then send shipping instructions to the distribution centres located throughout the country. In the houseware division, delivery can be made within 24 hours after the receipt of an order.

CIM directly connects this sales information and 280 manufacturing plants throughout the country which manufacture individual products as well as intermediate products. In the plant where the CIM operates various elements of data control from inventory control of raw material to shipping control of final products is centralized. At the moment, among 280 manufacturing plants, more

Table 1. Stages in the Development of Factory Automation

Stage	Aim	Action	Naming of automation stage	Elemental technology
1	Improvement of productivity at the level of working machine and the working process.	Automation in individual work and working machine.	NC machine ↓ FMC	NC machine tool automated selection and exchange of tools, automated loading and unloading of work, automated replacement of palettes, machining centre and abnormality surveillance system.
2	Improvement of productivity in the level of processing system and the parts.	Automation in the group of working machines and part of indirect work.	FMC ↓ FMS	Processing information distinctive automated processing system, roller conveyor, unmanned transport vehicle between the FMC's, automated control of jigs and tools, FMC group control system.
3	Improvement of productivity at the level of the factory.	Coupling with CAD/CAM, distribution system such as the automated warehouse, development and manufacturing, and control and manufacturing.	FMS ↓ FA	Automated whole process surveillance and control system, automated warehouse system, unmanned factory transport system, factory communication system.
4	Improvement of productivity in the level of the factory-head office and including marketing.	Coupling with marketing information and developing design and manufacturing activity, unified control of goods and information, and unification of control information and engineering information.	FA ↓ CIM	Communication network, LAN, MAP data base system, comprehensive management control technology

NC—Numerical Control
FMC—Flexible Machining Cell
FMS—Flexible Manufacturing System
FA—Factory Automation
CIM—Computer Integrated Manufacturing System
CAD—Computer Aided Design
CAM—Computer Aided Manufacturing
LAN—Local Area Network
MAP—Manufacturing Automation Protocol.

than 780 major plants are connected to the sales information system with an information network. In the near future, there is a plan to introduce a unified control system with CIM for all factories in the country.

As a result of the introduction of CIM to Kao, distribution stock decreased from 2·8 months prior to its introduction, to 0·7 months, while the turnover doubled without any increase in the number of employees from 4500.

Komatsu Limited (Construction and industrial machinery)
Since 1982, Komatsu Limited promoted FA by introducing more than 40 FMS's. Up to now, automation in its production department has been the centre of activity. However, from now on, the development and manufacturing departments will operate an integrated information system. As a result, CAD in the design department will be directly connected to the computer in the factory to enable design information to be immediately reflected on factory production lines. It will also promote the integration of information with the marketing department and construct a company wide CIM system.

To begin with, in the construction machinery division, the product codes and data bases of the manufacturing departments and marketing departments are united so that ordering information goes directly to the factory. At the same time, the marketing department can follow the production progress at the factory individually. With this unification the delivery time of products can be reduced drastically to a mere 2 weeks.

Also, the industrial machinery division is constructing a CIM system model plant. In this model plant, Manufacturing Automation Protocol (MAP) is employed to connect various machinery and equipment systems which forms FA and it is planned to complete the CIM system by connecting the factory LAN and MAP to the sales network information.

Mitsubishi Heavy Industries Limited
Since 1985, Mitsubishi Heavy Industries Limited has been promoting the introduction of a CIM system in its major plant of Takasago Works. In this works, automation and labour saving have been promoted vertically, namely, the design department integrated their CAD/CAM, at the same time the manufacturing department introduced its own FMS. It was estimated that an investment of ¥700m was made just to integrate these independent information systems. However, because of this unification, an estimated saving of ¥500m per year was achieved as information was shared and loss was reduced.

This company is also promoting the introduction of a CIM system in its 14 works located throughout the country. The CIM system that Mitsubishi is looking for is not the unified system for the entire operation by a dispersed CIM system which operates within individual operational units. The reason for this is the size of the individual works which can be equivalent to a big company; in addition they are built for each product category.

Although a dispersed CIM system is operated, an on-line information network, which connects manufacturing locations and sales offices all over the country, has been established. The company has a super computer which is basically used for engineering calculations, but it has started to build an information network system among the offices utilizing this communication line.

Yamazaki Mazak Corporation
Yamazaki Mazak Corporation, which produces machine tools, is promoting a CIM system which will connect over 30 locations at head office, domestic manufacturing sites and sales offices in order to shorten product delivery time and to minimize inventory using computerization of the entire work starting from receipt of order, designing, procurement of material, manufacturing and sales.

Information about an order activates the CAD system which then initiates the FMS of a stamping operation as it has an on-line connection with a CAD system terminal and thus, design and manufacturing are directly linked together. As a result the required time from designing to stamping and painting operations has been cut down from 3 months to 5 days.

An automated three-dimensional warehouse was built for assembly operation and the parts processed by FMS, with those procured from outside sources being stored in this warehouse before they were loaded onto a palette which combines together those required for each individual final product. Many unmanned transport vehicles carry these palettes to the work shop where the product is finished automatically on a just-in-time basis according to the plan.

The aim of this company's CIM system is to establish close co-operation between sales and production which fulfils the aim to 'Sell many products which can be sold in volume'.

NEC Corporation
NEC Corporation, which produces semi conductors and computers, completed an information network for individual works such as a CAD system, on-line system for parts ordering and receiving of orders, etc. in the 1970s—this was the first phase. The second phase of the information system in each of its plants was completed in the 1980s which covered designing, production control, manufacturing, etc., the company is now in its third phase.

The aim of the third phase is the improvement of employee's capability to be well prepared for the era of diversified products, internationalization, and the increasing importance of information processing. Orders are received from 37 overseas marketing companies and 150 domestic sales offices which are fed into the computer via an international VAN (Value Added Network). These are then transferred to plants as an order where the products are produced. In the plant, delivery time for particular customers is determined by the production system already established in the second phase. Sales personnel are able to learn of the delivery time through their terminals thus improving the effectiveness of the marketing activity.

A number of advantages already have been observed in various areas, such as reduced production lead time and improved adaptability in meeting customer needs, as well as a substantial reduction of inventory through the unification of manufacturing and marketing.

Toyota Motor Corporation
A distinctive feature of FA in Toyota Motor Corporation is not to supervise and control production workshop equipment and groups of robots by a host computer, but to adopt a system where 'Information processing of each production process' is thoroughly enforced; for example, a radio transmitter with the memory of production information fixed to the body of the car gives the instruction to the industrial robots. Also, it has adopted an international standard of MAP (Manufacturing Automation Protocol) in its key communication network so that the robotics and control equipment built by different manufacturers are uniformly controlled by the computer.

This system is a real-time system different from logical FA or CIM. Using this system, a sudden change of ordered model by the customer (currently, up to 4 days prior to its production) can be accommodated with flexibility. As it is a dispersed system to each process, substantial room is left to make human hand changes, unlike an unmanned factory. The management has its own viewpoint, namely, 'Even with CIM system, it is an over investment to fully automate production and to connect machines with an information network.'

This firm has already completed unification of marketing and manufacturing information and is currently extending the manufacturing information network to its 400 components manufacturers in order to construct a 'Electronic Just-in-time System'.

Success and Failure Factors in FA/CIM Introduction

According to a mail questionnaire survey on CIM (1988) conducted by Nihon Keizai Shinbun, Inc on major manufacturing companies in Japan, it was found that the FA/CIM movement was expanding among whole industries such as electronics, electrics, machinery, automobiles, chemicals, food, etc.

Among valid answers from 93 companies, 91 concluded that CIM is 'an essential technology to strengthen the international competitive edge and to survive', while 68 companies said 'presently, CIM system is partially introduced or being introduced'. On the other hand, problems such as shortages of system engineers to build CIM systems, were identified and there were still many problems to be solved.

(A) The following factors were found to lead to success in introducing FA/CIM systems:

(i) FA needs to be systematically integrated into the strategy of the enterprise. This involved clarifying the reason for introducing the FA system in the first place; then establishing an effective implementation strategy. The effect of FA varies considerably depending on the category of business, the structure and culture of the individual enterprise. As can be seen in Table 2, (the answers to the questionnaire) there are objectives that cannot be achieved and many companies have several aims with similar weight.

(ii) The needs of a FA system in the plant must be analysed and evaluated cautiously and thoroughly, in order to clarify the objective and identify all the problems to be solved.

It is essential to establish a plan for the careful introduction of the new systems. It is also important, not only to have strategic discussions throughout the entire corporation, but to list and review the following points (Table 3) that have an important influence on the extent FA can contribute to the expansion of production capacity and how FA can

Table 2. Objective of CIM introduction

(1) Important five goals
Reduction of lead time (69%)
Adaptation to small volume, various types production orders (52%)
Improvement of productivity (38%)
Rapid transfer of order information (37%)
Reduction of inventory (36%)

(2) Others
Production cost reduction (31%)
Reduction of indirect labour (30%)
Reduction of product development time (29%)
Improved and stabilized quality (26%)
Unification of individual systems of OA, FA and etc. (21%)
Unification of SIS and etc. and lower system of FA etc. (20%)

(From answers to questionnaires.)
Note: More than one answer could be given.

Table 3. Needs to introduce FA system

(1) Expansion of production capability
☆ Speedy and accurate work
☆ Switching work patterns, rapid change of product and accuracy
☆ Expanding, fineness, complication and higher-precision of the production system
☆ Product performance improvement, stabilization of quality

(2) Improvement of labour productivity
☆ Decreased dependence on skilled labour
☆ Improvement in working environment and quality
☆ Improvement of working efficiency and stability of employee
☆ Improvement of working safety

(3) Improvement of control level
☆ Improvement of adaptability of production in line with changing needs of the market
☆ Increased speed of the feedback function of control
☆ Reduction of unfinished products/work in progress
☆ Elimination of all losses such as raw material, service and labour

be integrated with the improvements of labour productivity and control level.

(iii) Systematically establish milestones in the process of implementing the FA system plan and fully inform the people concerned.

The FA system plan should not be handled in secret. It is necessary to examine the implications of the FA system throughout the factory by using the talents of all the employees. It is essential that the FA introduction area and its system are built systematically and reliably. The points that need to be checked are shown in Table 4.

(iv) Standardized parts. At the beginning, firmly establish a procedure to plan the development of FA production system design and arrange the points of fundamental design systematically to unify as far as possible the products or parts prior to the introduction of a FA system (Table 5).

Table 4. Check points

(1) Overall planning
☆ Clearly visualize the FA system introduction before starting work
☆ The system design of the overall factory should be well defined
☆ The situation of surrounding companies who support FA system introduction in the plant needs to be considered

(2) Product design
☆ Integrate system design with product development
☆ The system shall be based on a long range view of the product to be manufactured
☆ Review how the product design is to fit into the FA

(3) Production
☆ Standardize parts and establish appropriate groups
☆ Re-examine the whole process in order to ensure CAD/CAM consistency
☆ Rearrange processes where necessary
☆ Develop a special exclusive process and machines within the company
☆ Establish an effective controlling and operating system

(4) Personnel management
☆ Always train personnel for controlling and operating
☆ Establish a plan for effective utilization of excessive manpower

Table 5. Areas of standardization

☆ Make products and parts in series
☆ Make products and parts in modules and in units
☆ Make standardized and commonized products and parts as far as possible
☆ Make simplified products and parts
☆ Make products and parts with multifunctions

Table 6. Advantages and disadvantages of FA systems

(1) Advantages
☆ Increase in actual production capacity
☆ Reduction in production lead time
☆ Reduction of unfinished products in production line
☆ Reduction in duplicated investment on production equipment

(2) Disadvantages
☆ Limit the field of product development
☆ Greater costs when production line stops
☆ Huge investment in production equipment
☆ Increase in high level maintenance technology required

Table 7. Problems in management accounting

☆ How to solve a gap between the reduced life cycle of the equipment and legal amortization periods
☆ Increased investment on software and its accounting disposition
☆ How to express advantages and disadvantages which are difficult to quantify
☆ Trend to attach importance to payback period method
☆ Change of indirect cost distribution standards from direct working time to equipment operating time
☆ Increased difficulty to define costs by product because of the much greater element of indirect cost
☆ Increased importance of cost control in planning rather than operations
☆ Increasing requirement for simplified management accounting

(v) Evaluate the merits and demerits of the FA introduction and study measures to reduce the disadvantages.

FA is not a panacea, it has both advantages and disadvantages. It is important to predict and analyse in advance what is an advantage and what is not, so that action can be taken to reduce the disadvantages (Table 6).

(vi) Change of management accounting system. The introduction of a FA system will affect the management accounting of the enterprise. When an FA system is introduced, the attention sometimes focuses on the technical side only and insufficient attention is given to the control system side. If the control system does not adjust to the FA system, it will result in the effect of the introduction of the FA system not being measurable. Table 7 shows the points that create problems.

(B) Failure factors of FA system introduction.

(1) If the investment required for the equipment for the FA system introduction is very large a review of

management structure becomes unavoidable. If it is not well managed the investment will not be recovered.

In the case of FA system introduction, it is often the case that the system is technically perfect but economically of little value since engineering requirements have overriding priority over financial considerations even at the planning stage. Failure to get a proper balance between these two factors will not only result in failure of the FA system introduction but it may lead to the downfall of the company itself. Below are the check points.

☆ Is the equipment for FA system unnecessarily expensive because too much attention has been given to the engineering requirements?
☆ When establishing the composition of a FA system there needs to be an optimum combination of function and cost. Whether this has been done needs to be checked.

(2) It is said that FA system has the limitations described below. Unless action is taken to reduce these effects the FA system introduction will fail.

(3) Action to reduce failure.

The introduction of a FA system will fail unless action is taken to reduce the risk of failure, after making thorough investigation of the problem and

Table 8. Questions to avoid pitfalls

☆ Does the idea 'FA is God' prevail?
☆ Are too many dreams incorporated into the system?
☆ Has the system designer built a rigid system which cannot be modified easily later on?
☆ Has the education of workshop operators started well in advance of needing their services?
☆ Is the system introduction being made ignoring factory floor views?
☆ Is the person responsible clearly identified?
☆ Does the person have full power to provide effective leadership?
☆ Is there a gap between the position of top management and subordinates who are unable to catch up?
☆ Does the team consist of only one department?
☆ Is the team appropriately structured once established?

Table 9. Problems in introducing CIM

Problems and obstacles to introducing CIM

(1) *Human problems*
☆ Shortage of staff capable to make system designs and plans at corporate level (78%)
☆ Shortage of personnel for software development (69%)
☆ Need to train and change attitudes (54%)

(2) *Financial problems*
☆ Need for large investment in computers etc. (50%)
☆ Method for calculating benefits has not been established (38%)

(3) *Organization and control*
☆ Difficulties in co-ordination between departments (36%)
☆ Problems in developing an integrated database (34%)
☆ Problems integrating departmental systems (31%)
☆ Problems integrating protocols (28%)

(From answers to questionnaires.)

the obstructing factors at the time the FA/CIM system is going to be introduced.

According to the survey mentioned earlier, the biggest obstacle to successful FA system introduction is the shortage of talented employees and capable system engineers. If the shortage of talented engineers is the problem within the organization, there is an alternative that involves purchasing a package of FA construction work from a specialized engineering company that can provide these missing elements. However, even if this is the case, it is essential to retain appropriate human resources within the company so that it is prepared for future factory innovation.

Obtaining and sustaining talented engineers is an essential requirement if the introduction of FA system is not to fail.

References

Survey and study relating to a factory diagnosis system for the introduction of new machines for FA etc., *Japan Society of industrial Machinery* (1989).

FA Engineering, JMA Consultants, Inc. (1985).

CIM—Integrating manufacturing and sales, Nihon Keizai Shinbun, Inc. (1990).

Factory management—Special issue, Nikkan Kogyo Shinbun, Inc. (1989).

Dictionary of factory automation, Nikkan Kogyo Shinbun, Inc. (1987).

PART SIX

Increasing Employee Commitment and Productivity in Overseas Plants

Achieving Japanese Productivity and Quality Levels at a U.S. Plant

Kazuo Ishikure

This is a dramatic story of how one Japanese company changed the management system and corporate culture of a plant in the United States. After acquisition it was turned into a profitable plant. The Japanese management emphasized improvement of product quality: blue-collar and white-collar staff were treated equally: 'management by policy' was introduced. The results of these changes were a three-fold increase in production volume, a three-fold improvement in productivity, the number of defective products was reduced by half, all laid-off workers were re-employed and the plant, which had been making a loss, became profitable.

On 10 January 1983, Bridgestone Corporation of Japan (see Figure 1) bought a tyre plant in Tennessee, as well as inheriting both its active and laid-off work-forces, from an American tyre manufacturer. For the sake of convenience, this American tyre company will be referred to as Company 'A'.

The plant, located in a city just outside Nashville called La Vergne, was completed by Company A in 1973 for the production of truck and bus radial tyres (TBR). From 1978 to 1982, Company A pulled resources away from Research and Development and capital investment in TBR due to the high cost of operation. Between March and May 1982, two-thirds of the work-force was laid off, and between June and September 1982, the plant was shut down for 2 weeks per month. In consequence productivity, product quality, and employee morale all suffered.

In February 1982, Company A announced that the plant would either be sold to a prospective buyer or it would be closed. When the deal was consummated between Bridgestone and Company A in January 1983, a spokesman for Company A made an announcement stating 'We would have had to make investments of over $100m to stay competitive in the radial truck tyre market. Our analysts figured we could invest that money elsewhere at a much higher return.'

We compared the Tennessee plant in the first half of 1983 with a similar plant in Japan. The results showed that the productivity level of the Tennessee plant was less than one-third that of the Japanese plant. Also, the percentage of defective tyres produced in the Tennessee plant was far higher than in Japan as was the frequency of machine failure.

Quality—The Top Priority

Bridgestone bought the plant at the price of $52m. We started production from the evening the deal was signed, since we had agreed on the continued production of TBR with the Company A brand as one of the conditions of purchasing the plant. In order to continue production the plant's organizational structure went unchanged and within this structure we placed the administrative office. When I inspected this plant my first thought was that we would have to maintain mass production to utilize the large plant and make a profit. We researched the problem of low operating rate of 700 tyres per day and we came to the conclusion that it resulted from mediocre quality reputation. Field interviews were carried out by an outside market researcher and the results also supported this view.

The researcher visited 73 fleets, 103 tyre dealers and retreaders and 12 truck makers, carrying out 'image research' on TBR tyres by brand. The results did not rank the tyres made by Company A very highly. The report also concluded that image data were heavily influenced by the quality and performance of the company's radial tyres. We were positive that an increase in sales would result from the production of a high quality tyre. We set a goal to reach within 4 years whereby through improving quality we would produce and sell *four times* the

Kazuo Ishikure was formerly President and Chief Executive Officer of Bridgestone, U.S.A. He is a member of Bridgestone's Board of Directors and Auditor of Bridgestone Bekaert Steel Cord Co. Ltd., Tokyo.

Bridgestone Corporation, founded by Shojiro Ishibashi in 1931, is Japan's leading tyre manufacturer, having approximately 50 per cent of the market.
It is also the third largest in the world with marketing activities in more than 100 countries world-wide.

A.   Annual Sales — Approximately $6bn

B.   Twelve Plants in Japan

C.   Seven Overseas Plants Including Australia, Indonesia, Thailand, Taiwan and the United States (Tennessee) (Five Countries)

Although the name 'Bridgestone' sounds like a British or American company, it is a Japanese company. The founder Ishibashi christened the company with an inverted English translation of his own family name: *Ishi* means Stone and *Bashi* means Bridge.

Figure 1. Outline of Bridgestone Corporation in 1987

number of tyres being manufactured and sold at the time of acquisition.

The underlying policy of our company was 'quality is top priority' and the president's policy was:

(A) to produce tyres of the highest quality (to produce the best radial truck tyres in the United States)

(B) the tyres should be equal or better in quality than those made by Bridgestone in Japan.

The plant's slogan was: 'quality today will result in quantity tomorrow'.

Good Housekeeping—The First Step

When Bridgestone bought this plant, we felt it had not been properly maintained. Wastepaper, cigarettes, paper cups, bolts, nuts, nails, wood chips and so on lay scattered on the floor. Employees in the plant believed that cleaning up after the workers was the job of the janitors. We said that 'a clean workplace is everybody's responsibility'. We displayed actual samples of defective tyres containing foreign materials and pictures of the defective tyres in a show case near the dining hall. We also posted the amount of money lost due to foreign materials in tyres on the previous day and in the previous month. A sample notice might have read 'a loss of a $X was due to foreign materials'. Also, we held section–by–section cleanliness contests. As a result, the plant became clean. High quality products cannot be produced in an dirty workplace. They are the result of 'good housekeeping', the first step towards effective quality control.

The '4M' Approach

We used the '4M' approach in order to produce the highest quality tyres. *'4M' stands for Machine, Material, Method and Manpower.* On machines, we changed or improved about 530 items in the first 2 years. This was achieved by following detailed

plans. The two goals we wanted to achieve through updating the equipment were:

(1) to improve the quality of the product, and

(2) to decrease the workers' load.

Our attitude toward machine maintenance also changed, from *'expost facto* maintenance' (repairing a machine once it is broken) to 'preventative maintenance'.

As for materials, we used only brands which had been approved by Bridgestone's technical centre in Japan and made severe tests at the Tennessee plant before sending samples to the technical centre. Company A inspected all incoming raw materials and when they came across defective material, it was exchanged for good material. Bridgestone introduced the concept of quality control in the purchasing of raw materials.

Since good, consistent manufacturing process control leads to high quality products we visited the plants of our raw material suppliers and checked their quality assurance policies, manufacturing control and so on, and set guidelines for each supplier concerning the inspection of incoming raw materials.

Even if we inspect incoming raw materials very strictly, a practice which takes many man-hours, we cannot prevent the inclusion of substandard raw materials, so the institution of quality control methods at the material source brought an increase in productivity.

Company A's methods of producing tyres were changed to Bridgestone's methods. Of course, we had a lot of trouble in achieving these changes. Machines, equipment and most materials were different from the ones we used in Japan yet the test tyres were produced to the same specifications. Finished tyres, and their components, contained subtle differences when compared with the tyres made in Japan; so the desired level of quality could not be achieved, despite the fact that the tyres met the same specifications as those made in Japan. The number of test tyres increased and we had to increase the in-company tests. Meetings between Japanese advisors and American managers were held day and night in an effort to come up with effective countermeasures. After clearing many obstacles, we got test results which showed that the quality of the product made in Tennessee was equal to that which was achieved in Japan. The abrasion resistance of the product that Bridgestone made in Tennessee was superior to that which had been made by Company A by 30 per cent. *These results were achieved in the year following the buy-out.*

Manpower proved to be the most difficult problem. The improvement of machines, materials and methods was not enough to produce high quality tyres. It was also essential to instill the concept of quality in the minds of all employees. To achieve this we had to alter past behaviour patterns. 'Change and innovation' was necessary. We adopted the policies of TQC (total quality control) and MBO (management by objective) as the tools of management. We chose TQC and MBO as operating philosophies because they originated in America and so it is easier for Americans to understand them.

The Division Between Blue-collar and White-collar Workers

There was a wide communication gap between non-union members (salaried workers) and union members (hourly workers). Immediately after Bridgestone bought the plant, the union representatives came to my room and told me that they thought some of the salaried workers were not good for the company. 'We want you to discharge some of the managers, foremen and supervisors' they said. On the other hand, some of the managers, foremen and supervisors criticized the union members for being lazy. In order to bridge the gap between salaried workers and hourly workers, we emphasized that we were all members of the same family. Some changes were made. For example:

(1) we relocated some staff desks to the plant office,

(2) when staff worked in the plant they were asked to work without ties. It seemed that a tie was viewed as a sort of status symbol,

(3) we abolished reserved areas in the parking lot for some managers, and

(4) we discontinued a friendship party to which only the managers and their families had been allowed to attend. Instead we presented *all* employees with Christmas presents bought with the money budgeted for the party.

In order to improve labour–management relations and human relations in general, we asked a consulting company to conduct an opinion poll among the employees in October 1983 and had a management seminar to discuss the results of this poll. We spent an entire weekend at a hotel in the suburbs of the city of Nashville. There were 36 participants, including five Japanese. We divided them into five groups of about seven people each and they discussed questions which had been assigned to their respective groups. The discussions became so intense that time was forgotten and some groups continued until 3 a.m. We found through these discussions that human relations had been unsatisfactory in the past and mutual distrust had increased within the plant. We concluded that the problem which confronted us was how to establish good human relations, that is, 'mutual trust'.

Each group offered suggestions for the solution of these difficult problems. We discussed these and drew conclusions on each item. Top management then discussed these conclusions and decided upon measures to solve the problems. We divided the employees into over 30 groups, explained the measures to be taken, and began to implement some of them immediately. In 1984, all managers above the rank of supervisor and union officials were given a 1-day training course on the improvement of human relations with the consulting company's help. The trainees were divided into five groups and the training was conducted for 8 hours a day. It was done once a month for an entire year.

Interviews with the President
The president held 1-hour interviews with all managers who were above the rank of foreman and asked them about the company's problems, their personal difficulties and concerns, their suggestions for improving their workplace and so on. Three men, two V.P.s (one Japanese and one American) and I interviewed at the first meeting. Because there were three interviewers and only one respondent, we felt that there was some reluctance on the part of the respondents to disclose their true feelings. Therefore, I conducted the interviews on a man-to-man basis from then on. As for the supervisors, I did not have time to interview them on an individual basis so I interviewed them in groups of four or five. For 2 years, 1984 and 1985, I interviewed all men ranking above supervisor twice and asked for their opinions and proposals, many of which became useful for the improvement of plant management.

Training

At the time of putting 'TQC' into operation, we trained all of the managers, foremen and supervisors as well as all of the clerical staff, including secretaries. The main training activities in 1983 and 1984 are shown in Table 1. One thing we found out through the TQC training was that some of the supervisors and clerks were not so good at mathematics. Therefore we added 'The elementary mathematics course' to the training menu.

Table 1. Menu of training in TQC

Subjects	Participants	Note
Guidelines of TQC	All employees	Using the brochure *Guide to TQC* which was drawn up by the company
QC basic	Managers, foremen, supervisors	Studying the '7 tools of analysis'
QC intermediate	Managers	Lecture by a local university's professor
IE basic	Foremen, supervisors	

The Study Trip to Japan

'Seeing is believing. At any rate just go and see', we said.

We sent the first study group of division managers to Japan in April 1983 and continued to send plant staff above the rank of department manager and union executives for study trips of approximately 2 weeks in length through 1984. As 'seeing is believing', we expected them to notice and learn about the Japanese plant's cleanliness, productivity, discipline, and TQC activities. This is why we sent them to Japan. We thought that a one-way explanation from the Japanese side was not enough. Also, in order to adapt the newly acquired knowledge to the Tennessee plant, we also let the Japanese advisor, who worked at the Tennessee plant, go along. A plant manager, who had also been a plant manager in his Company A days, participated in the first study trip and reported on the management systems of both Company A and Bridgestone upon his return to America. The content of his report is summarized in Table 2.

Impressions of work methods and labour–management relations were also reported by the others participating in the trips. Their impressions are described in Table 3.

TQC Management—The Key Points

We would like to explain two of the points which we emphasized in TQC management.

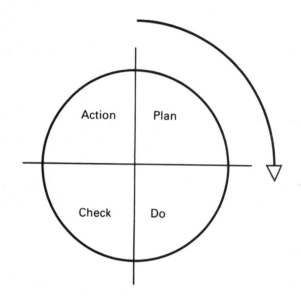

P-D-C-A

'P-D-C-A' became part of the daily work routine. 'P-D-C-A', also called the Shewhart cycle, means Plan-Do-Check-Action. Under the previous employer, the management had been in charge of 'planning', the workers had been in charge of 'doing', the supervisors had been in charge of 'checking' and the workers had also been in charge of 'action'. However, P-D-C-A has to be practised by all line members otherwise the improvement efforts will not be successful. Therefore, we asked all employees to adopt P-D-C-A and to practise it in their daily routines.

Table 2. Comparison of two management systems—plant managers' findings

Company A's method	Bridgestone method
1. No thought concerning acceptance for the next process	1. Next process is the customer 'The Customer is king'
2. Main QA activity is performed by staff departments	2. QA activity is performed by line departments with support from staff
3. Analysis of QA problems from EDP information	3. Analysis based on facts from actual process or product
4. When defects occurred, emphasis was placed on 'accept' or 'reject'	4. Main emphasis on product problems detection/disposition/prevention
5. QA/QC education mainly for technical staff	5. QA/QC education for all including line supervisors and workers
6. Standardization done mainly by the corporation	6. Standardization done in the plant with input from all members

Table 3. Comparison of two management systems—impressions expressed by American employees after visiting Japanese plants

| Impressions of Japanese and U.S. ways of working | |
United States	Japan

(1) People do not care what goes on in other departments
(2) All jobs are compartmentalized (each manager has his own little area of responsibilty)
	(1) More co-operation and communications:
	    (a) between staff and line
	    (b) between departments

If an objective is not achieved, people are afraid they may 'Catch Hell' Some people are afraid they may even lose their jobs	(1) Tend to set very tight and aggressive objectives (2) Never seem to be statisfied with the current status
QC circles won't work in the United States because money saved goes to the company and not to the individual	Team work approach Group activities Working together

Genba, Genbutsu

So far, decisions had been made based on written reports and not on actual situations. The staff members who had private rooms were called 'engineers' and the people under the engineers were known as 'technicians'. Based on data which had been collected by these two groups of employees, many meetings were held by the managers in the plant managers' private room. The subjects reported in the meeting were almost always the same. Consequently, anything not to do with these particular subjects was not considered during these meetings, even if it was important. There was a tendency to deal with everything in the private room which was far away from where things actually occurred—the production place (genba). In order to make plans based on actual working situations, we emphasized the importance of *genba, genbutsu*. An explanation of *genba, genbutsu* is given in Figure 2.

An oral explanation of *genba, genbutsu* was not sufficient, therefore we carried out on-the-job training repeatedly and persistently in order to teach the employees its real meaning. Also, since we wanted them to keep *genba, genbutsu* in their minds, we added 'see' and 'think' before P-D-C-A thus *our policy became 'See-Think-Plan-Do-Check-Action'*. Nowadays, all employees use the Japanese words *genba* and *genbutsu* as they are part of their daily lives.

Furthermore, they all understand the meaning of these two words quite thoroughly.

Mistakes and Misproduction

When we bought the plant, it was a rare occurrence when a mistake or problem was reported to us. Mistakes included the usage of the wrong raw materials, improper labelling, incorrect shipments from the warehouses, the inclusion of sub-standard products and so on. In February 1983, there were only two reports concerning mistakes or misproduction. This did not mean that errors had not occurred. Within the plant, the employees had not been totally open with the management for fear of being reprimanded over their mistakes.

However, from the point of QA, it was a serious mistake when inferior products were shipped to the customer. In addition, we could not solve the plant's problems under such circumstances. *Whether a mistake is trivial or not it must be reported without exception.* So, we encouraged the employees to report problems openly. We rewarded the people who did so with small gifts such as a ball-point pen. Through this type of encouragement, employees recognized that they would not be penalized by the supervisors even if they made mistakes. As a result, reports about misproduction increased rapidly. There were approximately 30 such reports per month in the last few months of 1983. Various kinds

---

Genba Means To Go and See the Place Where the Problem is Occurring

Genbutsu Means To Observe the Material or Product Itself With Defects

Usually a manager can get reports or information from his subordinates in his office. But sometimes this information is not sufficient to fully understand the scope of the problem. The actual site where the mistake took place and the materials involved is where the information stays. The old proverb says 'seeing is believing'; in other words 'seeing gives us more than 100 times the information that hearing gives'.

Figure 2. The meaning of *Genba* and *Genbutsu*

of mistakes were disclosed and we decided that our next step would be to establish a 'misproduction countermeasure committee'. This board consisted of employees who had made mistakes in the past, their co-workers, and the supervisors who were supposed to supervise them. We let the committee look into the real causes of mistakes and ways to prevent them from happening again. When we held a meeting to explain 'misproduction' to all employees we used the chart shown in Figure 3.

Also, we taught them that the customers, referred to at the end of Figure 3, meant not only the users of Bridgestone tyres but also the workers who worked at the next manufacturing process in the plant. The phrase that we repeatedly emphasized was *do not send defective components to the next step*. We also emphasized the necessity of *highly visible standards* as the method for preventing the recurrence of misproduction. This method's goal is to make it easy to distinguish different materials and their standards by using different colours and shapes. Figure 4 shows an example of the devices which we used to avoid errors.

The QC Circle

Before we created the QC circles, we completed various kinds of TQC training.

Reports which had been written by members of the first inspection trip to Japan stated 'QC won't work in the U.S.A.'. Therefore, we participated in the International Association of Quality Control in 1984. We wanted to let our people study how other American companies handled QC activities and also let them see how widely accepted the practice was. We also used a consulting company to educate the QC instructors. Of course, participation in the QC circles is not compulsory but voluntary. The number of QC circles gradually increased so we held meetings to present the TQC's activities three times in 1984. In the summer of 1984, the best QC circle, which had been chosen from among all the circles, participated in the 'all Bridgestone QC circle meeting' in Japan as a representative of the Tennessee plant. Ever since, we have sent our best circle to participate in this meeting each year. Participating

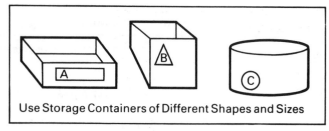

Figure 4. An example of devices to avoid mistakes

in the meeting has become a good incentive for all QC circle members.

Management by Objectives

The company's fiscal year is the same as the calendar year. Every year the president makes his preliminary policy statement in the middle of November and then allows plenty of time for several executives to examine it. After that, the president proposes it to the executive committee as a theme of discussion aimed at drawing up a final presidential policy statement.

The meeting is held annually at the end of December with staff above the rank of department manager attending. Then we distribute the policy statement, including many graphs, to all managers. Each graph indicates the following year's monthly budget and last year's results. The purpose is to explain the attainment of the target and to stress the importance of continuous improvement.

A policy statement which lists the budget or objectives, is usually under 10 pages, but the graphs and charts may occupy more than 40 or 50 pages, since there is a potential for misunderstanding if only written words are used for the explanation.

Our aim was that the policy file should be understood by everyone and the discussions should be based on a common understanding. We encouraged the staff to bring the file to their daily meetings. Each division manager drew up an implementation plan according to the president's policy statement. Department managers, who work under division managers, developed the items in detail, and drew

1.   Bridgestone Encourages the Reporting of All Errors in Production

2.   If We Are Aware of Problems They Can Be Solved By:

        (a) Discovering the Real Causes

        (b) Implementing Countermeasures to Prevent Similar Mistakes

3.   Bridgestone Encourages Negative Information and Constructive Criticism From Customers

Figure 3. 'Learn from mistakes'

up an itemized implementation plan. Figure 5 illustrates this process.

When we held the policy presentation meetings, we divided the employees into groups of 40–50 people so that we could explain to them in person the circumstances of the company, next year's budget, our future plans, and our goals, and provide the opportunity for questions and answers. We held the meetings after working hours so as not to interfere with production. In addition, we met with the union staff individually and explained the policy over lunch, where we could have constructive discussions in a relaxed atmosphere.

The Results

As a result of our efforts we achieved the following:

(1) *Quality*. The quality of the tyres improved remarkably and reached the level of Bridgestone tyres made in Japan. We were praised in surveys conducted by industry periodicals as making *the best TBR tyre in the business*. Our TBR tyres have been named as the best for the past 3 years.

(2) *Rehiring*. By the middle of 1985 we had recalled all the union employees who had been laid-off. When the last member was recalled, I called the union and commented on this achievement. The summary of what I said is as follows: '*Increases in recruitment and productivity go together. We have proved it.*'

(3) *Safety*. Safety levels have also risen and our company received *the 'Most Improved' award* from the U.S. Rubber Manufacturers Association in 1985. We also received it in 1986.

(4) *Improvement of performance*. Our achievements for the years 1983–1985 are as follows, in comparison to Company A:

(A) Production volume: about 3 times

(B) Productivity: about double

(C) Percentage of defective tyres: about half

(D) Energy efficiency: about a 40 per cent improvement.

As a result of these improvements, we made a profit in the latter part of our third year of ownership. It was a while coming. In December 1985, I held a party to celebrate our going into the black. On that day I invited all employees and their families to the cruise boat *General Jackson* which floats on the Cumberland River. Incidentally, the river flows through Nashville City. This is an extract from my speech:

Welcome aboard the *General Jackson*. Our plant has come a long way. Through your fine efforts and just plain hard work, Bridgestone's first U.S. manufacturing operation is now showing a monthly profit. For this, I would like you to join me in a round of applause. Not for me, but for you, and for every person sitting next to you. Because it was a team effort, everyone contributed. Not only the employees, but also their family members who accepted that their husbands or wives had to be away from home often on overtime

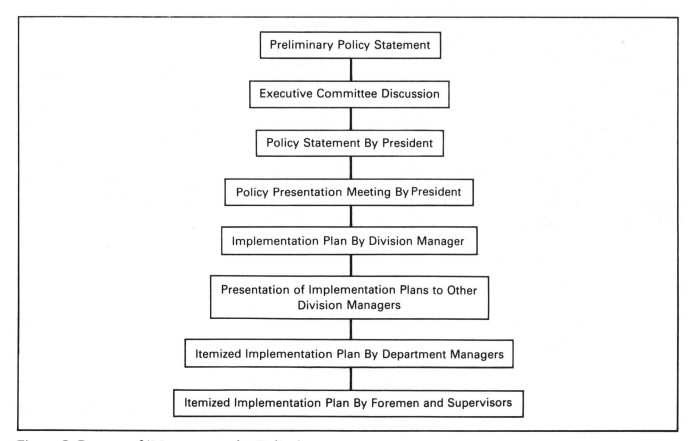

Figure 5. Process of 'Management by Policy'

work assignments. Therefore, I applaud you, employees and families, and the Bridgestone plant in La Vergne, Tennessee. As I stand here today, I notice *we are in the same boat*. Both with Bridgestone and with *General Jackson*. This is most symbolic . . .

I had often used the phrase 'We are in the same boat' during my tenure at the Tennessee plant. When I repeated it while standing on board the *General Jackson*, everyone burst out laughing and applauding. Since that time I have always used that phrase 'We are in the same boat' at policy presentation meetings.

References

(1) Taro Ihara and Osamu Nishihara, TQC activities at Bridgestone Tire Manufacturing (U.S.A.) Inc.

(2) Mary Walton, The Deming Management Method.

(3) George Ruccio, QC Circle Presentation at an IAQC Presentation Meeting.

(4) Kazuo Ishikure, Establishment of mutual trust.

(5) Hideo Asano, Bridgestone in Australia.

How Sumitomo Transformed Dunlop Tyres

G. D. Radford

In 1989, Sumitomo Rubber industries will be celebrating the 80th anniversary of the foundation of Dunlop Japan in Kobe in 1909. The first tyres were produced there in 1913.

Sumitomo Rubber Industries (SRI) is justly proud of its long association with the Dunlop name. Sumitomo Electric took a majority share in Dunlop Japan in 1963, changing its name to Sumitomo Rubber Industries, but close technical and commercial links continued to exist between Sumitomo and Dunlop right up to the early 1980s. It was in 1983, during discussions about the renewal of technical aid agreements, that the Dunlop Board suggested to SRI that it might become involved in Dunlop's European tyre operations.

At that time the Dunlop Group was in growing financial trouble, and was finding the tyre operations an impossible burden to bear. Indeed it reluctantly decided not to re-finance the French company's losses, and consequently to allow it to go into receivership.

SRI was deeply concerned. It had a massive investment in Dunlop brand tyres, and could not contemplate the European tyre operations falling into the hands of competitors or other third parties. Moreover, it was conscious of the fact that the European operations had tremendous potential if they were wisely managed. It did not take SRI management long to perceive the inevitability of a takeover, and by mid 1984 they were already moving into Fort Dunlop in Birmingham. Their first move was to take charge of the Technical Division, which at that time was the centre of the Dunlop empire, supplying technology throughout the world. This was followed by taking over the manufacturing and selling operations firstly in France and, in January 1985, by the opening of SP Tyres U.K. Limited and SP Reifen in Germany.

SRI acquired the license for the Dunlop brand name for tyres throughout Europe, but not the company name itself except in France, where it bought the company lock, stock and barrel from the receiver. (SRI subsequently bought Dunlop Tire Corporation in America in 1986.)

What Has Changed in the Four Years Since SRI Took Over?

From the start Kyohei Yokose, at that time Vice Chairman of SRI and responsible for European operations (he is now Chairman of SRI), forecast that the European operations would be profitable within 3 years. This was a bold statement, considering the depressed state in which they were taken over, and the fact that losses in the U.K. alone were running in excess of £20m per year.

In the event Mr Yokose's forecast was, if anything, conservative. By the end of its second year SP Tyres U.K. Limited had reached breakeven and since 1987 it has been operating consistently in the black.

How Was This Transformation Achieved?

It is perhaps worth remembering that SRI did not enjoy the advantages generally associated with Japanese investments in Britain—greenfield sites, tax concessions, government grants, careful selection of personnel and single union deals. SRI had none of these. It took over a declining operation, with ageing plant and equipment, and a completely demoralized workforce split among nine different unions. No government help was sought nor offered. Such a prospect would have daunted the bravest of foreign investors, but not the tough SRI Board.

There were some immediate grounds for confidence. Under the Tory government, then in its second term of office, the economic climate in Britain had been steadily improving for some years and was expected to go on doing so. Perhaps more important was the change on the industrial relations front. The militant days of the seventies were over,

G. D. Radford is Chairman and Managing Director of SP Tyres U.K. Limited at Fort Dunlop, Birmingham.

and it was apparent that unions were beginning to adopt a more pragmatic and flexible approach.

The fact of a foreign takeover of the business was also a significant catalyst in turning it round. Many years of bad news, axed budgets, lack of resources, and cut-backs in personnel had reduced people at all levels in the old company to an almost catatonic state of despair and apathy, mixed with total insecurity. The dramatic news of a Japanese take-over came as a traumatic shock which changed all that.

Gone immediately was the uncertainty about the future, the spectre of bankruptcy disappeared and it became clear that, in one form or another, the business would survive. SRI were not asset-strippers, they were a major manufacturer committed to the tyre business and to the Dunlop brand. At the same time, however, the new owners, because they were foreign, were unlikely to respond to government or union pressure if they subsequently decided to walk away from the business, and much had been reported about the different and stricter way in which Japanese companies operated.

So even before the new owners set foot in the place, there was not only an expectation but indeed an acceptance that radical change would occur. This was accompanied by an underlying assumption that the Japanese knew how to run a successful business, so it was in every sense worth giving it a try. The first hurdle, receptivity to change, was therefore overcome almost before we commenced operations.

Capital investment had for some years been completely inadequate to the needs of the business and SRI lost no time in drawing up a carefully phased programme for the upgrading and renewal of plant and equipment. This programme was totally dependent on outside finance, as even the most optimistic forecast indicated that it would be some years before the new company could hope to become self-financing. For the first, and by no means the last time, we witnessed the ability and inclination of our new owners to take a long-term view of the business, and to ensure that its recovery was in no way undermined by a lack of resources. At no time was it suggested that the capital investment programme might be modified on the basis of short-term results.

This capital investment, which to date amounts to some £50m, and is scheduled to continue at or above this level for the foreseeable future, was oriented entirely towards quality and production efficiency. There was to be no increase of actual capacity, except as a consequence of higher productivity. And from now on, quality and productivity improvement would be the focus of our struggle to restore profitability. Increased sales and better prices should, of course, follow, but they were too much subject to market forces and short-term fluctuations. If we wanted to be sure of survival, we had to guarantee it in the areas under our direct control, such as costs and overall efficiency. Any other improvements, for example in market share or sales margins, would be a bonus.

Hence each year tighter quality targets were set, and a drive for productivity improvements of not less than 10 per cent per annum commenced. A formal programme of cost saving activities was also pursued, covering everything from energy to material waste and efficient plant layout.

Together with financial investment we also benefited from the Japanese skills in production efficiency and their meticulous attention to detail. Their ability to identify and analyse a problem with painstaking precision paid off handsomely through the support of a handful of Japanese production advisers at our two main plants in Birmingham and Washington. A continuous programme of rationalization was instituted alongside the introduction of new plant, and the emphasis was also switched from breakdown repair to a carefully organized schedule of preventive maintenance. There was a dramatic reduction in time lost on breakdowns.

The investment and production efficiency drive were backed up by a policy of improving the working environment, which we familiarly refer to as the '4S's'—seiri, seiton, seiketso, seiso—meaning sorting, orderliness, cleanliness, cleaning, or in plain English, good housekeeping. For the most part, the workers themselves enthusiastically conducted this operation. Each item of equipment and materials was allocated to its specific area, and kept there. Plant and equipment was painted in bright colours, and each operative became responsible for keeping his work area tidy and clean. Better rest room and discussion area facilities were also organized within the factory. In this simple, methodical way the whole working environment was transformed and became a more cheerful place. For the first time we could take visitors round our plants without fearing for their welfare, and without being ashamed of what they might see.

From the very beginning SRI identified communication as being a critical weakness in the old operation, and we undertook an intensive programme to change this situation. There had typically been poor communication previously, with Board members rarely speaking even to their senior managers. Factory visits were like a royal occasion, and about as frequent. It was symptomatic that when the new Board requested an early meeting with union representatives to discuss plans there was widespread concern about the possibility of a fresh round of redundancies. Management had only communicated bad news in the past, and worse still had relied on the union representatives to communi-

Table 1. The 4S's

Seiri (sorting): separating items into necessary and unnecessary groups, and discarding the unnecessary.
Seiton (orderliness): storing items in their proper place so that they are immediately available when required.
Seiso (cleaning): keeping the workplace and all items clean. It is said that 'cleaning is checking'.
Seiketsu (cleanliness): ensuring that people and their equipment are always clean and tidy to create a good working environment.
The 4S's are the first step in quality control and fundamental for continuous three-shift production. By identifying unnecessary or faulty items appropriate action can be taken so that each operator can work more easily and effectively.
Commented one operator: 'At one time you had to move all sorts of things to find the item you needed. Now you know it is there and this saves time.' Another added: 'The cleanliness of the shop is now beyond belief. This encourages the operators to be more tidy. . . They now feel they have something to work for.'

cate with the rest of the workforce. Little wonder if credibility was at a low ebb!

From the start, the directors of SP Tyres U.K. Limited set about improving communication. Each month they spent a half-day presenting and discussing the results with all senior managers. These managers in turn were required to undertake similar communications with individual working groups, and to involve all other managers and supervisors in the process, so that by a cascade system every employee was informed, and could ask questions. In addition directors made it their business to participate in lower level meetings wherever possible, and three times each year held larger communication meetings, involving some 250 employees (10 per cent of the workforce) in discussing the results and forward plans. The management walkabout was strongly encouraged in order to shorten lines of communication still further and obtain direct and immediate feedback on how the business was doing, rather than waiting for problems to be reported back through 'proper channels'. Nor was the new management afraid to get its hands dirty working alongside other employees in a team effort to get the job done. 'Player manager' has been a term often used to describe management's role.

Naturally we also instituted quality circles and suggestions schemes, initially with the same dismal results achieved by so many similar experiments. What we had failed to realize was that the climate was not right. At the start, the suspicious and demotivated workforce, with little or no faith in management, was simply not receptive to the idea of quality circles. Management probably lacked conviction too, and failed to provide the necessary training and guidance for them to succeed. As confidence and motivation have improved, together with the whole working environment, we

have experienced little difficulty in involving people at all levels in problem-solving groups.

Suggestions have also flourished, and when we achieved an annual average of one suggestion per employee we felt we were really making progress, until informed that our colleagues in Japan were producing 200 suggestions per employee. So we are still working on it. We make scaled awards for all suggestions, and special additional awards for any patentable ideas. We also make a 'Suggestion of the Year' award. The return on such schemes is enormous, but so is the administrative effort involved. For the scheme to be effective, each suggestion must receive a rapid response, otherwise interest declines immediately. Many suggestions require detailed investigation and particular problems arise in the technical area, with a backlog of suggestions quickly piling up. The only way to handle this is by spreading the load, and permitting first line supervisors to evaluate less complex suggestions and make the appropriate awards.

The concept of teamwork is fundamental to every Japanese company, and the emphasis is very much more on the team than on the individual decision maker. Through a process known as 'nemawashi', or 'preparation of the roots', ideas are canvassed and opinions sought so that a consensus gradually develops and the final agreement or decision making becomes very much a formality. In this way not only is everyone concerned with the matter involved in the decision, avoiding future conflict and ensuring maximum communication, but wider and deeper consideration is given to the subject and violent clashes between individuals are avoided, preserving harmony and team spirit. Naturally this process takes time, and can be frustrating to those accustomed to swift and individual decision making. It does seem to work, however, in most situations, and a more thorough approach to planning avoids the need for many previously 'urgent' decisions.

The team concept necessarily embraces also the conditions of work. It is difficult to cultivate the idea of 'everybody being in the same boat' if the distinctions and privileges of status are everywhere apparent. Separate canteens were long since abolished, as were segregated car parks, and on-site management wear the same uniform as everyone else. There was initial resistance to this idea, especially among some older managers. To them it smacked of regimentation and loss of status. Fortunately they accepted the need to break down barriers and destroy the 'them and us' concept which previously inhibited co-operation, and by many it is now considered an honour rather than an imposition to wear the Company uniform.

When we started we had nine unions, and even today there are still seven. This initially meant that there were large discrepancies in pay and conditions not only between different categories of employee, but between employees of similar category on different sites. Much time and effort has been dedicated over the last 4 years to the closer harmonization of pay and conditions, and although further progress still needs to be made, it is no longer unthinkable that there should be a single annual negotiation involving all parties.

Our unions so far have taken a fully responsible attitude, and after their hesitant initial response have supported most of the changes which have taken place. It was clear to them that management was maintaining its promises, and that their members could only benefit from the strengthening of the company. One of the principal benefits was that with increasing job security one of the major obstacles to flexibility and the acceptance of change was removed.

Teamwork and improved communication go closely hand in hand, and play a significant role in improved motivation. Another important element of this mosaic has been training.

SP Tyres has a very modest training budget, and only one training officer. This may be a surprise to those in government and business circles who appear to judge training effort by the size of the budget. The explanation is quite simple, Most of our training is in-house, conducted by managers and supervisors themselves. We do not of course exclude external training, which is often necessary in specialized subjects or for the input of new ideas. We take a totally pragmatic view on this matter. But we do find that our own managers can best relate the training to our own circumstances and needs. There are additional benefits—the trainer sometimes learns as much as the trainees, and the training session provides yet another opportunity for contact and communication. As far as possible we assemble multifunctional training groups to encourage communication and understanding between individuals who might otherwise not meet each other.

Within our first 3 years, every single one of our employees had participated in at least one training course, some in many more. Our forward training programme foresees this activity continuing even more intensely in future.

Our SRI colleagues firmly believe in the principle that 'seeing is believing' and have generously arranged for many of our employees at all levels to visit their factories in Japan. This has provided an invaluable first-hand training experience for those involved, who have invariably returned with new ideas, convinced that they too could apply what they had seen. Often they were also keen to show they could do it even better! This spirit of pride and competition between production units is encouraged world-wide. The trends and results of all sister factories are regularly displayed on the shop floor.

The ultimate focus of all our activity is the end user of our product. The basic philosophy of SRI is 'gemchi gembutsu'—keen awareness of customer needs and prompt action to satisfy them. As customers become more sophisticated and enjoy a wider choice, the only basis for a long term and mutually satisfactory relationship is quality. Primarily it is the quality of the product which counts. The tyre business is notoriously one of 'distress purchase' i.e. most customers, except motoring enthusiasts, derive little or no pleasure from buying tyres. On the contrary, most private users are rarely conscious of having tyres unless something goes wrong, or they wear out. So the quality of a tyre, which is frequently abused and undervalued by its user, is a critically sensitive matter. There is precious little recognition for getting it right, but the dangers of getting it wrong range from lost customers to lost lives.

It is not surprising therefore that we dedicate so much time, effort and financial resource to the constant control and improvement of quality standards. We have found ourselves pursuing a parallel course with vehicle manufacturers, who are also looking for ever tighter standards of quality and uniformity, not to mention all-round performance, from their tyres.

Not many years ago quality control meant increasing the number of inspectors at the end of the line to sort out defective products. Now our total effort is on prevention and 'getting it right first time' . Under this system each operative is carefully trained to do his job, and encouraged to take a personal pride in his workmanship. He considers the colleague who receives the partly processed material or product from him to be his personal 'customer', whose satisfaction is every bit as vital as the end customer's. So each operative must check his own work and not release it unless he is sure it is right.

This concept led to the early introduction of SPC (statistical process control) and lot control, so that each process can be carefully monitored and each item traced throughout the entire work process. Training was given in these and other quality procedures, and contributed much to the job satisfaction of the workers involved.

It was apparent to us, however, that the concept of quality was applicable beyond the strict limits of the product. We supply both products and services to our customers, whether internal or external, so that everyone in the Company has a customer to satisfy at some stage in the chain. For instance it is just as important to supply correct invoices as it is to supply good tyres, and a courteous and helpful reply to a telephone call or letter can have a significant effect on customer loyalty.

For this reason, we decided that it was essential to create a common set of values, and a common language, throughout the whole company. This we are trying to do through a programme we call Total Quality (TQ). We called on the assistance of an outside consultant to help us organize and launch this programme, which is intended to become a permanent way of life for everyone in the company. Our ultimate goal is 'zero defects' and we are training every single employee in the concept and the techniques involved. The approach is structured, to ensure that results match good intentions. Everyone will have improvement targets and their success (or failure) will be closely monitored.

What has been Achieved as a Consequence of all this Effort?
Today, with 30 per cent less people, our factories are producing over 40 per cent more units, but we still have a long way to go in order to match our Japanese colleagues. The factories are also much happier and cleaner places than they used to be, and there has been a resurgence of confidence and motivation throughout the entire workforce. We can now promise our employees a job for life. They also enjoy a profit-sharing scheme.

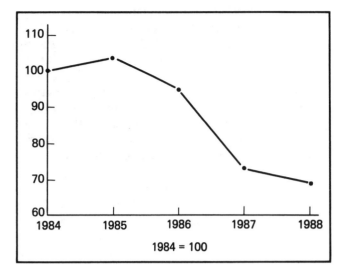

Figure 3. Waste level

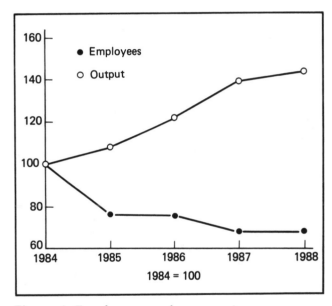

Figure 4. Employee numbers vs unit output

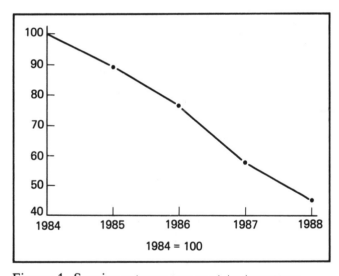

Figure 1. Service returns per cent to turnover

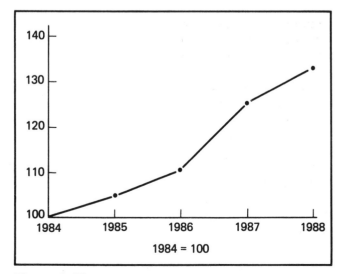

Figure 2. Turnover

In the market place our quality image has improved, together with our market share, and we are key suppliers to all major vehicle manufacturers in the U.K. For the benefit of any cynics, who believe that Japanese investment in the U.K. is an umbrella for increased Japanese exports, it is worth noting that a higher proportion of our product range is now manufactured in Britain than 4 years ago, and SRI has also opened up additional export opportunities for us.

Perhaps the most significant improvement has been at the bottom line. Before the takeover, the U.K. tyre operations were losing in excess of £20m per year. In 1986, our second year of operation, we achieved an operating profit. In 1987 this became our first post tax profit, and in 1988 our profitability again increased sharply.

This achievement has resulted from the strong and

successful combination of Japanese and British expertise. The Board itself is evenly divided between Japanese and British directors, though with one exception all executive responsibilities are British. A dozen or so Japanese 'advisers', including the directors, are based with us, assisting principally in the technical and production areas, though the Japanese directors have a European rather than a purely U.K. role. For the rest, most of the managers and other employees worked for the old Dunlop company, which makes their achievement all the more remarkable.

It is evident from our experience that success depends not so much on investment in machines as in people—caring about them, training them, and motivating them by helping them to realize their full potential. We believe we have only just begun, and that the next few years offer us an exciting new challenge.